To Reni,

with best wishes

Antonia Fraser

She's No Lady

She's No Lady

Arvonne Fraser

INTRODUCTION BY GARRISON KEILLOR

Edited by Lori Sturdevant

NODIN PRESS

Library of Congress Cataloging-in-Publication Data

Fraser, Arvonne S.
    She's no lady : politics, family, and international feminism / by
Arvonne Fraser ; edited by Lori Sturdevant ; foreword by Garrison
Keillor.
      p. cm.
    ISBN-13: 978-1-932472-64-6
    ISBN-10: 1-932472-64-9
    1. Fraser, Arvonne S. 2. Women politicians--United States--Biogra-
phy. 3. Feminists--United States--Biography. 4. Women in politics-
-United States--History--20th century. 5. Minnesota--Biography.
6. Democratic-Farmer-Labor Party--History. 7. United Nations
Commission on the Status of Women--Biography. 8. Feminism-
-International cooperation--History--20th century. I. Sturdevant,
Lori, 1953- II. Title.
E748.F79A3 2007
305.42092--dc22
[B]
                                    2007034685

All photos from private collections except where noted.
Design and layout: John Toren

Nodin Press is a division of Micawber's, Inc.
530 N. Third Street, Suite 120
Minneapolis, MN 55401

to Don and Bonnie

Acknowledgements

This book would never have been written without the loyal support of my husband, Don Fraser, who is also good at finding typos and factual errors. This book would never have been completed without Lori Sturdevant's and E. Richard Larson's skillful editing and encouragement. During the long journey of writing and revising, the late and lamented Paul Gruchow, and Patricia Hampl and Patricia Francisco, generously welcomed me into their writing workshops at the University of Minnesota. Their perceptive comments and wise counsel kept me on task. Thanks also to my much-younger classmates in those workshops who, with good humor, taught me that some of my idioms were archaic and that I was actually writing history. Earlier, I also benefited greatly from Loft classes and workshops, and treasure my many friendships made there. Eternal gratitude goes to Terry Saario and Mary Pruitt for their insightful readings and comments. Tom Fraser's close editing occasionally put his mother to shame.

I can never thank Garrison adequately. Who wouldn't be honored by a shy young man who turns up to help you out one day and some forty years later he's still helping you out. Only now he's a celebrity, sends you messages through his weekly columns and emails when on location. With friends like him and all those above, one is blessed. And then there's Norton Stillman of Nodin Press, an added blessing, about whom everyone who deals with him agrees. John Toren was patience personified when dealing with the pictures—and lack thereof. I had to explain that Don and I decided we didn't need wedding pictures because we would remember the event—and we have, for fifty-seven years.

Finally, I owe Jerome (Jerry) Liebling, eternal gratitude for superb photography, including the picture of the younger woman on the cover, and most of Don's early campaign pictures. I did look like that once, but at least I can still smile.

Contents

Editor's Note

I first interviewed Arvonne Fraser during a long, anxious and ultimately disappointing evening for her family. It was September 12, 1978—primary election night. Though the outcome of the contest for the DFL nomination for the U.S. Senate between Don Fraser and Robert Short would not be known for hours, Arvonne was politician enough to be discouraged by what she was seeing at 10 p.m. She knew Fraser's Twin Cities vote wasn't large enough to assure victory.

At the fringe of an animated circle of friends and family stood a young female reporter, whose byline Arvonne recognized as one who covered religion and women's issues. I was hanging around the family's hotel suite to collect "color" for the election story being compiled in the Minneapolis Tribune newsroom.

"C'mon," Arvonne said in response to my request for a brief interview. She led me to the relative privacy of a bedroom, plopped down on the bed, propped her petite frame up with pillows, invited me to perch at the foot of the bed, and encouraged me to fire away.

I was immediately won over—as I know every reader of this book will be, too.

The direct, open, generous woman I met that night almost 30 years ago is the same one readers will meet on these pages. She may be "no lady," in the prim-and-proper way her mother intended. But Arvonne is an archetypal county-cum-city Minnesota woman, the sort to whom her friend and admirer Garrison Keillor refers when he speaks of a place where "all the women are strong."

It may not have been ladylike to do an election-night interview on a bed. But it was the unpretentious, pragmatic, accommodating thing to do just then – so of course, that's what Arvonne did. I don't remember what she said that night. But I remember being impressed with her intelligence and spirit, and wanting to get to know her better. I'm extremely grateful to have had that chance through the years, most recently as the editor of this book.

– Lori Sturdevant

Foreword

The sons and daughters of Minnesota are bound by a lingering loyalty, even the ones who moved away to warm places and got deacclimated, we recognize each other in foreign places, no need for a big maroon M on our fronts, and we often take comfort from each other. I know I have. I have been trapped in the mineshaft of a New York literary cocktail party and a voice nearby says hi and I turn and a woman says, "We're from the Range," and now I am rescued. We wend our way to a quiet corner and talk English. This happens again and again and it makes me feel that I belong to a tribe. We have suffered many dislocations and our writers have failed to defend us but we exist and we know each other.

I could try to describe what I mean by Minnesotan but we were brought up to be modest and now here is a book that exemplifies the tribe and what we are good for. In my Minnesota, Arvonne Fraser is a classic heroine, a farm girl who learned to pull your share of the load and mind your manners and don't feel sorry for yourself but who rebelled against the social dictates of Main Street just as Sinclair Lewis's Carol Kennicott did and felt the irresistible pull of the big city and escaped to Minneapolis during World War II to work in a war plant and wound up at the University where she came under the spell of Hubert Humphrey and became his campaign secretary and got enmeshed in the hurly-burly of politics and married a Democrat and embarked on a life of steady commitment to the cause, while raising a brood of children and managing her husband's campaigns to serve eight terms in Congress.

My first glimpse of her was at the Fraser for Congress headquarters in a storefront in north Minneapolis in the summer of 1966 where I reported for duty as a volunteer. Arvonne stood at her desk near the front door, a short stocky woman, black hair cut short, phone in one hand, cigarette in the other, talking in a clear level voice just short of a bark, several small Frasers clustered around her, and as she talked, she pointed me toward a table where a dozen volunteers were stuffing brochures ("Keep Fraser Working For A Strong America") into envelopes. I sat down and stuffed.

Arvonne was an original, then and now. She was warm-hearted, enjoyed company, could be wickedly funny, had a big laugh, was gracious about Please and Thank you and Excuse me, but she was clearly in charge and always looking around and nothing, absolutely nothing, escaped her eye. She spoke directly and there was no passive-aggressive in her, nothing apologetic or coy or coquettish or whimsical or demurring. Arvonne skipped the big wind-up and got to the point. I wrote some campaign literature for Fraser and back it came with her marks on it: she was not a hesitant editor. There was, back then, a certain passive resistance to the idea of a woman running things and Arvonne simply ignored it and moved forward. She was committed. When you were around her, you learned what the word "commitment" meant. I was not committed. I was a bystander, a tourist, still am, but Arvonne had a clear vision of a society that invested in its own people as if they truly mattered. She could've run Cargill or taught Jane Austen or designed buildings but she had landed in politics and she seemed to have no regrets about that.

She and Fraser—around the office, she was Arvonne, he was Fraser, even Arvonne called him Fraser—had the luxury of running in Minneapolis, a diehard DFL district, and often against sacrificial opponents. The Frasers always ran hard, but a safe seat comes with a price. You lose touch with the changing currents; you stay anchored in place, while the shoreline shifts. Maybe you lose the urge to do battle, to rise up on your toes and cry out, to face down the hostile crowd and appeal to their better angels.

Fraser ran for the U.S. Senate and lost and it was a terrible loss. He was stoical about it and so was Arvonne but to the rest of us, Don Fraser was a sort of political saint, a serious, thoughtful, curious, dedicated, intelligent, self-deprecating, and profoundly decent man who was a credit to the voters of Minneapolis. They elected a man to Congress who spent a lot of his time thinking about things that pay no quick political dividend. If the U.S. Senate is meant to be a contemplative body, Fraser was the man for the job. He got sand-bagged in the DFL primary, picked himself up out of the dust, and became a popular mayor of Minneapolis for a decade.

Arvonne took one run for public office herself and came up short and walked away unscratched. Having raised her brood, she launched a midlife career in the cause of international women's rights, doing the hard work, traveling, writing, attending the meetings, digging the potatoes, serving as U.S. Ambassador to the U.N. Commission on the Status of Women, and all to bring women's rights under the protection of international law and thereby change the world. And when the winds shifted and it was time, she came back to the University to write and teach. She had a whale of a time doing all this. She suffered the loss of two daughters, an irreparable hurt, unspeakable, and she has grieved but seems never to have despaired.

I didn't care for the title of this book. Arvonne is a great lady; Jane Austen would've been proud to know her. But I was moved by the writing. You'd expect a political woman to write her life story in the form of a treatise but instead she has given us a memoir of intense descriptive power and authenticity that place it among the classics of the genre. Most political memoirs are written by winners, as trophies, or by candidates as campaign materials, but Arvonne isn't running for anything and she has seen cataclysmic defeats, and this memoir is simply to say that she knows who she is. It's the first book I've read that gives a true sense of the DFL, and so it's an important document in the history of Minnesota and good reading for people of any political persuasion.

And it has given me a small crucial insight into my old friend, which is this: Arvonne's voice never changed. She lived in Washington for years, she was a dignitary, she traveled the world, but she kept her voice, which is present throughout this book, and it is the voice of a Minnesota farm woman. That is what I found fascinating about her in 1966 and find astonishing now. She met all those people, could talk officialese, knew all the acronyms, wielded some power and influence, and yet down deep she is related to my aunts who threw the dishwater out the back door, who cleaned chickens, who scrubbed the kitchen floor, and who, in the gentle twilight, sat on the steps and told us children everything we wanted to know about the history of our family.

– Garrison Keillor

She's No Lady

Arvonne in her milk-route clothes.

Chapter 1

From Lamberton to Timbuktu

My grandmother's favorite expression for an impossible distance was "From here to Timbuktu." She never expected anyone she knew to get there. It was her metaphor for places far beyond the long horizon where the limitless sky met the rolling prairie of southwestern Minnesota.

I always wanted to know what was beyond that horizon. But Expectations for farm girls in the late 1920s were limited. You were supposed to grow up, go to school, find a job for a while, then get married and settle down. Settling down meant having children and being content with what life handed you. Conveying and reinforcing those expectations was incessant as in "Settle down, be a little lady," my mother's admonition when I was being too boisterous as a child. Later it was "Be a good girl." I couldn't settle down. Some horizon always beckoned. There had to be more to see, do, and try. I didn't know what was beyond any horizon, or how I would get there, but I wouldn't settle for what life handed me.

Maybe it was that expansive sky, or the ever-changing weather that made me restless. On the farm we read that sky for signs of approaching weather. We looked out the kitchen window at the weather vane on the windmill to see which way the wind was blowing. Had it changed? Our skins and psyches were attuned to change. Winter blizzards were exciting. The north wind howled, snow stung your eyes so you turned your back to the wind as you plowed through drifts. Inside, we watched the red liquid in the outside thermometer fall below zero. A south wind meant warmth and sunshine in summer. East winds or no wind didn't feel right. Summer storms came from the west, sometimes abruptly, sometimes with a stultifying, breathless gray sky turning ominous. Even small children could feel something was going to happen. We watched the overcast sky as angry gray and black clouds appeared, roiling overhead, buffeted by unseen winds, then waited for the first gust of wind to hit our bodies, turning quickly to keep the swirling dust out of our eyes. Then, a crack of lightning, the smell of rain. Children were taught to count "one thousand one, one thousand two, one thousand three" between a crack of lightning and the thunder clap to determine how far away the lightning had struck. As a farm child, the ever-changing weather, that big sky, the long horizon and my grandmother dominated my world.

One of my early memories is of a sunny summer day. I was alone in the farmyard, the hot sun blazing down on me. Nothing moving, no sound. Even the chickens were quiet. It must have been noon. The sun was directly overhead. I couldn't have been more than four or five years old. I stood there, realizing with a start that I was totally alone under that huge sky. An epiphany, some would call it; perhaps it was the moment I realized I was an individual, a person all by myself. Nobody was there to tell me what to do. I stood a minute or two, motionless, frightened but savoring the experience. I was totally alone. Nothing terrible happened. I could do whatever I wanted. I don't remember what happened next, but the memory of that moment's thrill lingered.

Some of our neighbors and all of our ancestors came from places far beyond that long horizon outside Lamberton, Minnesota. Grandma knew about Denmark. Her parents came from there and she spoke Danish to them. Others in our area spoke German, Swedish or Norwegian. Men who came to visit Grandpa or my Dad taught me to count in German. When I went with Grandma to the Brown County Fair or, years later, to Vienna, Austria, the words spoken around me sounded familiar but I didn't understand what was said. Grandpa DuFrene, who lived 150 miles away, spoke French. This was good background for international work.

All my schoolmates spoke English although some said "dese, dose and dems" for the common definite pronouns. Sometimes we mocked them, I'm sad to admit. At school we studied what went on beyond our horizon. At home we listened to adult conversations and learned quickly that distant markets and politics impinged on us. Men listened to the grain and cattle markets on WNAX, the radio station in Yankton, South Dakota, or WCCO in Minneapolis. The chant of the announcer was like that of auctioneers, understandable only to the initiated. Mothers and grandmothers were more concerned about egg prices. They traded eggs for groceries in town, children in tow. Grain, cattle and eggs were shipped out by train. If the harvest was good, we took trips to the Cities—Minneapolis and St. Paul—or drove up north to see Grandma and Grandpa DuFrene before school started.

The divide among neighbors was between those who concentrated only on the ground and the weather, who expected to stay put, and those who looked—and sometimes went, temporarily or forever—beyond the horizon. I was among the latter. I did the expected things. I went to school, worked for awhile, got married and eventually had six children, bowing not only to family expectations as well as my own inclination .Coming from a big, extended family, I enjoyed the security of that part of my life . But in time I also traveled far beyond the boundaries of post-war rural expectations and conventions. For my grandmother, Timbuktu had been merely an expression. I actually *went* there.

It was 1978. My youngest child was almost sixteen, and my oldest had graduated from peddling the *Washington Post* and working on Mississippi River barges to practicing law. Those in between were trying to do what I had urged them: "Find what you like to do and then figure out how to get paid for it."

I went to Africa that year with "Miz Lillian," President Jimmy Carter's mother, as part of my first post-marriage full-time regular job. An Agency for International Development (AID) colleague had learned Mrs. Carter was to be awarded a medal by FAO, the Food and Agriculture Organization in Rome, for her Peace Corps work. He convinced the White House that extending her trip into the Sahel, the area devastated by drought in sub-Saharan Africa in the 1970s, would be good public relations for U.S. aid to developing countries.

I was invited to accompany her. It was a trip of time warp.

Arriving in our small Air Force jet at the tiny, windswept airport outside Timbuktu in the nation of Mali, we were driven into what had been a bustling intellectual and market center in the fifteenth century. The airport road to town was lined with silent men on camels, their heads and necks swathed in startling, indigo fabric as protection from the blowing sand. They stood sentinel as a tribute to us, representatives of the United States, for the tons of grain and meal our nation had sent them during their drought. "We saved their lives," our State Department guide said.

I knew about drought, about rains that never came. The1930's Midwest drought devastated our farm community. The dry air of Timbuktu was familiar, making the 100-degree heat tolerable. The men on camels had the same sad eyes I had seen on my father, grandfather, and neighbors when our crops wilted. In the Sahel the crops died.

As we entered this famous old city, a small, wistful crowd stood quietly around an unidentifiable monument eroded by eons of blowing sand. They simply looked at us. We didn't wave, although our car caravan had all the aspects of a parade. In this somber, isolated place, smiling and waving to people recovering from near starvation didn't seem appropriate. We simply proceeded slowly to the famous well. Timbuktu is an oasis. It had been an important stopover on the cross-Sahara trade route. Camel caravans in the fifteenth century brought Islam to Africa. A significant Koranic university was established, scholars mingling with merchants who traded gold, horses, salt, and slaves.

Beside the well, staring at us forlornly, was another grandmother, with a small child beside her. I recognized the white enameled pail with a tiny blue line around its rim beside them. We had used pails like that on our farm. I noticed the grandmother's well-worn rubber flip-flops, evidence that some modern commerce reached this desolate place. The child had no shoes, nor was she as thin as the grandmother. They had come for water, I was told. I gasped, felt like vomiting, seeing that the open water beside them was covered with algae. That's not a well, I thought, it's a polluted slough. Did they drink that water? They couldn't. Did they have to use precious firewood for boiling it? I turned away, speechless.

We were hurried on, into a building made of banco, the local version of adobe. Cool air emanated from the building, whose thick walls resisted the blazing sun and the cold desert nights. Across the doorway hung an Oriental carpet. Had it been transported across the desert years ago, along with Islam? Inside, at the near end of the official receiving line, were a woman and her young daughter, clearly Americans in freshly laundered cotton dresses. The wife and child of an official or with a relief agency, I assumed.

"What are you doing here?" I asked brightly, for she was the first American I had seen since arriving who was not a member of our party. I shook her hand eagerly, hoping to get a sense of what relief workers were doing to assist the families eking out an existence in this now decimated city.

"Saving souls," she said proudly. *That's the last thing these poor people need*, I thought, but I bit my tongue, smiled, and nodded politely. Politics had been my trade, now diplomacy was. I moved quickly up the receiving line to the reception room. Bare, except for more brilliant carpets covering the floor and the wide ledges around the edge for seating. There was no furniture. A large opening in the north end of the room revealed the relentlessly blue sky.

The Tuaregs, the local people, are beautiful. Tall, thin, and handsome, the waiters' fine-featured dark faces contrasted sharply with the stark white aprons covering their shabby pants and shirts. Diplomatic receptions require something to drink, but my traveling companions and I were shocked to see the trays laden with ice cold Coca Cola and champagne. *In this place?* My face must have revealed my thoughts.

"Flown in from Paris," my Africare colleague whispered, contempt in his voice. We took our drinks eagerly—for we were thirsty—but with shame, and stood awaiting the speeches.

"At least they didn't feed us," another colleague observed when we were on our way again. "I don't think I could have swallowed one bite, all those hungry people outside."

"Don't be so hard on your hosts," our State Department officer said. "They were doing their best. They don't get many visitors here and, after all, she is the mother of the president of the United States. They were trying to honor her and our country properly."

During the drought years of my childhood, life was difficult but we never went hungry. Some farmhouses were abandoned and all of them needed paint. One despairing neighbor hung himself in his barn. But Minnesota was outside the Dust Bowl. We had spring rains and enough water underground, clean water that windmills and hand pumps pulled up for people and animals. Though farm prices were low, most farmers could harvest enough to keep their families and the townspeople eating regularly over winter. Pasture grass kept the cows milking, though some of my schoolmates came to school with lard instead of butter on their lunch sandwiches. Young men sometimes had boils on the back of their necks in winter from lack of decent nutrition and baths. Children came to school in worn but clean clothes. Our Minnesota drought was nothing, I mused, compared to what I had just seen. But drawing analogies between how people cope with life makes the world a smaller place. Timbuktu and Lamberton weren't so far apart after all.

In the twenty years following my visit to Mali I traveled from the Arctic Circle almost to the South Pole, from Minnesota and Washington to Vienna, Austria and back more times than I can count. I flew to Jakarta, Paris, Rome, Stockholm, and Buenos Aires. Once I flew from Tokyo to London across the North Pole and backwards in time. Grandma would have been amazed, but then she was born at the end of the nineteenth century. I am living in the twenty-first. She saw women get the vote; women now lead our Minnesota Legislature and the U.S. House of Representatives.

I have been part of the massive changes of the twentieth century. Born at home under a kerosene lamp, I sit typing emails to friends around the world. Perhaps because of that big sky and horizon, I take the long view and welcome change. I like both storms and security. I wanted children, lots of them, but not until I was ready and had the right father for them. I was ready for the new women's movement when it emerged, and turned my talents and experience to it. Defying expectations, taking risks, and seeing what I could do beyond near horizons became my sport. I found it satisfying, most of the time. It's thrilling to imagine the possibilities that await my grandchildren—and you readers. This is my story. I wrote it to encourage other women to live fully and write theirs.

Chapter 2

Grandma's Girl

"The year that nothing happened" is what 1925 was called in a book I once read. Calvin Coolidge was sworn in as president and immediately took a vacation. The federal budget was three billion dollars—an astronomical amount to my poor parents. Not that they were paying much attention to the federal budget. A 1924 snapshot in Grandma Skelton's old photo album (lower right) shows them in tight embrace, Dad smiling at the camera, Mom with her eyes closed, enraptured. They're standing in a farmyard, a windmill in the background, a scruffy farm dog at their feet. Dad has on a dark suit—his only one, I'm sure. Mom is wearing a Roaring Twenties

flapper dress and stylish shoes, her thick red hair bobbed. She always did love clothes.

Her one-room country schoolteacher's salary bought the wool coat she is wearing in another picture. This time she and my dad are standing beside a Model T Ford, his arm around her shoulder. Again, there's his smile below a '20s wool cap with visor, and belted overcoat. She's somber. The cloche she's wearing hides her eyes. Everybody knew them as Shorty and Phyl, the best dancers in the community.

They were married in February, 1925, in Redwood Falls, Minnesota. I was born on September 1 that year, the child my mother didn't want but Grandma did. Low-waisted flapper dresses helped camouflage my mother's pregnancy until the school year ended. She kept her maiden name. Revealing their marriage, to say nothing of her pregnancy, would have resulted in her being fired as a teacher and they needed the money.

The 1920s were not good years for farmers. Farm prices were low and living was hard. Winters were long and dark. Electricity had not yet arrived and houses were lit by kerosene. and heated with wood, corncobs or kerosene—kitchens and dining rooms only. Homemade quilts and wool blankets kept sleepers warm in frigid bedrooms. Water was carried into the house in galvanized pails by wives and children. Behind every house was an outhouse with an outdated Montgomery Ward catalog for toilet paper. Farmers in our part of Minnesota kept horses and a sleigh—a wagon box on heavy runners—to get to town or to the neighbors in winter. Horses pulled plows and cultivators as the farmers worked their fields. Only the major roads leading to and from the small towns were graveled; the others were dirt or mud in the spring.

I know nothing about my parents' wedding. They never talked about it; I never asked. I was fourteen when Donnie, one of my young twin uncles, mentioned their wedding date, and I was shocked to realize I was born less than seven months later. Nobody ever said I was premature. Dad always pointed out my birthplace—a tiny, abandoned house—when we drove past it. He was proud of

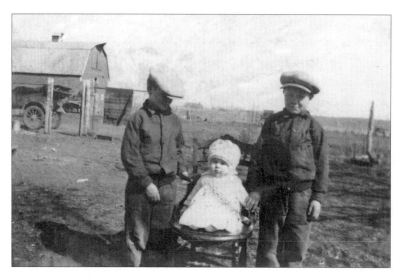

Arvonne with twin uncles Darold (left) and Donald

their hard beginnings. Like many others of its kind, that house is now gone, plowed over, a fertile field marked only by an abandoned driveway. Mom was usually silent as Dad reminisced.

But my most vivid memories of my early childhood are of Grandma Skelton and quiet Grandpa. Dad and his nine siblings called her Ann, for she was their stepmother. I was told there had been a real grandmother who died of the flu on Christmas eve in 1918, not a year after she had borne the twins. A prominent memento of that grandmother was a black and silver plaque, the words in Swedish, hanging above the dining room door. I pictured that other grandmother as coming from the Old Country, like the old ladies I often saw sitting quietly in farm kitchens or in the back seat of the car when the Old Man drove to town. Members of the older generation—especially those from the Old Country—were always referred to as Old Lady or Old Man Holznagel, Fredrickson or Pfarr.

Nobody would dare call my grandmother Old Lady Skelton. She was a presence, a woman in her own right. A tall, swarthy, brown-eyed Dane, born in the United States, she was the childless widow of a World War I veteran. She married Percy Skelton, my grandfather, in 1921 when she was thirty. He was 43, a widower with ten children. She brought some money with her, kept it as hers, installed a telephone and a radio in his farmhouse and brought only the youngest three of his children home to live with her and their father. Four years later I was born. Dad was delighted with his new baby girl and, so the oft-told story goes, told Ann to send his young twin brothers over next morning to see her.

"Shorty has something new for you," Ann announced to the seven-year old twins the morning after I was born. "Eat your breakfast and then you can go over and see what it is." Expecting at least a pony if not a horse to ride—for Shorty loved horses—they gulped down their oatmeal, wiped their mouths on their sleeves, and rushed out the door to the barn. Grabbing a bridle off a hook, they ran across the small field separating the two farmhouses.

Ann Hanson Skelton

"Where is it? Ann said you had something for us," they called out, rushing into their older brother's house breathless with anticipation, the bridle dangling from Donnie's shoulder.

"Shh…Come in the bedroom," my smiling father said as he led the crestfallen pair into the only bedroom in the house. "You're uncles now. Isn't she cute? You'll have to help take care of her."

"A baby, only a baby? We thought you had something really good," Donnie, the more talkative twin, said, throwing the bridle on the floor in disgust while Darold leaned over the cradle.

"Has she got a name?" Darold inquired.

"Not yet. Phyl's thinking about it. You got any ideas?"

"Biddy, little Biddy," Darold responded, running his finger across my hand.

The nickname stuck. Officially I was Baby Girl Skelton, born in Charlestown Township, Redwood County, Minnesota, U.S.A., the first child of Orland Skelton, aged 22, and Phyllis DuFrene, 19. Only when I graduated from high school and needed a copy of my birth certificate. did Mom register me as Arvonne Delrae, memorializing her French heritage and my father's favorite uncles. Only teachers and schoolmates—and Mom when she was angry—called me Arvonne.

Shuttling back and forth between my parents' and grandparents' houses began two weeks after I was born and lasted until I went to kindergarten. My great-grandfather, a Civil War veteran and homesteader who had moved on to northern Minnesota, died, and Ann asked my parents to come over and take care of the twins while the rest of the family attended the funeral. When they returned, Ann would often say to my Aunt Helen, "Go get Biddy," and send her the quarter-mile down the road with the baby carriage. She'd keep me a week or more at a time.

My sister Bonnie was born fourteen months after me, Marilyn thirteen months later. Mom was always glad to have one less child "under foot," as she called it. At Grandma's I was the center of attention. "Grandma's girl, " she'd croon as she snuggled me on her lap. The twins tolerated me, their surrogate baby sister. The frilly white hat and dress pictured in photos Grandma took are her contribution to my wardrobe.

The large dining room and smaller kitchen were the focal points of my grandparents' house. We gathered for supper around the long oak dining room table, Grandma and Grandpa, Donnie and Darold, Aunt Helen and I. After supper, while the twins and Helen finished their schoolwork, I sat on a grandparent's lap or played with the twins—"bothered" them was their word. An oak china closet—which I now have—stood between doors to two small bedrooms. Filled with fine china dishes I was only to look at, they were a sharp contrast to what Grandma called our everyday dishes. One evening, Darold stood up while I was hanging on the back of his chair, and I fell into the rounded glass front of that china closet. I wasn't hurt,

Arvonne, Bonnie and Marilyn

and no dishes were broken, but replacing the rounded glass took six months because it had to be ordered from the Cities. Darold was punished, not I.

In the south corner of this room, near the kitchen, was a huge black horsehair sofa, the kind I imagine Freud used in Vienna. It was my favorite place to nap or lie lazily on summer mornings beside the open windows as Grandma chatted away in Danish with her mother over the telephone on the wall.

"I've got to talk to Mama," she would say as she twirled the crank, then asked the operator in English for the Hansen residence, shifting to Danish when her mother answered. Sometimes she'd let

15

me turn the crank and talk to the operator. "Central" the operator was called.

I could never understand why Grandma liked her mama so much. She and Old Man Hansen scared me. They lived in a dank old ramshackle house beside Charlie's Creek—we pronounced it "crick"—with Grandma's younger sisters. Old Lady Hansen didn't seem to like small children. If the gruff, forbidding-looking Old Man was home when we visited, I cowered outside in the car, joined by Grandpa who had nothing to contribute to the raging Danish conversation. The Hansens didn't have a car, only a horse and buggy. Later, as a schoolgirl, I'd hear that when the Old Man went to town and got drunk, the horse knew the way home.

I couldn't reconcile Grandma and her relatives. She was quiet; they were loud. Chris, her bachelor brother who lived with Ida Peterson, the local nurse and midwife who was not his wife, was to me a surly giant. He wore the farmer's uniform, blue-and-white striped overalls, denim or flannel shirt, and big work boots even on Sundays. A large red and black printed handkerchief hung out of his back pocket to blow his nose or wipe oil off machinery. He and Grandpa co-owned the threshing rig. They earned extra money threshing grain for all the farmers around. "Brother Chris," Grandma called him, reverence in her voice. He rarely talked to me. Instead, he often squirted luminous blue oil at my feet from the oil can that always seemed to be in his hand and laughed.

"If you aren't a good girl, the Gypsies will get you," was one of Grandma's favorite admonitions. Gypsies came every summer in their black cars, camping on the roadside, cooking meals over campfires, and eating while perched on the running boards of their cars. They stole chickens for their dinner, people said, and little girls if they didn't behave. They brought mystery and excitement to the community. I thought Grandma's Mama and sisters, and Grandma herself, looked like the Gypsy women but never dared say so. Grandma's skin was coffee-with-cream colored, soft as silk, a delight to stroke or softly pinch. Her deep brown eyes could look fierce or loving, depending on her mood. I still wonder what genes her ancestors carried.

Sometimes Grandma had "the blues." Depression we now call it, but depression to Minnesota children of the 1930s meant being "hard up," short of money. The word was pronounced as if it began with a capital D. When Grandma had the blues she would sit beside the kitchen stove, a vague, faraway look in her eyes. I could rouse her. If I gave her a little push, put my head in her lap, she'd smile, shake her head, get up from her chair and say:

"All right, Biddy, let's get to work." I learned early that work was solace and physical activity an antidote for depression.

When Grandma got dressed to go to a dance or on a trip she looked regal, her eyes flashing as she bustled around, smiling in anticipation. Her green wool outfit with fur on the pockets, bought ready-made in Milwaukee when she went with Grandpa to visit "the girls," my Skelton aunts, was my favorite. My grandparents' bedroom was a cozy, mysterious place. A special treat was being able to sleep with them, cuddled between those two adult bodies. The double bed sat flush against the side and back walls, with room enough for only one person to stand between them. The mirrored bureau with its starched white doily and Grandma's comb and brush, fragile little hair pins, and a few pieces of jewelry, entranced me. I jumped on the bed as Grandma changed from her flannel nightgown to her housedress or housedress to town clothes. Making faces at me in the mirror, her brown eyes sparkling above her sly smile said: "You really shouldn't be jumping on the bed, but it looks like fun." I was the indulged child at Grandma's, "spoiled rotten" my mother would say when I came home. "It takes me a week to get you back in hand."

Next to the bureau was a handy, substantial oak box on short legs. It served as the only chair in the room but the top had hinges that allowed it to open, revealing a round hole in another oak board, the predecessor of children's potty chairs. The front of the box opened out to allow the chamber pot, or slop jar, as Grandma called it, to be slid out for emptying and cleaning. In winter the room had a strange, acrid, not unpleasant odor that I always identified as Grandma's bedroom smell until I was old enough to recognize the smell of sex and urine.

Statuesque and *formidable* describe this grandmother of mine, but they imply a severity I never felt and only saw occasionally. Once, when she was particularly frustrated with Donnie, always slow about doing his chores, I saw her pick up a stick of firewood from the woodpile and threaten him with it. To me she was a tower of strength and delight; to the twins and their siblings she could be a stern, but compassionate, figure.

Grandma read the daily St. Paul paper and the Thursday *Lamberton News*, delivered by the rural mail carrier to the mailbox at the end of the driveway. When she and Grandpa listened to the radio news, I had to be quiet. Later, before the U.S. entered World War II, they kept a map beside the radio with stickpins showing the progress of Hitler's forces through Europe. It was my introduction to foreign affairs. I suspect now that Grandma had Danish relatives who were imperiled but she never mentioned them.

Chris's housekeeper, fast-talking Ida Peterson, was her special friend. Chris and Ida were a strange pair, she as cheerful as he was gruff. Was she Chris's common law wife? I knew they weren't married. Her two fatherless sons helped Chris on his farm. I learned early that people had different living arrangements. This was not a community of nuclear families behind white picket fences and sex was not openly discussed except about breeding animals.

While Chris and Grandpa sat out in the yard and talked, or worked on their threshing machine, Ida and Grandma would have a cup of coffee and a doughnut at the kitchen table and chatter away. An enameled coffee pot sat on the back of every farm house's wood-burning cookstove, ready for any visitor or the men when they came in from chores mid-morning. Grandma enjoyed telling Ida about her visits to Dr. Valentine in Tracy or her New Ulm doctor. I never knew her to be sick, but she kept various body parts preserved in formaldehyde in Mason jars in a corner of the dining room buffet, prized remnants of her and others' operations. She chuckled with delight over my discomfort when she took out the jars to be admired.

More fun was the front room, the parlor. Unlike the dining room's bare wood or the kitchen's dingy, nondescript linoleum, it had a patterned wool rug. My dead grandmother's piano stood in one corner. A Victrola graced the other, its large bell shaped speaker atop and records stored below. "Wind it up," Grandma would say, then help me put the needle ever so gently down on the record.

"Careful now, don't scratch the record or break the needle." Then she'd encourage me to dance. Used only in summer, in winter this room was her refrigerator/freezer, her mouth-watering divinity and fudge kept in tin containers atop the closed phonograph. Aunt Helen and I scooted through that room clutching hot water bottles on the way to our cold bedroom beyond, not daring to raid the candy containers.

Grandpa preferred music and baseball to farming, though he rarely complained. Rooted on his eighty acres, he played the banjo, violin, piano, and drums, and served as caller for square dances. One of my earliest memories is of sleeping among winter coats with fur collars in a room over a dance hall. Music and smoke pervaded that room, but I felt secure and happy snuggled among the coats, my bed until the dance was over. Winter evenings at home Grandpa would stand beside the kerosene heater and play the banjo or fiddle for us. Sometimes he'd do a jig, accompanying himself on "the bones"— dried cow shinbones sawed into four-inch strips. His large, deft fingers clicked them rapidly, encouraging laughter from his audience. On lazy summer days, between cultivating and harvest, after dinner—the noon meal—he taught me to chord on the piano. His stories about his childhood—his cruel homesteading father, his walking miles to have grain ground into flour, how the town moved after a flood—imbued in me a love of history. Warm summer evenings out in the dark yard, he held me between his knees as he squatted among neighbors negotiating over whose crop was ready for threshing, who would help whom on what farm. I didn't realize it then but collaboration and administrative skills were what I was witnessing.

Grandma was a different kind of teacher, explaining what she was doing and why, announcing what we were going to do next. Teaching me management skills, it would be called today. One of her constant worries was that the bank in which she had money would go broke. She had good reason. Among the papers found after her death was a depositor's agreement on a certificate of deposit in her name dated February 4, 1922 for $489.60—the equivalent of about $5000 today— from the Lamberton State Bank. The bank had been closed by order of the Minnesota Superintendent of Banks. Payment on the certificate was extended for two years while the bank was being reorganized. This, of course, was before the Federal Deposit Insurance Corporation. No wonder some afternoons Grandma would say, "Get ready, Biddy, we're going to the bank." She would change into her town clothes, and off we'd drive to neighboring towns.

"Don't put all your eggs in one basket," was her motto. A shrewd businesswoman, she lent money to her husband's children for their various enterprises and spent it on things she wanted—clothes, houseplants, a canary, its birdseed and cage. I learned early that women handling money brought them a measure of independence and respect. After each harvest my sisters and I made a special trip with Mom to pay Grandma off, with interest of course. My children now laughingly refer to doing business with the Bank of Mom.

Travel was my grandparents' respite and reward after a year's hard work and a good harvest. I visited Estherville, Iowa, and Sioux Falls, South Dakota, long before I could place them on a map. Summer Sundays Grandma would pack a picnic lunch, bathing suits and towels, and off we'd drive forty miles west to Lake Shetek. New Ulm, forty miles to the east, was where Grandma bought hops, caps, and bottles to make her beer. She took great pride in her beer and dandelion wine, unconcerned about Prohibition. Winter nights we'd sometimes jump at a loud explosion and then laugh as Grandma grabbed the lamp and ran down the cellar steps to see how many of her bottles had popped and were broken. Mom disapproved, but she and Ann were friends, despite their differences. Neither woman ever talked about women's suffrage although women got the vote only five years before I was born. Mom did mention with admiration the WCTU, the Women's Christian Temperance Union, the organization that brought the country Prohibition. Only years later, when I became interested in feminist history, did I learn the WCTU also organized and funded kindergartens, community libraries, and assisted in the suffrage campaign.

An aerial view of the farm, circa 1960

Preparations for Grandma's occasional Sunday dinners began on Friday. I was taken home then, returning Sunday noon with my parents and siblings. Mom and the other women would arrive with their dishpans carefully covered with a flour-sacking towel to keep flies off their contribution to the meal. A white, highly starched cotton or linen tablecloth covered the everyday worn oilcloth. Grandma carried in her steaming roast duck, goose, or chicken, crying "Out of the way, it's hot." Set in the center of the table, it was surrounded by bowls of mashed potatoes and the brown gravy I hated; string beans, peas, or beets; the inevitable Jell-o salad with tiny marshmallows if the donor could afford it; pickles and relishes; bread, rolls, butter, jellies, and jam. All were homemade or homegrown.

The men were served first, taking their plates and coffee out into the yard to talk about the crops and machinery. After dessert Grandma would bring out her prized Kodak, a rarity among farmers then. After I became an active feminist, looking at a picture of the bevy of women at one Sunday dinner, I realized they were what we feminists called a women's support group. Grandma would never have called herself a feminist, but her marriage was a partnership of equals, and she certainly maintained her independence.

"Time to feed the chickens, Biddy," she would say, grabbing her heavy ragged sweater off a hook by the kitchen door and donning it over her apron. Buttons gone, she pinned the sweater together with a large safety pin. Bundling me up, she'd hustle me out into the yard, laughing as her ducks, geese, chickens, and guineas swarmed around us, eager for food and water. Towering among her flock, she'd pick me up and plant me out of harm's way, saying "Watch out for the geese, they can bite." The warning was unnecessary. The geese were taller than I. With a wide swing, she would toss cracked corn in a circle, laughing as her poultry scrambled for it. After refilling their watering pans, we moved on to the hen house to gather eggs. Reaching under a hen on a nest, she'd pull out a warm, newly-laid egg for me to feel before she put it in her pail. On the way back to the house, she'd admire her guineas, elegant black-and-white speckled creatures, and laugh as her Bantam rooster strutted around among the hens. The guineas and Bantams were her luxury, unusual birds. I don't think we ever ate one.

When she wanted a chicken for dinner she would grab an unwitting rooster by its legs and say: "Out of the way, Biddy. Stand back," as she wrung its neck with a vicious twist, chopped its head off with one swish of the sharp axe kept securely on a bloody stump of wood, and throw the rooster aside. We watched the poor thing dance headless, blood spurting from its neck until it fell over dead. Picking it up by the legs, she shook out any remaining blood and hung it high on the fence, away from the barnyard dog. On her back porch, she dunked the bird in hot water and plucked off its feathers. In the kitchen she dissected the homely, naked thing, savagely pulling out its innards.

"Look, Biddy," she'd say with a smile, displaying the undigested corn and bits of gravel in its gizzard.

She attacked her huge garden with equal relish. Growing popcorn, watermelon, and flowers alongside the staple vegetables reflected her view of the world—mixing the exotic among the mundane. Life shouldn't be dull. As she cooked and baked, I savored the freshly-fried doughnut holes. The smell of freshly ironed cotton or linen still brings her instantly to mind.

Late afternoons I tagged after the twins, Donnie and Darold, as they did their chores. One of their jobs was filling buckets with grain. The granary door was fitted with boards taken out one by one as the level of grain diminished. Once, when the supply was very low, I leaned over the low boards and fell head first onto the cement floor. I remember seeing stars and was carried into the house, unconscious, by the panicked twins. No doctor was called. I revived and survived with cold compresses on my head. Years later, being examined at the university health service, the doctor asked when I had had a concussion and chuckled when I recalled the incident. Grandma's thirty-ninth birthday was a shock to my ego. I usually sat between them in the car's front seat, straddling the shifting lever. This night, coming home from the Hansens', Grandma sat in the middle, snuggled up against Grandpa. I had to sit on the outside, feeling like an outcast. I don't remember where I slept that night.

Much better were her Christmases. The tree was loaded with small white candles in tin holders, and it dazzled on Christmas eve when the candles were lit. My sisters and I sat at a safe distance devouring Grandma's peanut brittle that Mom was sure would spoil our teeth. Surely a pail of water stood handy in case the tree caught fire but I don't remember that. Even small children were taught the dangers of fire.

One winter our house *was* damaged by a kitchen fire, and Grandma kept my sisters and me—then aged 5, 4, and 3—for weeks until the house was repaired. Christmas morning, we were ecstatic. There were toys, a small table and chairs, and a box of crayons and coloring books. Dad never enjoyed Christmas. Painful memories of his mother's death clouded that holiday. Mom always served him oyster stew that night, what his mother had served on Christmas eve.

Ann Aanonsen Hansen Skelton, in her own way, trained her stepdaughters and me to be independent. My aunts resented her at first, but she was loyal and supportive, sending the older girls money when they needed it. She knew her limits. She would have been overwhelmed by teenaged step-daughters. They continued to live with or near Skelton relatives, working for their board and room while they attended school. She welcomed them home for short visits, sometimes longer, "until they could get on their feet again." She accepted life and people as they were, but coddled only small children.

Every fall "Grandma's bum" stopped for a night. After selling her needles and a few other goods from his pack, he had supper with us, sat and chatted through the evening. He slept in the haymow, was given breakfast the next morning and walked off down the road. I thought of him as an old man because of his beard, worn black suit and hat. Years later Grandma received a letter telling of his death in Minneapolis. Apparently she was noted for showing this Jewish merchant special kindness.

I don't know how much of my preschool life I spent with my grandparents. There is no longer anyone alive to ask. I only know they and their house dominate my early memories. Today I can visualize my poor young mother, two weeks shy of twenty years old, stuck alone in that tiny farmhouse with me, a baby she hadn't planned on. She had loved school, graduating at age sixteen. With a year of teacher training, she taught in a one-room country school and spent a summer working in Minneapolis, which she enjoyed immensely. She loved the man she married. He was charming and intelligent, but uneducated. She had to be lonely in a new community over a hundred miles away from the mother she venerated and the sisters she adored. She felt shamed. She had had to get married. Anybody who could count knew that. Shame to her was a terrible thing. She withdrew, coped as best she could. Within four months of my birth she was pregnant again.

I suspect she said to herself that Ann took better care of me than she could. With me gone she could read, sew, and write letters to her mother and sisters. These were the things that gave her pleasure, not me. I wasn't neglected. She willingly shared me with Ann, who never had any children of her own. That's probably why I never bought the cruel stepmother stories of fairy tales—or fairy tales for that matter.

Chapter 3

Mixed Messages

By 1935, when I was ten years old and a schoolgirl, living with my parents and two younger sisters, both the drought and the Great Depression were in full force, but Franklin D. Roosevelt was president, preaching hope. We weren't poor; we were "hard up," Mom said. Poor meant you were never going to make it; hard up meant too few bushels per acre that year and loans from the bank and Ann to carry us through to the next harvest. We were better off than most, renting richer, more productive river bottom land, running the town's mn his spare time. My sisters and I had no worries. We were well fed and clothed, told to behave, and sent outside to play when we were done with our chores. Summer meant freedom, running barefoot in shorts, cooling ourselves by splashing in the cattle drinking tank below the windmill and going swimming evenings with Dad in the Cottonwood River. It rarely rained. On the hottest nights, the thermometer in the 90s, sleeping outside in the yard was an adventure.

We made a game of counting the bums, as we called them, who appeared atop or at the bays of boxcars on the freight trains that passed our house. Dad told us the bums were just people riding the rails west looking for work, following the harvests. When a train held hundreds, we counted only the Negroes or the women. For two summers in a row, the same genial blond University of Pennsylvania football player got off a train and worked at our place during harvest. He said he was lucky, got his room and board and kept in shape doing anything anybody would pay him for, and earned enough for his next year's tuition. Dad bragged about having a college man working for him.

Mom sewed for neighbors. Rarely paid in cash, clients brought her vegetables from their gardens or helped her during canning or butchering season. Barter and recycling were words I learned later, but witnessed early. Mom saved and reused everything. Her sewing scraps became quilts, old clothes became rags or rugs. Good strips of worn cotton or wool clothes were sewn together into large balls. When she had enough cotton balls, we rode along to town to deliver the balls and watch the woman who made rag rugs on a loom for fifty cents apiece. Wool balls became rugs that Mom braided winter evenings.

"Don't let me forget," Mom would say, talking about the woman who made the cotton rugs. "We have to take her a pint of cream or a loaf of bread. She's really hard up." The message about helping the less fortunate was clear. Mom talked as she worked, drumming into our heads messages that would last a lifetime: "Keep busy. Don't waste time. Save the bacon grease. The cloth strips have to be sewn together on the diagonal or the rug won't lie flat. Waste not, want not." Leftover food was fed to the pigs or the yard dog.

I'm still a Depression child. Recycling became ingrained, mandatory. Putting newspapers, cans, paper, cardboard in separate grocery bags ready for city pickup gives me a feeling of pride. When someone throws an aluminum can in the office trash, I cringe and retrieve it if I can. I don't figure on the backs of used envelopes as Dad did, but my grandchildren accept the fact that their coloring paper and Grandma's "scratch paper" has printing on the other side.

We lived on an economic yo-yo. If Dad's cattle deals at the South St. Paul slaughterhouses went well, Mom brought home presents. My adult pleasure in leather gloves was born with the little leather gloves my sisters and I got after one trip. I still feel chagrined at how proudly I showed off those gloves at school. Most of my classmates were children of poorer farmers or townspeople who lived above the family store, with grandparents, on the edge if not *in* real poverty. I did have enough sense not to express my shock when a classmate announced that lard was good lotion for chapped hands. This girl, whom I disliked, lived alone with her mother, her father unknown, and I was supposed to be nice to her, Mom said, because she and her mother had a hard life.

In good times, Mom had hired girls, daughters of neighbors, paid $2 a week plus board and room. We especially liked Carmen who made fudge and caramel popcorn for us when our parents were away. I didn't know it was a treat she never got at home. Nor did I know that in bad times Mom had to decide between buying a white or black spool of thread with her egg money that week. Dad always had a hired man. When new ones ate so much we thought they'd burst, Mom told us quietly never to comment. They didn't get enough to eat at home.

When we moved to the Roth place, the first thing Dad showed us was a stain in the living room ceiling. "Bootleggers," he said, in an awed, amused voice. "They had a still upstairs and it leaked." That gave the house a special aura. It was our connection with the mysterious, lawless world of Dillinger and Al Capone. His prized console radio—the result of a successful deal—sat in the east corner of the living room. During broadcasts of Joe Louis's prizefights and about the Lindbergh baby's kidnapping, Dad invited neighbor men over to listen to our radio, always making sure he had an extra battery handy in case the old one ran low at a crucial moment. (We didn't get electricity until 1943, a result of Roosevelt's Rural Electrification Program.) My sisters and I couldn't avoid these newsworthy events but we much preferred the Shirley Temple or Tarzan movies we saw in town on Saturday afternoons for a dime.

The house on the Roth place had two parts, the old and new. I never learned when each part was built. I now assume the old part was a homesteader's house; the new when some farm family prospered. The old part contained the kitchen, a downstairs bedroom and the "other room," an all purpose/family room. Every year after Christmas the newer part—dining and living rooms with bedrooms upstairs—was closed off until late March to save fuel. Only the hired man slept in the frigid upstairs bedroom. One summer I discovered I could climb up on the roof of the house from the upstairs porch. Hiding between the peaks of the old roof and the new, my feet braced against one peak, my back against the other, I read *The Bobbsey Twins, The Five Little Peppers and How They Grew* or the latest Big-Little Book I'd bought with spending money I earned doing special chores. It was my secret hideout.

Long before I knew about Virginia Woolf, I had a room of my own, albeit open air. (See photo, page 2) I could lie there, read, or simply watch fluffy, white clouds against blue sky. I also could look out over our grove of trees, across the fields, down to the river and beyond. As Emerson would say, I had the long view. I still crave one, selecting houses, offices, and airplane seats from which I can see large segments of sky. On my rooftop I avoided Mom and the jobs she always had ready for me. I'd hear her call "Biddy, Biddy, where are you?" I didn't answer, knowing she'd soon give up. She would think I was out in a field with Dad, down at the river or over at the dump. It wasn't worth her time to find me. Half an hour later I'd sneak downstairs and out the front door, and then nonchalantly wander in the kitchen door.

The dump, next to our farm, was our summer playground. Even during those hard times it was amazing what people threw away—dishes, bottles, pots and pans, stoves, ice boxes, wrecked cars, washing machines, rags, and mounds of ashes from wood stoves. There my sisters and I scavenged items for our playhouse—a space between four trees—or sat in junked cars pretending to drive. With neighbor kids, we played king of the hill on the ash heaps. It was a dangerous make-believe world, smelly but enticing. We were careful about rusty nails because we had been told horrible stories about people with lockjaw. Tetanus shots were a thing of the future.

One evening about dusk I cut my foot badly. Seeing blood gushing out the bottom of my foot, I screamed. Dad came running and jumped over the low barbed wire fence to rescue me. He carried me back to the house where Mom was ready with hot water and Lysol in the enamel washbasin. While my foot soaked she ripped a piece of worn sheeting from her ragbag for a bandage. That injury cramped my style for weeks. Hopping around on one foot, soaking the other for what seemed like hours, I was sup-

The Skeltons: baby Kenneth with (left to right in foreground) Marilyn, Arvonne, and Bonnie.

posed to sit quietly while Mom changed the bandage and made new poultices. These were bits of stale bread soaked in milk, her remedy against infection. I have often wondered if that bread and milk was a precursor of penicillin.

"Don't be such a big calf," Mom would say in her contemptuous voice as I squirmed and winced when she took off the old bandage and applied new poultices. No crying allowed. Her dream had been to be a doctor but her bedside manner left something lacking. It was the wound she loved tending.

The summer before I turned eleven, I joined the family work force, becoming a proud member of our milk route's delivery team. Up at sunrise in the cool mornings, pulling on a cotton shirt and bib overalls, I shivered with anticipation. Riding on the running board of the old black Model T Ford that was our delivery vehicle, I felt grown up, superior to my sisters and schoolmates. The back seat of the Model T had been removed and thrown in the dump to make room for the metal milk crates filled with gleaming bottles of milk and cream. I soon learned the choreography. Jumping off and on the running board of the car as the driver inched down the street, you grabbed full bottles, ran to a porch step, checked the empties for the requisite number of orange tickets, deposited full bottles, picked up the empties and ran back to the slowly moving truck. One misstep and I would be flat on my face in the graveled street. Tripping on a cement porch meant a scraped arm or knee and/or a broken bottle and cut hand.

One poor widow outsmarted me by tearing tickets in half, counting on my youth and haste not to notice. Mom discovered the deception but said the woman was "dirt poor." She waited until the woman wanted to buy another book of tickets and then called on her. A hired man driving the delivery truck wasn't so lucky. Once, when he made an insulting remark, without thinking of the possible consequences, I whacked him on the back of his head with the empty bottle I had in my hand. He complained later to Dad who laughed and told him he probably "had it coming." Then I heard him bragging to his friends about how his girl didn't take backtalk from anybody. Mom scowled and said, "Good girls don't do things like that."

It was a conflict of wills, my mother and me. I was a "tomboy." She wanted "nice girls." She never went to town without changing her housedress for "town" clothes. I refused to wear anything but overalls or shorts and a top at home and when I went to town. I hated housework and preferred milking cows to helping make supper. But her constant stories of her ancestors, of home and her family in Long Prairie, belied the conventions she tried to instill in her daughters. With admiration in her voice she often told us stories about her grandmother DuFrene, an orphan, probably part Indian, she said. I pictured this young Indian girl journeying across more than a thousand miles of wilderness from Quebec to Shakopee, Minnesota. This great-grandmother, we were told, cooked in a lumber camp and decided to marry our great grandfather "because it was easier to cook for one man than for twenty." With delight in her eyes, Mom told us about this grandmother's dancing on the dining room table as she sang French songs to her grandchildren when their parents were away. This contradicted all Mom's stern admonitions about proper behavior. And she seemed proud of our great-grandfather who, upon arriving in New York from a small town outside Paris, spent all his money on patent leather shoes and a Panama hat, the latest in styles of that day. All money gone, he stowed away on a boat up the Erie Canal and onto the Great Lakes, arriving at the lumber camp in Shakopee. So much for Mom's warnings about not wasting money on frivolous things.

And then there was her own family, whom she adored. Thirteen siblings, with number ten named Anna Versary in honor of the DuFrene grandparents' fiftieth wedding anniversary. Hardly conventional. Aunt Merry (pronounced Marie) built her own house. It was sturdy, artistic, and tasteless. Each door of her handmade kitchen cabinets had a different scene painted on it. Somewhere in the background was Uncle What's His Name, totally overshadowed by his energetic, gregarious, red-haired, red-faced wife, who dressed in home-sewn satin and lace dresses whenever we visited. She must have worn overalls when she built the house. Uncle Erle, number fourteen, tailored his own pants, and built a two-story tree house beneath which he fixed cars. Unmarried Aunt Florence had a baby whose fatherhood was a mystery, at least to the child's cousins. Hardly the role models Mom had in mind for us, but no criticism or laughter allowed.

In 1939 we moved upstream along the Cottonwood River to a farm Dad bought. Although he loved farming, it is seasonal and he was restless, always the entrepreneur or dealer. He sold the milk route and built a sales barn at the edge of town. Every Saturday, except in summer, horses, cattle, machinery, even household goods were sold there at auction. Driving out to South Dakota, proud in his tan Western Stetson hat, he bought horses to admire for a week before reselling, and cattle to feed and sell. The auctioneer came for a fried chicken and mashed potatoes dinner at noon on sale days. Mom rushed from kitchen to dining room and back serving food, while Dad sat eating and expounded about politics and the upcoming sale.

An avid Farmer-Laborite, Minnesota's dominant political party then, Dad saw no contradiction between making money and supporting liberal candidates and causes. His excitement about politics infected me early. I was his eager audience. But I hated how hard Mom had to work over those meals, and developed a deep aversion to cooking and serving food for people beyond family. In high school and college when teenagers sought part-time jobs, I didn't even consider working as a waitress.

Summers, Mom had even more mouths to feed. In addition to my sisters and me and our two brothers born in 1931 and '41, three or four cousins—children of working parents—came to stay with us for weeks. This meant extra beds to make and clothes to wash.

"An educated woman, working like a dog," was the sad comment my New York cousin made about my mother years later. My sisters and I thought having cousins around was glorious. After our morning chores we were free, except for doing dishes after meals and tending the littler ones. We swam for hours in the dammed-up river at the bottom of the hill, played ball in the front yard, took Bonnie's Shetland pony and cart out for drives, or got in the car and drove over to Grandma's. Mom was glad to have us out of her way. Grandma gave us lemonade and cookies but she didn't take in groups of grandchildren.

My uncle Darold, then Dad's hired man, taught me to drive the summer I turned twelve. Each day, returning from delivering milk, I begged him to let me drive on the gravel road home. Finally, he relented. Things went fine on the straightaway but our lane—a ramp, only a car width wide—required a sharp turn. I missed it. We charged up the almost 90-degree bank, the car stalled, the engine killed and we rolled, unharmed, back down into the empty road. Darold bent over laughing. Recovering from the shock and mortification, I giggled too. Darold made me back up and try again. I made it on the second try. When Dad heard about the incident he smiled, always proud of my daring and accomplishments. Mom was aghast, but pleased I wasn't hurt.

Soon I was sent on errands, driving lunch to the men in the field or to town for whatever was needed. I ducked my head low whenever I saw the town cop. Dad reported with a sly smile that the cop said he saw this driverless car going down Main Street. The morning of my fifteenth birthday I marched, exultant, into the bank and was issued my driver's license. No driver's test in those days. Soon I was driving trucks and tractors, for Pearl Harbor was bombed in 1941 and all the hired men were off to war. My days of summer leisure were over. I became Dad's hired man. The worst time we had was with soy beans, the newly introduced crop. I was perpetually stopping and starting the tractor as Dad sat on the binder trying patriotically—while swearing a blue streak—to serve the war effort. The new crop wasn't very compatible with older harvesting machines.

Despite World War II, the demands of farming, and helping Mom with her washing and my baby brother, I never missed a day of school. It was my delight from the day Uncle Phillip took me by the hand and escorted me to kindergarten in the spring of 1931. Phillip, Mom's brother, lived with us, attending Lamberton High School while earning his board and room and a little spending money. "One less mouth for Grandma DuFrene to feed," Mom said. My heart pounded as he led me up the school sidewalk, through the heavy oak door that clanged when it closed, and down into the bright basement kindergarten room. The polished wood floors gleamed and the place smelled of Lysol and floor wax. Cleanliness is godliness, we learned in Sunday School.

My kindergarten had as many teachers as students. The Lamberton Consolidated School of which Dad was so proud, included a Normal Training School. Its students conducted a half-day kindergarten six weeks every spring to practice teaching. After one year of Normal these students would have jobs—a precious commodity then—teaching in the one-room country schools still prevalent around the state. Teaching reading was the crucial element of teacher-training, so we were taught to read in kindergarten. I thought it more fun than the sandboxes. Dick and Jane were a different world. They lived in town. The father went to work and the mother stayed home and wore an apron. Spot, the dog, was nothing like our grungy farm dogs.

"Run, Spot, run. See Spot run."

Years later I would be among those challenging the sexism in that reader. But in kindergarten, learning those beautiful black words was as close to ecstasy as I had known in my young life. Running my finger under words on the book page was a sensuous act.

I adored the male teachers who would hoist us up on their shoulders and run around the room singing songs we were learning, or play with us during recess. When Miss Holm, the teacher training director, came to observe, we had to sit quietly. It didn't take me long to notice that only the good readers were called on to read for Miss Holm.

In grade school, nothing pleased Mom more than my bringing home school papers and telling her what I had learned. Rushing in the door, I would proudly hand her my good papers. Turning from sink or stove, she wiped her hands on her apron, sat down for a minute, looked at my papers and complimented me on how well I did. I might be a tomboy and Grandma's girl, but I was as enthralled with school as she had been. Mom never talked about her teaching, only her learning. She sometimes conjugated Latin verbs as she swept or scrubbed floors, proudly declaiming the opening sentence of her Latin book, "All Gaul is divided into three parts" in Latin.

My sisters and I were not being educated to be farmer's wives or country school teachers. Dad was determined that his girls would get a good education, even though he hadn't finished eighth grade. The role models for us were the Skelton girls, Dad's sisters who finished high school despite their mother's death. They then went off to Sioux Falls, Milwaukee, or New York and got jobs, married, and kept working even when they had children. Aunt Bernice, especially, was held in awe. She went to college on the insurance money she received after her young husband was killed in a car accident. College! It was a goal nobody else in the family had ever achieved.

The town's teachers were our other role models. These single women were admired. Married women were not allowed to teach. Our teachers were better educated than the townspeople; they spoke and dressed well, and were earning their own money. They and the school superintendent were highly visible figures, for the school was second only to the bank as the town's preeminent institution. Teachers were outsiders, ripe subjects for gossip. They had to guard their reputations. Town families competed to have them as boarders, a means of distributing the wealth and achieving status. A single woman in her own apartment would have been raw meat for the town's gossips, so they lived as paying guests of town families, revered, respected, and watched.

I no longer remember the name of my first grade teacher, but I learned an unexpected lesson that year, and still resonate with those falsely accused. On a dare by a classmate, I peeked in a boy's lunch box after he had gone out to play. Someone tattled, said I had stolen something, and Mr. Keller, the superintendent, came across the street to our classroom that afternoon. It was a momentous event. He was said to take a strap to students. Without mentioning my name, he gave us a lecture about stealing. I knew I was the accused but I held my ground. I went unpunished, but could tell the teacher didn't believe me. I mentally crossed her off my list.

The two Miss Zielkes who taught second and third grade were a study in contrasts. Lucille was the stereotypical quiet prude with her fine brown hair pulled back into a bun. One day she led me into the cloakroom, the long, dark adjunct to our classroom where unruly children were sent as punishment. Bending down over me, she whispered that I should tell my mother to lengthen my skirts because when I leaned over, my panties showed and that wasn't really very nice, now was it. What saved her reputation for me was that she talked about the 1932 presidential election and held a mock election in class. I supported Roosevelt passionately and wore my campaign button on the school bus because Dad said Roosevelt would lead us out of the Depression. Hoover had run the whole country into the ground and was no friend of the farmers, he said.

Laura Zielke gained the respect of our whole class when one unfortunate wet his pants during a spelling bee. As the puddle grew larger, students gasped, suppressed giggles, and watched in horrified silence. Unperturbed, Miss Zielke opened her bottom desk drawer, drew out a rag, and began mopping up the floor. With her back to the class, she explained that accidents happen and Billy could take his seat now.

During second grade I began wearing glasses. Mom had a cousin whom we sometimes visited in St. Paul whose good friend was an optometrist. He sold Mom glasses for me but it was my sister Bonnie who really needed them—and got them later. I never questioned Cousin Ethel's relationship with the optometrist. She went downtown to lunch with him every day, talked about him all the time. Herman, her husband, didn't seem to mind. This unusual arrangement just was. Hazel, another city cousin, a beautiful, smartly-dressed single working woman, had her own apartment in Minneapolis. Her boy friend came to stay with her every weekend but they couldn't marry. A traveling salesman, we were told. His mother wouldn't let him marry Hazel because he was a Jew and she was a Catholic. I accepted Ethel's friendship with the optometrist as normal and hated that mother who wouldn't let her boy marry Hazel.

My class moved up the broad, varnished stairway that squeaked deliciously to Miss Mickelson's fourth grade. She introduced her motley collection of small town and farm kids to symphonies on a wind-up phonograph and talked about the lives of composers. I resonated more to her interest in history and biography. We all knew life was tough, and winters cold. She made us feel, deep in our bones, what it must have been like for the first Frenchmen to explore the Minnesota River, which our own Cottonwood River flowed into, and how vitally important the help of the Indians was to their survival. It was also during my year in Miss Mickelson's class that Sacajawea, the Indian woman with her baby who led Lewis and Clark up the Missouri and on to the Pacific, became my heroine.

Miss Nienow and our *Weekly Reader* took us to the world beyond our farthest horizons. Emperor Haile Selassie of Ethiopia became my hero with his battle against Mussolini and the Italians. Miss Nienow probably understood that the boys in our class would be fighting Mussolini and Hitler in a few years. A mental health lesson came next with our sixth grade teacher's moods and unrestrained temper. The day she lashed out at a meek, kind-hearted classmate, screaming that she didn't care if his dad was on the school board, he was going to get an F in arithmetic, I was appalled .. You don't demean people in public. But she was our authority figure. The whole class sat frozen before her irrationality. She disappeared in the middle of the next school year. A nervous breakdown, it was whispered. By that time our class was across the street, in junior high, segregated by sex and rocking—or is it reeking—with adolescence.

Gone was the carefree elementary school playground where the boys and girls played kittenball together, climbed the monkey bars—underpants showing, for we always wore dresses—and slid down the fire escape. I gulped my lunch of peanut butter and jelly sandwiches and then rushed to my friend Helen Olson's house. I must have been a bother to her mother, showing up every day. I listened with horror as her beloved teenaged Bobby—a "spoiled brat," my mother called him—kept insulting her, demanding money to buy another balsam wood airplane model. I should have felt sorry for this mother, but I didn't. I couldn't comprehend women who didn't stand up for themselves.

The Olsons' apartment above the store had a big unfinished space at the back where I organized a girls' club. This gave me my first taste of excitement at organizing and presiding over meetings. We accomplished nothing. The meetings were our game. I did appear before the town council a few years later to request more recreation facilities for teenagers. The town dance hall, just off Main Street, was rarely used. I suggested it would make a great roller skating rink. The council members heard me out, but to no avail. That wasn't the last time I had an idea that went nowhere, but I wasn't discouraged.

During the 1930s and 1940s the small town of Lamberton, population 750, was like most small towns, but had a bigger school. Grocery stores, a bakery, and a variety store, which some people called the five and dime, lined the two blocks of Main Street with the bank holding the most prominent corner. Auto and implement dealers were closer to the highway at the edge of town. I knew that town like the back of my hand after delivering milk to most of the houses. I liked the smell of new rubber tires that permeated Homer and Lucille Pacquin's apartment above his tire shop. Mom felt sorry

for Lucille, a quiet, lovely,
dark-haired woman who
had few friends in town.
She was the only Catholic
living above Main Street
and had come from the
Cities. Once I overheard
Lucille tearfully tell-
ing Mom that the priest
complained every Friday
when she went to confes-
sion because she only had
two children. At the time
I didn't think that was her
fault and wondered why
she cried.

The Skeltons, when Arvonne is in high school:
back row, Arvonne and parents; front row, Kenneth, Marilyn, abd Bonnie

Homer's tire store was
two doors away from the pool hall, a dark, mysterious place that
smelled like men and beer when you walked by. Women and children never went in that pool hall. I watched the men come and go,
wiping their mouths on the backs of their hands as they emerged
from that forbidden door. Wilt's ice cream parlor was far more invit-
ing with its gleaming black and white tiled floor and marble soda
fountain. Summer Wednesday and Saturday nights were our nights
on the town. Dad warned us, in a rare stern voice, to stay on Main
Street, never go into the town park after dark. Bright streetlights
and the farm women sitting in the cars parked along Main Street
were girls' protection. When the nine o'clock whistle blew we were
supposed to get in the car and wait for Dad. Nobody locked their
cars—or houses. Crimes happened in cities. The one man in town
who went to jail had impregnated his daughter, but they were poor
and didn't know better—at least that was the impression we girls
were given.

One winter Saturday night when my schoolmate Evelyn
Bittner's grandmother was gone, Evelyn told me about the bottle

of apricot brandy the grandmother kept in her closet. I suggested we find it and have a taste. Evelyn stood by the bedroom door to warn me if she heard her mother coming while I rummaged among the old-lady-smelling clothes and found the bottle in a shoe box. Brandishing it as if I'd found hidden treasure, I unscrewed the top and took a sip. It tasted sweet, but had a bite to it. I urged Evelyn to have a nip, using a term I'd heard men use, but she didn't dare. Her mother was a strict Methodist, but I felt daring, defying mothers and the Methodist minister for whom I had nothing but contempt.

He was a round little stern-faced man in a shiny black suit and tie. Shoulders and head thrown back, belly up front, a frown on his face, he looked like a duck in his swallow-tailed suit, His demeanor said : "Don't defy me, I'm a man of God." I didn't like his meek wife either, but felt sorry for her, married to a man like that. She cried when she taught the Bible class Mom made me attend Saturday afternoons one year. I studied her more than our lessons. Why did she cry over Bible stories? How could she live with that man? When she got sick, the gossip was that she was taken to the Mayo Clinic in Rochester and that she had a brain tumor. Nobody ever saw her in public again. Neighbors reported that she just sat in the pastor's residence in a rocking chair, looking out the window.

How could a man treat a woman like that, I wondered. She was a captive. And he a minister? I had nobody to talk to about how I felt. You didn't question religion, not in a small town, not with Mom. Dad often said he didn't know if there was a God, that churchgoers weren't any better than anyone else, some of them worse. For instance, old Mr. _____ went to church every Sunday but cheated all his customers and Old Lady _____ prayed all the time but used to beat her kids with a stick.

Religion ended for me one Sunday school morning when I was in eighth grade. Our teacher's gray hair was blue Sunday mornings from her Saturday beauty shop visit. The bluing wore off and kept her hair from yellowing before her next visit. The lesson was on brotherhood. In response to a question she said: "I think you can carry this too far. I don't sit down in the streetcar in the Cities if the only seat left is beside a black man." I couldn't wait to tell Dad. He hated hypocrites.

Moving across the street from the 1898 grade school to the newer junior and senior high meant subtle and manifest discrimination, segregation by sex though the word sex was never uttered out loud. Girls had to enter the north door, boys the south. Only the very daring ever used the forbidden door and we exited fast. Assignment to manual training or home ec classes reinforced the message that girls and boys were now different. When a girl mysteriously left school and town we all knew why but never uttered the word pregnant. No sex education in our classes. We learned watching animals.

In seventh grade I announced to my friends that I was going to have five children—all boys. Men had more fun, I decided. Dad drove miles to baseball games many summer evenings and would never take me along.

"You can't go with all those men," Mom decreed. Don't ask stupid questions, her voice said. My feminist education continued with my father's contempt at the way some men treated their wives and children. Old German-immigrant farmers were his special target, possibly a holdover of the anti-German sentiment during World War I, although he was also contemptuous of the discrimination against the town's Austrian baker during that war.

"They keep their girls out of school when they need help at home, and make the boys quit after sixth or eighth grade to do field work. Then they buy those boys a farm and find them a hardworking wife," Dad often said, scorn in his voice. Comments like that always followed his pointing out farmsteads with large, freshly-painted red barns behind small, scruffy-looking houses when we were driving along country roads.

I couldn't understand men who kept children out of school, or kids who hated school. To my sister Marilyn, school was drudgery; to me it was a great adventure. I loved the smell of chalk on blackboards, discovering new worlds, ideas, how things worked. English, history, Latin, physics, something new all the time, transporting me far beyond home and Lamberton. The endless sky outside our schoolroom windows symbolized the broad expanse of knowledge and opportunities that were mine if I got away and searched for them.

I envied Dad's freedom to roam and to think and say what he liked. He came and went as he pleased, and didn't seem to care much what others thought. From him I heard that a California man named Townsend had a plan for old age pensions, and up in North Dakota there was a group called the Non-Partisan League that fought for farmers. Dad believed labor unions were good, fought for decent wages, and that Floyd B. Olson, our Farmer-Labor governor, could be president one day. I assume now that he subscribed to the Farmer-Labor Alliance newspaper or had friends who did. We were all proud when a Lamberton farmer got elected state treasurer on the Farmer-Labor ticket.

I don't know when Dad's serious drinking started but by the time I was in high school the whole family was on edge. During the long, bleak winters, after his morning chores, he took off, ostensibly buying or trading. If he was fairly sober when he came home, he would sit at the kitchen table and talk about what he'd seen or bought in South Dakota or at the Walnut Grove sale barn. Mom bustled around the kitchen, filled and refilled his coffee cup, started a meal.

The evenings he didn't come home for supper seemed endless. Each afternoon on the school bus I began to worry. Would his truck be in the yard? Would he be out in the yard, out in the barn working, or in bed? What would Mom be like, look like? We lived in awful silence and suspense. Fewer visitors dropped by; there were no more Sunday dinners.

We lived a pretense. If his truck wasn't in the driveway when we arrived home from school, Mom might say he'd gone to a sale in South Dakota. We could relax, have a free evening. If nothing was said by the time we'd finished reading the paper and doing our nightly chores, the tension would rise, everybody waiting, pretending not to. Mom would slow supper preparations, forget to ask whose week it was to set the table, and then finally call from the kitchen, "time to eat."

After a quiet supper and the dishes done, my sisters and I would wander into the dining room to study. I sat at the dining room table so I could see the road, watch car lights appear at the crest of the other hill, waiting anxiously to see if the car turned into our lane. Mom sat quietly sewing or knitting, her eyes averted or her back to us. About eight o'clock I put my little brother Grant to bed and read him a story. Later, in the quiet of my room I listened for cars on the road. I could tell by their speed if one might turn in our drive, and would breathe a quiet sigh of relief when car lights shown in my window. He was home. He might be drunk but he was safe. I could sleep.

One morning the awful silence was shattered. I woke up to loud voices downstairs. Usually they were quiet, supposedly keeping their secret from us. Tempted to cover my head with a pillow, I also wanted to know what was going on. I could tell Mom was, as she would say, "beside herself."

"Where is that check?" she demanded. "Don't tell me you lost it? You couldn't have drunk it up. You and your drinking....You're going to send this place and this family to wrack and ruin....Where did you have it last? Look in all your pockets." I could hear her pacing, from bedroom to kitchen, through the hall to the dining room, round and round in her anger. She seemed unconcerned about our hearing them. Perhaps she was making sure we could.

Finally Dad's deep, slow voice: "It's right here someplace. I know I had it...twelve hundred dollars and something...good money." He was trying to placate her.

"You better find it. I don't want to be the one to go in to the bank and say you were drunk and lost it." Her voice changed with her words.

"What are we going to do? When are you going to quit staying out all night, getting soused after a sale. You should know better. We have all these kids and you can't come home with a check we need desperately. What were you thinking of? Or have you quit thinking?"

On and on she went, the floodgates opened, all her reserves gone. Finally I could tell she was crying. From the sounds I knew she was in the dining room, now sitting on a chair because her voice didn't move around. I imagined her thinking "What on earth are we going to do? Why can't he stop drinking?"

Finally I heard him come out of the bedroom and say disgustedly: "Here it is. It was in my pocket. Now are you satisfied?" Soon the kitchen door slammed and I knew he'd gone out to the barn. I assumed to tend his livestock. I didn't know then he kept bottles out there. My children told me that years later, marveling at how many bottles they found. As soon as they were old enough to understand I told them about his drinking.

I heard Mom get off her chair and go out to the kitchen. It was safe to get up. I banged a dresser drawer to signal to my sisters that I was up and getting dressed. I clomped down the stairs for breakfast. Mom was busy setting the table, making our school lunches, her back to me.

"Can you get Grant up and dressed?" she asked, trying to make her voice sound normal. Pulling a handkerchief out of her apron pocket and blowing her nose, she said her sinuses were bothering her. I knew better. Relieved that I didn't have to stay in the kitchen, I went off to change Grant's diaper, get him ready for the day. I took my time. I wanted to get out of the house without talking to Mom and not face my sisters before we all ran down the lane for the school bus. I played with Grant, fed him breakfast in the dining room, then grabbed my lunch and books and ran out the door.

When I was a junior in high school, Mom called my sisters and me down to the kitchen after we'd gone to bed to announce she was leaving. He'd been drunk for days, she said, and was now in bed. The bedroom was always his retreat. We never saw him stone drunk. She was taking the bus to the Cities the next morning. She'd get Ann to keep Grant. She didn't know when she'd be back. She sat slumped over the kitchen table, crying. I felt the bottom falling out of my world.

She came back three days later with a new dress and hat and a bad case of eczema on her arms. The pattern kept repeating itself. For weeks he would be fine, at least not visibly drunk. Then he'd be gone or in bed or home but out of the house. Somehow he still made enough money to satisfy the bank and Mom. The war was on. Farm prices were up. When there was work to do he stayed sober.

Even now, I can't stand waiting, and expect the worst when someone is very late. They've had a car accident, are hurt, or dead. I alternate between anger, fear, and despair. I pace the floor, preparing myself for the worst and for how I will cope. I had to learn to depend on myself. No wonder Mom had urged me to take typing and shorthand so I could be sure I could support myself. She was explaining her own life.

Ruthless was a descriptor someone used for me during my 1977 government security check. I checked the word in a dictionary: "no compassion or pity, merciless." Maybe. I learned to steel myself, to escape when confronted with disasters I could do nothing about. I adored my father, and the feeling was mutual, but now he was two people. One was the drunk. The other a man who doted on his children, was fascinated by people and politics, could make anything grow, loved horses and making deals. I lived suspended, waiting for him, and increasingly, waiting to leave. My parents had nurtured and supported me as best they could and would go on doing it, but even before I left home, I knew I was on my own.

Arvonne's high school graduation picture

Chapter 4

New Pastures

Sliding eagerly into the driver's seat of our black Ford the morning after high school graduation, I was ready for the real world, "the Cities," Minneapolis and St. Paul. Goodbye farm. I'm off to sidewalks, streetlights, a life on my own while my male counterparts went off to war. I was not valedictorian of the 1943 class of Lamberton High School, but who cared? I earned good grades and edited the school newspaper. My new suitcase was on the back seat, Mom in the front. She was eager to deposit me in my rooming house and visit her city cousins. Dad and my siblings stood beside the car. My family doesn't kiss or hug. We congregate, stand quietly and smile. With one last grin at them, I flipped down the sun visor, waved and started down the lane, shifting smoothly from low to second to high gear. I could feel Dad watching. He told everyone I could double clutch a truck as good as any man.

Monday morning I'd be at the trade school my parents had enrolled me in, living in a Women's Christian Association dormitory in downtown Minneapolis. With a war on, the trade school salesman had assured my parents there would be plenty of jobs waiting for me. I had money and check blanks in my purse, along with Mom's list of city relatives I must call and visit, especially "if you get into trouble." That meant losing my purse, getting lost, running out of money. Getting pregnant wasn't my worry. I dated little in high school, was contemptuous—a defense mechanism?—of classmates who went steady. Seventeen years old, I raced sixty miles an hour to my future with the sun glistening on the morning dew across the thousands of acres of oats, soybeans, and corn flanking Highway 14.

Three hours later, we entered Dunwoody Hall's spacious lobby with its worn Oriental carpet and massive, polished oak front desk. A brownstone mansion, it now housed country girls like me making their way in the city. Its wide, imposing staircase connoted fancy balls and elegant manners. Suddenly I was no longer the grinning, super-confident graduate ready to take on the world. This wasn't like the 4H dormitories on the State Fair grounds where everybody felt lost and laughed about it. This place told me I was the farm girl new in town.

An attendant showed us my third-floor room, Mom chattering away as she did when she was nervous. Why couldn't she keep quiet as she did in the car? I could figure things out by myself. I wasn't a baby. *Just leave me alone, get me to my room where I can look out the window, see where I am and decide what to do next*, I said to myself. Upstairs it looked more like a dormitory: worn dark green linoleum on the long hallways, rows of doors, muffled voices and radios playing, printed notices in black frames outside the bathroom door. Women's smells, cheap perfume, soap, and talcum powder. The attendant knocked at a door, listened, then rattled a long key in the lock and ushered us in to a small room. Twin beds, cots really, two small dressers, a small table for a desk, and one chair for two people? White curtains covered the window that overlooked an alley, its cheap tan shade pulled half-way down.

Questions raced through my mind. Where would I put my books? When would I meet my roommate and what she would be like? How much time would I need to get to Brown Institute on Monday morning? It was within walking distance, on 12th and 3rd Avenue, not too far from here, but where exactly? My new alarm clock would have to go under the bed. There was no bedside table.

"Lunch is being served in the dining room," our guide said, glancing at her watch as she handed me my room key. "Always leave your key at the desk whenever you go out." Turning to my mother, she said, "You're welcome to stay for lunch too. Guest tickets are available downstairs at the desk, a dollar each."

"My relatives are expecting me so I'll just run along," Mom said. She was as eager to leave as I was to have her go. Her independent daughter could cope as she had done during her summer in Minneapolis, twenty years earlier. How many times had I heard her, while scrubbing a floor or cooking a meal, extol my sisters and me with stories of that wonderful summer, her summer of freedom the year she turned 18? Now she could hardly wait to spend the weekend with her favorite cousin, Mildred Paquin. With her usual, "be a good girl," she was off.

In the almost empty dining room, I gulped down a bowl of watery soup, a soggy egg salad sandwich on spongy white bread, and a glass of milk. Anxiously, I kept checking my pocket to make sure I still had my room key. I had to remember to leave it at the desk. I had to remember my room number when I picked it up. Slyly I perused the room. My meal over, my dishes bussed—I had read the sign—I turned in my key and walked out the front door hoping I looked more competent and resolute than I felt.

There was Dayton's, two blocks to my right, the department store Mom led me through every time we came to Minneapolis. I could orient myself between it and the Foshay Tower with its thirty-nine stories stretching to the sky. It could be seen from anywhere. I would find my way around. I remembered numbered streets ran one way, avenues another. I had to remember Dunwoody Hall was at 10th Street and LaSalle, three blocks west of the Foshay Tower. I started walking, determined to orient myself. Passing a drugstore, I bought a candy bar, always my solace. Savoring the sweet chocolate, I studied my fellow pedestrians. Tall, short, fat, thin, some looked rich, others poor, some happy, others not. I walked around blocks in an ever-widening square, turning right at each corner until I'd memorized that block, then across the street and right again at the next corner. My mental map began to take shape . Soon I found Brown Institute, my trade school, and breathed a sign of relief. I knew where I had to be Monday morning at nine o'clock. Mom had said my cousin, Phyllis Padrta, was also at that school and could show me around.

The next Friday evening a homesick girl stepped off the Greyhound bus in Lamberton. "I knew you'd come home," Dad said. "How was it?" His small smile said he was glad to see me. He had worried about me. And he was sober. Nervous and slightly ashamed for coming home so soon, I couldn't stop talking.

"Well, I'm learning Morse code. Dit, dit, daaah, dit. That's f, one dit is an e, and they put me in the advanced typing class. In ten weeks they told us we'd all have jobs at some airbase. Phyllis and I walk together to school in the mornings and my roommate, Dorothy Pofahl, is lots of fun. It gets real hot in our room sometimes but we keep the window wide open all night. The food's not bad and I've met some of the other girls. One night this week some of us are going to take the streetcar out to Lake Calhoun to swim." I couldn't stop talking, relieved at being back on familiar ground. My sisters hung on my every word and looked at me with awe.

In seventeen different ways that weekend I said it was all wonderful, never admitting I had walked the two blocks to the public library one evening intending to apply for a library card and didn't have the courage to approach the severe-looking librarian at the front desk. Seeing my sisters' eyes glisten as I described the Hennepin Avenue movie theatres, I didn't tell them I hadn't seen the inside of one yet. My parents probably suspected my non-stop talk was covering up my loneliness, but in our family emotions were private, not discussed, to be hidden. You did what you had to, suffered in silence and didn't complain.

By Sunday morning I was talked out. Home was old hat. I itched to get back on the Greyhound bus with a package of Mom's cinnamon rolls and cookies to share with my roommate. I had another new dress Mom had made me in my suitcase and more of my books. I would go to the library, get that card. One evening Dorothy and I could go to a movie. Trade school was easy, no homework. We were through at four each day. Dorothy knew about an agency that got you babysitting jobs. You took a taxi to and from the job and they paid you for that too. I would earn extra spending money. I would write letters to Uncle Darold, now in the Navy. I was refreshed, ready for the wider world again.

Restless and disloyal as late teenagers are, Dorothy and I moved over into Pillsbury Hall on Second Avenue the next month, another glorified rooming house in an old mansion. Spending our babysitting earnings on movies, Cokes, and popcorn, the weeks passed quickly. I was good at Morse code, found the office procedures class easy and increased my typing speed to eighty words a minute. The faculty dangled the Civil Service test before us daily, implying it was our ticket to exotic air bases where women were needed to replace military clerks.

"Congratulations. You passed with high scores and there are openings at the Cleveland air force base," Mr. Evenson, a slight man we all knew was 4-F—not fit for military service—told me the day our test scores were announced. I walked around the rest of the week picturing myself sitting in a control tower with a blue Ohio sky around me, guiding airplanes through their take offs and landings, handsome Air Force pilots and navigators in their dashing uniforms coming in to ask me out on a date just like in the war movies I had seen.

49

Two days later it was: "I'm sorry, Miss Skelton, but we just learned they don't take anyone under eighteen years of age. That's really too bad. You did so well on the test." Without a pause he added, "But they do need people in the Northwest Airlines plant at the St. Paul airport."

Why didn't they tell me I was too young before I took the test? They should have known. Mom and Dad had spent good money to send me to that school. Were they taken in by a smooth-talking salesman? I remembered the afternoon I had gotten off the school bus to find a strange man in our living room. My parents proudly announced they had signed me up for this trade school. I never told them that earlier I had sent off to Vassar College for a catalog. Even before that catalog arrived I knew aspirations like that were a fanciful dream.

Swallowing my disappointment, I listened carefully as Mr. Evenson told me what streetcar and bus to take to get to the Northwest Airlines plant and who to see about the job. I was not too young to work the swing shift, three to eleven p.m., in a huge hangar across the Mississippi from downtown St. Paul. I didn't need Morse code or even typing skills. World War II was in full force. I would be helping the war effort, he said.

The next afternoon I was installed in a small, unpainted wooden cubicle beside the plant's time card machine. As shipping and receiving clerk in this huge airline hangar converted to a war plant, my job was to record incoming shipments of parts and supplies with an electrified pencil on a screen, a new invention. Where my data went I didn't know. Mouths were shut in wartime. Signs posted around the hangar implored you not to talk about your work or what your plant was making. I never asked what those older men and women were doing. I could see they were working with metal parts at benches. I didn't go beyond my proscribed perimeter, ate my bag supper at my desk, and took the bus back to downtown St. Paul. There I transferred to the midnight streetcar, opened my novel and rode the ten miles back to Minneapolis. I walked the two blocks of deserted streets to my dormitory unafraid. I had a job, was decently paid. I was on my way—but to where?

I was the only office worker in the place. The other workers, all machinists, talked about their lives, not their work, as they greeted me each morning and punched the time clock. The women were Rosie the Riveter types in their gray coveralls, their husbands overseas or working in another war plant. Once they invited me to a supper hour birthday party, white cake with frosting squeezed out of their sugar rations. At least a decade older than I, they had their own worries and families to care for. Everybody was on hold, working furiously, waiting for the war to end.

One friendly deliveryman, a short, jolly, dark haired fellow, turned out to be too friendly. The term sexual harassment hadn't been invented yet but I, like most women, encountered it. We were silent about it for decades until Anita Hill went public with her experience in 1991. This man leaned over my back one afternoon as I was sitting at my desk and grabbed my right breast, squeezed it and, murmuring, rubbed his grizzled beard against my cheek. I was aghast, felt violated, but had sense enough to give his fat belly a hard punch with my left elbow and what Mom would call a dirty look. Neither he nor anyone else bothered me again.

Once a week I took the section's time cards to an office across the airfield and brought paychecks back. One week the time clock beside my desk—a glorified name for my plywood table—didn't register times correctly. The workers complained, showed me the problem, so I simply wrote the correct times over the printed numbers, thinking nothing more about it, and delivered the time cards as usual. The next week an imposing group of men in suits and ties, accompanied by the frightened-looking female payroll clerk I delivered the cards to, appeared at my cubicle with grim looks on their faces. The whole plant grew quiet, watching as two burly managers crowded into my tiny space, their underlings hovering outside. One man showed me the altered time cards, holding them as if they were dead rats, and asked, in a commanding voice who had made the alterations.

"I did. The machine was stamping the times all wrong. We called but nobody came to fix it so I marked in the right times," I answered, thinking any idiot could see those stamped times couldn't be right. My adversaries looked at each other, then at the machine on the wall. The men took turns picking time cards out of a slot, studying them, then putting them back. They looked crestfallen. Had they expected to uncover a conspiracy, perhaps browbeat me into finking on a whole hangar cheating on its hours? Silly waste of time, I thought. It was my first lesson in mindless bureaucracy, but far from my last. After this incident, the older workers quit treating me like the new kid at the plant.

I enjoyed the unusual hours, three to eleven, at first. It felt almost like a paid vacation. I slept late, enjoyed my coffee in the quiet dormitory living room as I read the newspapers. I roamed the public library, went to museums, explored the two cities. I didn't have time or need to babysit strange children for spending money. The fact that I couldn't talk about my job impressed my roommate and others. But after a few weeks I was bored, the days long and lonely. I am not a shopper. In wartime there was little to buy or even look at. I began taking the Como line, the long way to work, stopping for lunch at my Uncle Phillip's house. The big brother I never had, for he lived with our family a year or two, he bragged to me about his work.

Norma, his wife at home with a baby, was also lonely. She enjoyed having someone to talk to the days Phillip didn't come home for lunch. One weekend she introduced me to her sisters, Verna and Evelyn, from Velva, North Dakota. They lived with their mother in a house near the University campus. Mrs. Gilbertson, their energetic mother, was taking advantage of the housing shortage and ran a rooming house. Knowing her mother could use an extra bit of rent money and I more company, Norma suggested I move in with them. I was assigned the top bunk in what had been the living room. Verna had the lower one; Evelyn and her mother shared the downstairs bedroom. The dining room and kitchen were the family rooms; the upstairs was sublet. I felt honored at being accepted as housemate by women who had known Eric Severaid, the admired national radio newsman, who also came from Velva. Evelyn, a nurse, entertained me with hospital stories and made sly comments about her friend, an unhappily married man. All of them read voraciously and attended university events. It was the first female-only, intellectually oriented household I had encountered. I liked the taste of the occasional rum and coke offered by Norma or her sisters after dinner and began reading the more serious literature they recommended. Their forays on the university campus intrigued me, opening up a world nobody else had told me about. I knew about the University Experiment Station near our farm but had never ventured onto the campus I now lived near.

One day I read a University of Minnesota ad in the classifieds section of the newspaper. It promised good jobs immediately after graduation. The war had decimated its student body which I now assume was the reason for the ad. Tuition was only $25 a quarter, with part-time jobs available to help pay for board and room, the ad said. With Norma's encouragement, I enrolled spring quarter, nine months after graduating from high school. With my swing shift job, I took morning classes. Elated to find that my high school record and the required English exam put me in advanced composition, I also signed up for Spanish 1, to meet the foreign language requirement, and a sociology course.

In my weekly letter home, I announced what I had done. Mom wrote back that Dad bragged to all his friends about my being at the University. I pictured him at the implement dealer's or in a bar carrying on about it. His delight in me was always expressed second-hand. In my hearing, he laughingly told others about my spreading machine grease on the car seats, messing up the water pump, or avoiding the town cop. Mom's letter also said I should write checks for my tuition and books. I had written checks for years on my parents' account for groceries, machinery parts, gas, whatever they told me to buy. I never signed a signature card. Small town banks knew their customers. The check blanks I was given when I left home were "just in case." Now I had permission to write them for what I wanted.

I had no goal or vocation in mind. I knew what I didn't want to be: a teacher or a nurse. School to me was for learning, not for

grades or a vocation. The university course book had far more interesting courses than I would ever be able to take. The war meant
you didn't have to look for a job. Someday I would graduate and
then I could think about what I wanted to do. There was little room
to study at the Gilbertson's so I soon rented a room in St. Paul near
Norma and Phillip's and the inter-campus streetcar line. The Northwest Airlines job lost its appeal so Phillip found me a late afternoon
job at a nearby foundry that two friends of his managed. Evenings I
baby-sat for faculty families that lived nearby. After the cherubs were
in bed, I studied.

My first day at the foundry I stood open-mouthed, fixated on
the huge cauldron hanging at the far end of the monstrous room
with molten metal bubbling in it. The dangerous red hot soup boiled
above white-hot coals in a mammoth hearth. At the other end of the
room, men and a sprinkling of women worked at machines making forms into which the molten metal was later poured. Big men,
wearing heavy leather aprons and hats with Plexiglass face masks,
lined the forms up slightly to the front and below the cauldron. The
whole place turned deathly quiet during the late afternoon pouring.
One false move by the men, using spearhooks to guide the cauldron,
might burn them alive. If there is a hell, I thought, working near that
hearth must be what it's like.

My job was to collect production cards from each machinist
late afternoons, take them to the office and record the information.
With legs like jelly the first day, I edged around the cavernous room,
giving the hearth a wide berth. Each machinist welcomed me, the
new girl, with a smile and a nod and handed me their cards. Two
thirds of the way around the circle of machines, a craggy-looking,
unshaven blond man in greasy denim shirt and jeans paid no attention to me. When I spoke to him he didn't answer. I yelled louder
over the machinery clatter. Finally he turned and made wild motions with his fingers, stared menacingly and shook his head as if he
didn't understand who I was or why I was interrupting his work.
Fearful, I pointed to the cards in his breast pocket and with a nod
of comprehension, he handed them to me. The odor of sweat and

steel filings in my nostrils, I walked the oily path to the next man, an equally fierce-looking character. They scrape the bottom of the barrel for workers in wartime, I thought to myself.

"I'm the new production clerk. I need your cards," I yelled over the racket. He also ignored me. Waiting a few seconds, I repeated my request in an even louder voice. Still no response, but the machines were quieter. Worried now, I stepped forward and gingerly touched his arm. He turned abruptly and gestured madly, pointing to his mouth and ears. His crooked mouth moved, as he slapped his chest, then pointed to his machine as if to say: "Can't you see I'm busy, quit bothering me." I stood transfixed. No audible words emerged from his slowly moving mouth. His fingers kept moving in strange patterns.

My face must have expressed my consternation. The man broke into a big grin, pulled his cards out of his leather apron pocket and with an exaggerated bow handed them to me. The machine clatter had stopped. Everyone was watching. The workers broke into laughter and started clapping. I blushed, hung my head and moved to the next man.

"You were set up," he explained with a grin. "They're deaf mutes—both of them. Good workers, nice guys, but they can't hear or say a thing. They were in on it. We all need a good laugh once in awhile." I smiled sheepishly, thanked him and moved on, relieved that I had survived my initiation. I had never seen sign language used before.

Each day I toted up production data beside a co-worker who collected cards from the sand core makers. I substituted for her occasionally and found those complex, intricate sand structures intriguing. They were true works of art. I wasted one worker's time questioning him about the whole process. My co-worker found it boring. We worked alongside a pretty blonde receptionist-secretary-bookkeeper who never ventured near the production floor. Sometime that summer my co-worker saw all our bi-weekly paychecks, and discovered that the secretary was paid ten cents an hour more than we were.

"It's not fair," she complained, pounding the ladies room sink with her fist and almost in tears when she told me what she had learned.

"We work out on the floor with all those guys...get dirty, smell like the foundry when we're done, could get hurt..." Her voice trailed off. She was neither good looking, nor slim like the secretary—and neither was I. That ten cents an hour pay differential galled us. One Friday afternoon just before quitting time, knowing we wouldn't have to face anyone in the plant until Monday, we gritted our teeth and, with uneasy smiles, marched into the manager's office and confronted him. Neither of us knew anything then about equal pay laws or the term sex discrimination, but we felt wronged. We got our ten cents an hour. The managers wanted no trouble. We emerged from the building feeling victorious, as daring and accomplished as those burly men on the pouring floor. I learned later the company kept two sets of books, one for the government, one for the owners. Not everybody was a patriot. Some years later my uncle's friends went to jail. The double set of books was discovered.

World War II raged in Europe, North Africa, and the South Pacific. I read the papers, followed the war, but it affected me most in that there were few datable men around. I was enraptured by the university, and especially Mr. Monachesi's sociology course. This tall, suave, erudite man in immaculate grey suit, his thin hands gesturing as he lectured, shared his knowledge as if he were conveying a blessing on us. He rarely smiled but his intense interest in his subject confirmed my view that learning was an end in itself. I read every word of the text, sat in rapt attention, and was rewarded with my first college A.

Among eight thousand students—primarily women—I talked to few, made close friends with none. Happy in class, awed by most of my professors, I was almost ecstatic as I perused the shelves of Wilson library. Over lunch in glossy, new Coffman Union, I read my assignments, then took the inter-campus trolley to work, and walked back to my room. Supper was often an apple and a candy bar eaten while studying.

English 5—an advanced composition course—compensated for my bare social life. My high school newspaper column, published in the weekly *Lamberton News*, had given me great satisfaction. Collecting thoughts on paper, which I thought of as talking to potential readers, was much easier than speaking in class or to other students. I was overeating, gaining weight. Too many Baby Ruth candy bars, deluxe size. When baby sitting I stole—there's no other word for it—food from the family's refrigerator. Norma hid her mouth-watering brownies but I found them when sitting my little cousins. Mornings I walked the ten blocks to city limits—saving a dime—to catch the inter-campus streetcar, had a cup of coffee and a roll or two in Dinkytown. At lunch I sometimes splurged on pie while reading *The Daily,* the student newspaper.

On some gray mornings during fall quarter 1944 I found myself in tears, walking down the dark streets at seven a.m., books under my arm. I didn't know what was wrong. I just felt sad, directionless. I hated getting fatter and fatter. And I had a new responsibility-my sister Bonnie. She had followed my lead, enrolled at the University, and was bereft. She'd found a dull job at Montgomery Ward in St. Paul and roomed with a Lamberton woman she didn't much like. Housing and money were both short. I couldn't tell Bonnie my troubles. She had her own. The university and the Cities were too big for her. When we met at the Union for breakfast I could see she was sad and scared. I had to cheer her up, keep her going, while keeping a stiff upper lip, as Mom would say, about my own troubles.

By the time I got to the streetcar stop my tears dried up. I couldn't cry publicly. I had talked myself into facing the day. I didn't know then that physical activity, putting one foot in front of the other over and over again, was a way to work out of depression. Twenty-five years down the road, a psychiatrist would tell me that. I also didn't know how strong the attachment between Bonnie and me would become, that she would be my support as much as I hers over the next sixty years. Being our mother's daughters, we coped, kept our troubles to ourselves. Skelton girls were expected to do something with themselves. No moping allowed. After all, tThere was a war on, men were getting killed, as Grandpa always reminded us if we dared complain.

We were privileged, attending one of the premier institutions in the country. Many of its faculty had national reputations. Numerous faculty members moved on to Berkeley, Columbia, Harvard, or Yale. They didn't impress Bonnie. She left for Mankato Teachers College and I was alone again. Beneath my excitement over my classes the nagging question was: where do I fit in? When am I going to graduate, get married, have children, and settle down? I didn't worry about finding a job. World War II meant jobs found you. By winter quarter, I discovered you didn't have to take required courses sequentially. I indulged myself in electives. Political Science 1: Government and Politics with Evron Kirkpatrick and Humanities in the Modern World with Alburey Castell were my favorites. I was on familiar, exciting territory in the political science course. I had heard Dad discuss politics all my life. Professor Evron Kirkpatrick, his blond hair, shiny face and glasses glistening as he stood on the lecture platform, made government the noble thing Thomas Jefferson, Thomas Paine, Benjamin Franklin, and my father thought it should be. After many lectures, our row exploded with political talk as Ben, an impassioned black student raised his voice and arms, his face animated, and railed about whatever moved him that day. I was enthralled. As the energy wound down and students moved out into the hall, I reluctantly gathered up my notes and books, wishing I had Ben's courage and ability to speak in public.

Alburey Castell, the philosophy professor who designed a new humanities course, exuded intellectual excitement. His ability to convey complex ideas in simple language awed me. He started us with Voltaire's *Candide,* then on to Rousseau, Tom Paine, Goethe, and Wordsworth, ending the year with Tolstoy's *War and Peace.* We were urged to question and critique. He gave us sections of Adam Smith, Karl Marx, and Walter Lippman as examples of social critics. Philosophy, he taught us, was "to explore…to disclose or lay bare the ultimate presuppositions upon which men (sic) of sincerity are trying to act." Students were challenged—no, required—to think. To some, that was subversive activity. Years later, when I asked Don's secretary why she didn't go to the university as did her brothers, she responded that her mother, an evangelical Christian, thought the university "a bed of Reds." Too dangerous for girls, apparently.

Maybe that mother was right; the University wasn't all about learning. Spring quarter, 1945, the campus began being invaded by returning veterans, their tuition, living costs, and books paid by the GI Bill. In my Dior-inspired long green checked dress, made by Mom, I swished around the campus, across the mall, as intent on getting a man as a degree. Good girl that I was, getting a man meant marriage. I had dated a few men, but never seriously.

Bill Aguirre was movie-star gorgeous but had a slight limp, making him unfit for military service. We worked together at Northwest Airlines. A gentle, intelligent workman, we had long discussions about the differences between his life as a Mexican-American and mine. He expected when the GIs came home his job prospects would lessen, but somehow he'd always find work, marry some girl from his neighborhood, have children and live out his days in St. Paul's old Mexican neighborhood. When my liberal DFL friends later decided to put a freeway smack through his neighborhood, decimating it, I worried about him and his community but did nothing. We drifted apart but I kept his picture for years.

A blind date led me to a marriage I knew was wrong. Like others, I got caught up in the postwar marry-and-settle down fever. He was a veteran, six years older than I, working on his Ph.D. in chemistry, and a friend of Verna Gilbertson's and her new-veteran husband. And I was hungry for sex and a social life. Through them I met his friends, Russ and Dorothy Frazier. Dorothy was secretary to a politically active labor leader and the whole group was interested in politics. From her job Dorothy had inside information I didn't get reading *The Daily*, although it was full of information about the new Democratic-Farmer-Labor Party. The two old parties had merged and the campus was alive with political activity that I followed but didn't know how to engage in. My new social group discussed ideas. I was tired of being alone and smitten with the group.

Within a few months my blind date proposed. I accepted. He sent me to Planned Parenthood, a diaphragm my engagement ring. I never considered a wedding at home. The bridal shower Mom held for me was traumatic enough. I felt fraudulent, accepting all the pots, pans, Red Wing pottery dishes and silverware. I took my future husband home one weekend that summer and escaped back to the Cities as fast as I could.

A judge in City Hall married us in early September, 1946. I was 21, an adult. We went to classes, studied, went to bed. On the GI Bill, we saved money, two thousand dollars in three years. It wasn't all bad, especially at first. The small apartment atop a bungalow with long, high windows was cozy. Our little living room was lined with book shelves, his and hers. His mother came weekly to clean the apartment, do our laundry. Saturday nights we went to movies or to our friends' houses for drinks and conversation after dinner. The University was our focus, books our haven. I knew nothing about chemistry, his field, and cared less. His interest in politics was peripheral, I soon discovered.

Some days I cut classes, wandered home slowly, went to the library. Graduation seemed eons away. I passed time, waiting, but for what? The GI Bill money more than covered our expenses. I worked in offices summers, assumed I would find a job after graduation and work until he finished his Ph.D. We would live where he found a job, then start a family. But that was three years away. I coasted along.

"Get your ass off my chair. Don't touch my desk," was the first confirmation of my uneasy feeling about this marriage. He supported my efforts to get a degree but had little interest in my classes or studies. I made my own study space, buying a second-hand chair like the ones we had in classes, with a wooden reading and writing arm and storage space for books underneath.

"You looked like a whore, leaning against the lockers, smoking," was another shocking comment he greeted me with one day after classes. I had started smoking to lose weight before I met him. I quit meeting him after classes, went to the library or home early and enjoyed studying in splendid solitude. Within a year I began dreading his return home. In public everything looked fine. We studied, lived separate intellectual lives. Occasionally he would talk about his childhood, his absent father and his Army life, which he had hated. I listened but was preoccupied with my own dilemma. After a year of married life I knew I had made a horrible mistake and began contemplating divorce, but told no one. I had had practice at silence and pretense in family matters.

I immersed myself in my classes. I had switched from Spanish to French as a foreign language and again found my two years of high school Latin useful. The emphasis was on reading the language, not conversation. I became enthralled reading the journals of the eighteenth-century French explorer LaSalle at Wilson Library, mentally following him down the Mississippi, and, not incidentally, passing the time. My American Studies seminar was another respite from my domestic troubles. Being one of only six students studying with Henry Nash Smith, a challenging, distinguished professor who soon went on to Berkeley, gave me a semi-weekly intellectual high. I began riding the streetcar downtown with a male classmate, continuing the seminar discussion until we reached the transfer point and went our separate ways. Simply riding with my classmate would have infuriated my husband. I never told him. In a strange way, adversity strengthens me. My inner conflicts about this mistaken marriage made me stronger and more self-confident. I didn't have to put up with such treatment. I had been out on my own for over three years. I had survived by myself. I could do it again. The decision was up to me.

The university had a special liberal arts program allowing students to graduate without a specific major if they took extra credits. I took an eclectic array of classes that included Gregg shorthand, taught in the business school. I simply assumed that since I didn't want to be a nurse or a teacher, I would find work in an office that interested me. One day in an urban affairs class I became so excited about the topic being discussed that I burst out with a comment in front of fifty other students, my first post-lecture comment in almost three years of classes. Impressed by my vehemence, the professor asked why I'd never spoken up before. I shrugged my shoulders, felt my face redden and never admitted that my passion about the subject—and probably my stupid mistaken marriage—had finally loosened my voice. It was not the last time that would happen.

As I neared graduation, I decided that I wanted to work in politics, the labor movement, or the university. I assumed I would start as a secretary. Perhaps because I was raised on a farm where everybody was part of the enterprise—even the children—I looked at secretarial work as being part of an organization. I didn't think of it as typing, filing, answering the phone or doing clerical work, but being part of a whole, a cog on a wheel. I had been around farm machinery enough to know that if a cog broke, the wheel was damaged. I wanted to be part of something I cared about.

The previous summer I had signed up with a temporary office help agency, and found each new assignment a refreshing learning experience. What did this company do? How did it do it? How did what I was doing fit in the whole enterprise? Would I like to work here longer? Much later, when I managed campaigns and directed offices, I couldn't understand—and didn't tolerate long—people who thought of their work as only a job.

In the summer of 1947, Dorothy Frazier, my friend who was secretary to the regional director of the Committee of Industrial Organizations' (CIO) political office, hired me as her assistant. Rod Jacobson, her boss, was a force in the cabal that was struggling for control of the newly-merged Minnesota Democratic-Farmer-Labor (DFL) Party.

The old Democratic party had been devoted to President Franklin D. Roosevelt. Though Minnesota had traditionally been a Republican state, the home-grown Farmer-Labor Party had been dominant during the 1930's under the leadership of the charismatic, very liberal governor, Floyd B. Olson, an attorney who spoke Yiddish and well as English, having grown up in a Swedish and Jewish neighborhood. But Olson's legacy was corrupted by his successor, and following the death of Roosevelt in 1945, Minnesota reverted to its Republican leanings, except in the two major cities.

A year earlier, in 1944, the moribund Farmer-Labor Party had merged with Minnesota's Democratic party, and Hubert Humphrey was elected mayor of Minneapolis under its banner. The merger of the two parties as the DFL gave a generation of young people who had experienced the Depression and yet emerged victorious from a world war a sense of new possibilities. We had seen despair turn to accomplishment and thought anything was possible. But within the DFL there was conflict between traditional liberals and more radical socialists, who, in the pressure-cooker of the nascent Cold War, were deemed to be dangerous "Reds."

Under Humphrey's auspices, a local chapter of ADA, Americans for Democratic Action, had been formed to take on the challenges of riding the newly-merged DFL Party of its Communist influence and nurture a more modern brand of liberalism, including not only rights for labor but also for minorities. The liberal-minded and politically active elements of the labor movement, exemplified by the CIO and the United Auto Workers union, were crucial in this battle for control between the old Farmer-Laborites—some of them Communists—and the new group headed by Humphrey and his young colleague Orville Freeman, a Marine veteran, now a Minneapolis lawyer. The fight was generational as well as political. It was young vs. old, liberal vs. conservative, Communist vs. anti-Communist, and it carried national, and even international, implications. The labor movement itself was in the midst of a similar generational battle. The old American Federation of Labor (AFL) resented the upstart CIO, even though both organizations were staunchly anti-Communist.

And here I was, the starry-eyed liberal college student, blithely typing and filing in the midst of a maelstrom playing its part out on the 5th floor of an old downtown office building.

I have no recollection of the substance of what I or anyone else did in that office. All I recall is that a parade of notables whom I had read about in newspapers made their appearance there, one after the other. Rod Jacobson, with whom I may have had ten words during that summer, embodied for me the daring and dedicated labor leader—a latter-day version of the labor leaders I had read about in assignments for my American Studies and political science classes at the university, who had struggled to form unions and gains rights and some sense of economic security for workers. A gruff, heavy-set, very intelligent man, Jacobson exuded power and determination. His deep voice resonated throughout the office as he greeted, cajoled, or gave orders to the unending stream of important visitors. The fact that he was visited by United Auto Workers officials from Detroit—people who actually worked with the famous Walter Reuther, head of that union—kept me agog for days. My father, an avid Farmer-Laborite, had talked endlessly about the "sit down strikes" in Detroit during the 1930s and the famous 1934 Teamster strike in Minneapolis.

I also knew something about ADA, the new national liberal organization that Mayor Humphrey, Walter Reuther, and Eleanor Roosevelt were spearheading. Both Dorothy and Jacobson were deeply involved with it at the local level. Though I was a passionate observer to these remarkable goings-on, I was not an active participant in those days. My husband's skepticism and my own lingering farm-girl-come-to-the-city mentality limited me to my classes, work, and home. As a romantic liberal idealist, I could immerse myself in reflected glory simply by coming to work in the morning, but my political life remained vicarious.

Apparently whatever tasks I was assigned in the CIO office, I did tolerably well despite my awe at the surroundings, for just before my university graduation in early June, 1948, Dorothy called to ask if I would be interested in a job as secretary-receptionist in the Humphrey for U.S. Senate campaign office. Would I?! I felt it the grandest opportunity of my twenty-two-year life. I had dutifully voted DFL in the 1946 election, but to be part of the exuberant and effective

DFL mayor's campaign for U.S. Senate was almost beyond my comprehension. Humphrey's name was in the newspapers almost daily. Mayor since 1945, he had made a crime-ridden city safe and given Minneapolis—recently labeled by *Nation* magazine the American "capital of anti-Semitism"—the first Human Rights Commission and Fair Employment Practices Act in the nation. Single-handedly he had broken the "no coloreds here" barrier in downtown hotels. His speeches were endless but electrifying, filling audiences with aspirations and hope spiced with pragmatic realism. He was my candidate. I knew nothing about campaign organizations and didn't even know that campaigns actually had paid staff, but my problem of what to do after graduation was solved.

Getting off the bus at 4th and Hennepin my first day of work in the campaign on a lovely mid-June morning, I forgot my marital troubles. I felt like throwing my arms up toward the clear blue sky and yelling out my delight. Instead, I swung happily down the street in my new green-and-white-checked cotton dress—one more of Mom's creations—my high heels clicking on the sidewalk. Over and over in my mind I chanted: "I'm off to work in the Humphrey campaign. I'm off to work in the Humphrey campaign." My husband could slave over his damned thesis; I was going to be part of the most exciting political event in the state. I sat alone with the phone in the cavernous campaign office, minding the store, while the rest of the staff was off at the DFL state convention deciding who would control the party.

Chapter 5

This Time for Love

The 1948 DFL convention battle was between what came to be called the party's left and right wings. The right wing—though still definitely left of center politically—supported the Marshall Plan to restore Europe from the shambles of World War II. Left wingers were radical Farmer-Laborites and former or concurrent members of the Communist Party, who opposed the plan and supported Henry Wallace for president instead of incumbent president, Harry Truman. While foreign policy and the presidency were the defining issues, the fight was over who would control this new party and whether it looked forward or back. It was a vicious fight—too vicious, I later believed, but I held my tongue. I was too new to express an opinion. The ringing endorsement of Humphrey for U.S. Senate against the incumbent Joseph Ball, a Republican, was the only issue on which there was unanimity.

I identified with the right wing, often labeled the "university crowd," and its labor union supporters. This university crowd included students and recent graduates, among them many veterans studying on the GI Bill, and liberal faculty members from the University of Minnesota and Macalester College. Humphrey had been in the political science departments of both the University and Macalester before becoming mayor. Art Naftalin had left the University to become Humphrey's press person in the mayor's office. Orville Freeman, the DFL party chairman, and Gerald Heaney, a Duluth attorney and activist, were recent graduates of the University of Minnesota Law School. Dorothy Jacobson, chairwoman, was a Macalester professor. I was up to date on this fight because the leadup to it was reported heavily in *The Daily*, the university's student-run newspaper.

When the campaign staff returned from the convention, the office was abuzz with the fallout of that fight and I absorbed all the gossip. As receptionist, my job was to "man" the phones and meet, greet and screen every person entering the office. "Lincoln 0731," I brightly answered every call. I quickly learned who was who and who I could put on hold. Shirley Filiatrault, the consummate political secretary, was my immediate boss and kind trainer/mentor. Her office was part of the inner sanctum from which Art Naftalin, Orville Freeman, and Darrell Smith, a lanky United Auto Workers official from Detroit, managed the campaign. A day or two after the state DFL convention a good-looking, dark, curly-haired young man in a blue seersucker suit and crumpled white shirt, his tie askew, ambled up to my desk. *Fraternity boy*, I thought, my hackles and political antenna up a bit. *Wonder what he wants?* I assumed all fraternity boys were Republicans. But he looked directly at me, as if I were a real human being, not simply a receptionist.

"I'm Don Fraser," he announced in a friendly enough voice and engaging smile. "Who are you?"

I recognized the name, had read his letters to the editor in the *Daily*, and about him as a law student active in the American Veterans Committee and the Americans for Democratic Action. In my cool, professional voice, I answered:

"I'm Arvonne Skelton Morgan, the new receptionist and secretary here."

"Well, I work here too. Where's my desk?"

"Probably there," I said, pointing to a cubbyhole with no door, about twelve feet square, that was shared by young male campaign staff.

My desk was at the office entrance, the old newsroom of the newly-defunct afternoon daily, the *Minneapolis Times*. Filled with tables for volunteers who came in to address and stuff envelopes—and talk politics—the large dingy room had bare light bulbs hanging from the ceiling and boxes of campaign materials lining the walls. I felt this was close to paradise, dirty walls and all. My political science and history textbooks had never mentioned campaign offices but in my social and intellectual history class we were taught to look behind the facts of history.

As receptionist and assistant secretary to senior campaign staff, I was the funnel through which a great deal of information flowed and junior supervisor of campaign mailings. I soon learned I could ask Fraser—working a few yards from my desk—for help in responding to difficult phone calls or complex mailings and not bother Shirley in the inner office. On rare quiet afternoons when others were out campaigning, Fraser would draw up a chair, put his feet up on my desk and talk. He wanted to know what was on Humphrey's schedule, when national labor or political leaders were arriving, and anything interesting I had heard answering the phone. In return he told me about campaign events outside the office and we'd discuss how we were going to get the next big mailing out on time and which volunteers actually worked and who just hung around, wasting others' time.

Fraser and Tom Hughes, a dark-haired, blue-eyed, irreverent young man with an engaging smile, treated me as an equal member of the campaign team. They made sure I got to know the other young campaign workers including Fritz Mondale, the irrepressible Second District field man. Opening the mail one day, I was shocked to find Mondale's weekly expense report written on toilet paper, accompanied by a note saying he knew the report was worth about as much as the paper it was written on, and regretted wasting a stamp. The campaign was always short of money. Fraser and Hughes—men in the campaign were called by their last names—awould occasionally invite me and other young women volunteers out for lunch at a nearby café and always saw that my husband and I were invited to major campaign events in the city. Sometimes we went.

One of my most difficult assignments was to keep track of the junior staff members so they could be reached by Humphrey or senior staffer when needed. Fraser was the rare one who checked in and out regularly. Too often he was across the street at the coffee shop advising a legislative candidate he had recruited and I'd cover for him. He took August off to study and take the bar exam but was on call to work when other staffers were working major events out-state. Those days he pleaded with me to manage the volunteers so he could study. I shared his delight when he announced he had passed the bar exam.

On July 14, when Humphrey gave his civil rights speech at the Democratic National Convention in Philadelphia, all work stopped. Staff, volunteers, labor leaders, and party activists gathered in our big room, milling around until that distinctive voice came over the radio. We listened breathlessly until he finished with his famous line, "out of the darkness of state's rights, into the sunshine of human rights." At that point cheers of "He did it, he did it" broke out. Smiles erupted, fists were raised triumphantly, backs slapped. (We didn't hug or kiss then in Minnesota politics.) Humphrey's name would be in headlines all over the country. We could hardly wait for the afternoon papers. The phone rang off the hook with calls from all over the country. Going home on the bus I smiled, recounting the nationally-known people I had talked to that day.

Election night was equally glorious. Our headquarters was jammed with people awaiting the returns, some proudly bringing in their precinct results, others glued to the radio. My ear hurt from answering the phone. We weren't worried about President Truman, assuming he would lose as predicted. Our focus was on Humphrey. Fraser had quietly informed me earlier that he, Tommy Hughes, and others who had preferred William O. Douglas over Truman, had dumped Truman literature on a Mississippi River bank north of the city instead of peddling it in DFL precincts as they were told to do. When the news broke that Humphrey had won, I shivered with excitement as I answered congratulatory calls from Governors Adlai Stevenson of Illinois and "Soapy" Williams of Michigan; UAW head Walter Reuther, and other national figures. We had taken Minnesota from the grip of the Republicans. I was asked to join Humphrey's Washington staff but declined. I had a husband in school. Fraser occasionally drove my husband and me home from post-election parties that lasted long after midnight. Like many students then, we had no car.

After the election, Tom Hughes and I moved a block down 4th Street to staff the new DFL party office in the Midland Bank Building that Orville Freeman, as party chair, had opened. Down the hall from Freeman's law office, it was a step above those of the Humphrey campaign even with the old campaign furniture. Answering phones, keeping Freeman's schedule, typing and sometimes editing his speeches, and maintaining lists of party faithful was my job. Humphrey's election had been a triumph for Freeman and the right wing of the party. Now this young Humphrey/Freeman group, whom some called the "diaper brigade," was bent on building a strong party that would field good candidates and win elections. One of my major tasks was mimeographing and mailing out notices of state DFL central and executive committee meetings and press releases. Pre-TV politics depended on the printed word. I felt at the center of half of Minnesota's political universe, Republicans being the other half.

Fraser joined Freeman in the young law firm known then as Larson, Loevinger and Lindquist. This new firm of World War II veterans was organized around the premise [belief?] of Fraser's father, long-time dean of the University's law school, that lawyers were obligated to contribute time to public service. Politics was considered noble public service, but it was to remain an avocation, not a livelihood. Depending on it as a career put you at the mercy of contributors.

As Freeman often joked, after a couple of drinks at after-meetings socializing, there were only two subjects worth discussing: politics and sex. This was not yet the sixties. Sex wasn't discussed in mixed political company, only joked and laughed nervously about. Young DFLers with hormones raging maneuvered for power and played the mating game, sometimes surreptitiously. Marriage was an important qualification for elective office; divorce was anathema. Propriety was important to both Freeman and Humphrey.

Fraser found politics more exciting than being the junior member of a law firm. Almost every day he strolled down the hall or called, suggesting Tommy and I join him for a break in the basement coffee shop. Tommy—his warm, effervescent nature making his surname too formal—knew Fraser wanted the "the inside scoop." What county or district officer or labor leader was giving us trouble or quietly helping Freeman in his unannounced quest for the governorship? Who was looking to run for party or elective office? We knew his questions without his having to ask them.

"Found the courthouse yet?" I teased Fraser one afternoon, recalling his joke that they didn't teach in law school where the courthouse was. Bantering with these two bright, interesting men was more fun than I was having at home with an intense, jealous husband who demanded he be the center of my attention. When Grandpa Skelton died in a car accident in February, 1947, he had forbidden my attending the funeral. I went anyway. Now, in 1948, my joy at work was as evident as his frustration with his dissertation.

When the multilith, the kind of machine that spawned Kinko's, became the latest in office printing technology, Fraser convinced Freeman that the DFL office could be more efficient with it. Under Fraser's tutelage, I became a multilith operator. As we struggled together, adjusting pins to find exactly the right mixture of ink and water to produce decent copies, we laughed at who got dirtier, and Fraser quipped: "I got a law degree to do this?" In return for his help when the machine perplexed me, I typed stencils for him, sometimes after hours, succumbing to his plea that I could type so much faster than he, that he just had to have a few copies for a meeting that night, or had a client waiting in his office and "would I please…?

"OK. OK. How many copies do you need? But if that machine breaks down you're on your own."

If I was too late getting home from work my husband would be fuming. By then I hated going home. Much more pleasant were the diverse characters of the DFL—gruff, burly labor leaders, crusty farmers, League of Women Voters ladies, ordinary union members, county or district chairmen and chairwomen from all walks of life. They fascinated me. People such as Nellie Stone Johnson, the first black woman elected to public office in Minnesota, and Howard Y. Williams, an old Socialist once associated with Eugene Debs, were in our office often. This was heady stuff for a twenty-four year old who loved history and was awed by those who made it. I knew all the daily newspapers' political reporters by their first names and they knew mine.

As my husband became more morose and verbally abusive. I agonized over whether I dared leave him, and how. Over the summer of 1949, I began to plan. I found I could rent a furnished room close to downtown and decided I could support myself on the $125 a month I was earning. My husband and I had two thousand dollars in a joint savings account from my college summers' earnings. Could I legally take half and walk away? I decided to consult Fraser, pose a theoretical question. We were close friends. He invited me out to lunch occasionally and sometimes even paid for it. When he or Tommy ran short before payday, I lent them money. For my consultation, I picked an afternoon when Tommy was out, called Fraser and asked if he had time for coffee, saying I had a friend who needed some legal advice.

"Sure, meet me at the elevator."

We rode down the five floors in the ancient open-caged elevator with Oscar, the operator, who was everybody's friend.

"I'll buy," I said as we entered the inelegant shop, trying to cover my nervousness. "Consider it the fee."

"I thought you were bringing me a paying client. I'll never make a living this way," Fraser bantered back.

I led the way to a clean corner table. I didn't want anybody to overhear this conversation. We talked a bit about politics and then he said:

"So, what's the problem?"

"Well, this couple has a joint savings account. Can the wife take her half out and walk away from the marriage?"

"Legally she can take the whole amount," he responded. Looking down at his coffee cup, raising it, taking a sip, he finally looked up at me. His eyebrows a question mark, his brown eyes deadly serious, he asked:

"Is this you?"

My ploy had failed.

"If I answer that, will you promise not to tell a soul until I get out of town?"

"Lawyers keep confidences," he responded, his voice and face registering hurt. "Trust me."

I confessed, told him my plan. I would take off work the Friday before Labor Day, pack only a suitcase, take the Greyhound bus home to the farm and be back at work on Tuesday morning.

"I've rented a room across the street from Peg's. I'll be fine." (Peg Eichhorn was a dedicated university student volunteer, part of the Young DFL group. We both knew her well.)

"Be careful," he said very seriously, then added: "A bunch of us guys are going to Lake Okiboje over Labor Day. Tommy's going, and Bill Watters too."

"Don't get drunk and drown," I said, moving to lighter ground. I asked him to tell the other men during the weekend, relieved that I wouldn't have to make any kind of announcement. I understood he would tell Freeman and others in the law office. We both knew political people thrived on gossip—personal as well as political. No explanations would be necessary when we all returned after the holiday.

Labor Day was September 5 that year. For my twenty-fourth birthday, on September 1, Fraser ambled down the hall and shyly presented me with a copy of the latest liberal best seller: *The U.A.W. and Walter Reuther*. I suspected Tommy, an avid reader like myself, had selected the book. I blushed, asked how he knew it was my birthday. On its fly-leaf, were three inscriptions: Freeman's and Tommy's above Fraser's familiar scrawl that said: "Here's hoping for many, many happy birthdays for you—and with the thought that they needn't all be spent becoming an expert on our 'machine'." That book remains one of my treasures.

My plan worked. Soon after I got to the farm, the first of my husband's harassing phone calls began. Interspersed among them that weekend were daily calls from Fraser wondering if I was all right. I told him my husband's calls were a bit frightening but I wasn't worried. His bark was always greater than his bite, I said. All these calls worried my father because we were on a party line. I was disappointed. I had expected more support from him. On the other hand, I was surprised at how supportive Mom was. As I think about it now, each of my parents was probably viewing my actions through the prism of their own marriage.

Mom offered to drive to Minneapolis with a friend the next week. She would take all my possessions out of the apartment and bring them to my new place. I gave her my key to the apartment. She would undertake her mission during school hours when my husband wasn't home. I gave her a list of what I wanted and where she would find everything. I boarded the Greyhound bus late Labor Day afternoon a satisfied, liberated woman, although the term, "liberated," was years in my future. The move of my belongings worked fine; the harassing phone calls were endless.

In early October, Fraser sidled up to me at a meeting and quietly asked if I would like to go with him to a university football game the following Saturday and to a party at his house afterwards. I was astounded. Ten days after I returned from my momentous Labor Day weekend, Fraser had invited me to the play, *Mr. Roberts,* with Tommy, Kathy Pierce, and Bill Watters. I considered that an act of sympathy by friends event. This was different. The Saturday night Fraser house parties were major social events for the junior members of the Humphrey/Freeman group, the subject of gossip and intra-party envy. Everybody knew Dean Fraser had retired, was teaching in California, and that Don Fraser had taken over the big old family house near the university, sharing it with university law students who were DFL activists, and Tommy Hughes. An invitation to their parties was like an invitation to a prom. I wondered about the propriety of this but not for long.

It didn't start well. My husband's threatening and abusive phone calls at the office were one thing. I had become inured to cranks, could type or file with phone on shoulder, listen with only half an ear and murmur semi-intelligent responses until the caller exhausted himself. I never worried about my husband coming to the office. He didn't have the courage. It would be too embarrassing. Yet walking up 4th Street S.E. among the after-game crowd, Fraser and I were assailed from behind with quiet but sinister and obscene taunts. I jumped in fear, recognizing the voice. My husband was following us. It was our first personal encounter since I'd left. Fraser and I continued walking. I pretended the taunts weren't aimed at me. Furious and embarrassed, I looked down and counted sidewalk squares silently to keep my emotions under control. After a block or so, mild-mannered Fraser stopped abruptly, turned around and in the fiercest voice I had ever heard him use, said:

"If you don't shut up and quit bothering her, I'll baste you one."

Though he was only five-foot-eight compared to my assailant's six foot height, the threat worked. Our harasser ran into the street, grabbed the pole at the back entrance of a crowded streetcar and vanished. Fraser and I walked on in silence. I imagined everyone within earshot had heard what was going on, but as usual in tense or fearful situations, I remained calm until I saw my assailant run away. Then I began trembling, humiliated. Fraser said nothing, but at the next intersection, he took my hand as if to say, "It's OK. I'm here. Don't worry." My fears subsided.

It was a lovely fall day, leaves scrunching under our feet after we strolled through Dinkytown, the café and shopping center near campus familiar to both of us. We had graduated from the university the same day, he from law school, although he skipped the ceremonies to attend the DFL state convention that weekend, much to the consternation of his parents.

Arriving at the Fraser house, "Mother" MacIver, Fraser's housemate whose household manner earned him the title, put us to work immediately. I had heard stories about Dale keeping the house in order and protecting Mrs. Fraser's good things from the less-domesticated male inhabitants. Dean and Mrs. Fraser had left the house furnished as the dean's California appointment was for one year only. While MacIver and Fraser rolled up the Oriental rugs in the huge living room, I attacked the kitchen. Doing familiar household tasks was calming.

Fraser said not a word about the incident as we answered MacIver's questions about our afternoon at the game. His eyes said: "I won't mention it if you don't." Tommy arrived, regaling the three of us about his day with Freeman over a supper of take-out hamburgers and milk shakes. About eight o'clock he looked at his watch, announced with a grin that he had to take a shower, leaving MacIver, Fraser and me to clear the table and greet the first guests. I faced another hurdle. How was I to deal with the evening? Separated from my husband a bit over a month and dating already? What would people think? What would they say? Many political liberals were social conservatives, especially Freeman and Humphrey. I told myself to be discreet. I needn't be seen as Fraser's date. Who, besides the in-in group, would know?

Kathy Pierce and Bill Watters arrived shortly after eight. I could let other guests assume I came with them, was simply part of the crowd. The house filled up quickly. I soon learned these parties

Don and Dale ("Mother") MacIver

were in fact a political caucus without a printed agenda. Roz Eiser, a war widow with an adorable two-year-old girl, an ADA activist and Fraser's occasional date, acted as if my being there was no surprise. She was my friend as well as his. Later she told others she always expected Fraser would marry me. As host, Fraser circulated, always making sure I had a drink. MacIver and Tommy were equally attentive. I relaxed. All of the guests were friends or acquaintances.

Mid-evening a slightly older, single YDFLer from a suburban county began paying me more attention than I wanted. Maneuvering me into a corner, he asked me for a date, implying more.

I admired his politics but not his attention, especially since he'd had a few drinks. I sensed others watching. This guy is repulsive, I thought, throwing my head back and laughing at his persistence, desperately searching for a way to put him off. Fraser moved in, greeted my admirer and guided me to another conversational group. He must get tired of this, I thought, always saving me from some guy harassing or leering at me.

As the evening wore on, someone turned on the record player, and a few couples began to dance. I hadn't danced for too long. My husband considered it immoral, "sex in public," he called it. I suspected he couldn't dance and that was his cover. This night I couldn't resist the throb of the music. I hadn't gone to all those free wedding dances in Lamberton, been the daughter of the best dancers in the county, for nothing. Fraser pulled me into the circle of dancers and twirled me around the floor, smiling. He was a good dancer. We had more in common than the multilith. When a slow Glenn Miller record fell on the turntable, his arms felt good. Soon we were dancing cheek to cheek, holding hands between dances, and when a faster record came down on the turntable, we experimented with new steps and became the center of attention. Finally, tired but pleased with ourselves, we plopped down side by side on the sofa, his arm still around me.

I am into this much farther than I should be, I told myself. But it was too good to waste. I lowered my eyes, let my head fall on his shoulder and felt his arm tense a bit. I could see a number of feet through my half-shut eyes all pointing at me, could imagine some thinking:

"Oh ho, there's something going on here." Or worse.

"Tommy will take you home," I heard Fraser say, knowing it was as much for the rumor factory as for me. Saved again. Fraser didn't own a car. This incident would be talked about, but it would pass—or would it?

I figured if I behaved myself the divorce would go through with no contest. Earl Larson, the law firm's senior partner, had agreed to be my lawyer. The future would take care of itself. Yet late afternoons

I waited for Fraser to wander down the hall, casually suggest a drink or a hamburger after work. When he didn't show up, it meant he had another date or a meeting. All ears for gossip, I tried to keep my interest subdued. He still dated Roz, whose red convertible was only one of her attractions. I didn't discover until years later that when Freeman worried aloud at inner-circle meetings about having a divorced woman as his secretary, Fraser spoke up for me, emphasizing how valuable I was to the office. Roz also told me years later that Tommy and Fraser had agreed that they would see that I got home safely after work each evening because they knew my husband was stalking me. I was more naïve than they. I had spied him across the street one time when a group of us emerged from the Midland Bank building after work, enroute to a local bistro. I ignored him, considered him harmless, and was too delighted at being part of a crowd my own age to worry.

That explains why Tommy often invited me out for a hamburger and beer with Peg Eichhorn, Kathy Pierce, Bill Watters, or other friends who had gathered in the office, and then gave me a ride home. When Tommy was with Freeman outstate, Fraser and I might go out for a beer with a group or to a DFL meeting. Our formal dates were rare. We saw *Death of a Salesman*, played bridge once with a couple of his apolitical friends. We couldn't afford much more. Fraser earned less than I and, like Tommy, borrowed money from me. Both paid me back promptly. Tommy had car payments; Fraser a big dental bill. I was healthy and frugal. Mom still made my clothes and I had taken my half from that savings account.

One day after five o'clock when Fraser wandered in, a group of men were finishing a meeting with Tommy. He suggested we all walk over to the Nicollet Hotel bar a few blocks away for a drink. The sole woman in the group, I joined the men at the bar. The bartender approached us hesitanttly and, in an apologetic voice, said:

"No ladies at the bar."

Without missing a beat, Fraser retorted: "She's no lady," and turned to me with his devious smile. "She'll have a bourbon and ginger ale and I'll have a beer."

"I'll take a beer, too. A Miller's," Tommy announced over my shoulder before the bartender had a chance to utter a word.

Shaking his head, the bartender went off, made and brought back our drinks. The whole group smiled. A rule had been broken. Some rules were made to be broken; others not.

After my divorce was finalized, I began to date other men, and in early December I took a celebratory trip to New York. Fraser, Tommy, and other friends saw me off at the airport. It was an event. Few people took airplane trips in 1949. The plane was a renovated warplane, still painted grey. I needed that trip. Although I was secretly proud that I had admitted publicly I had married the wrong man, living with its consequences wasn't easy. I was skittish about what people thought of me. Talking about divorce and one's feelings was considered undignified. Vulnerable, with few I could confide in, I was losing weight for once in my life.

The divorce itself had been no contest. My husband didn't show up. He had quit his constant phone calls, and I had used my head. When the hearing was originally scheduled, Larson had a conflict and suggested Fraser could handle it. That's not very smart, I thought, my lawyer a guy I'm dating, and secretly in love with. I told Larson I would wait until his schedule was free. I sometimes think my deep friendship with Earl Larson, who later became a federal judge, began that day. Was he testing me? If so, I made the right decision; my judgment could be trusted.

Now I was a free woman, but not a totally happy one. Evenings without a meeting or a date, I devoured novels instead of food and began spending time again with my Uncle Phillip and his quiet wife in St. Paul. Occasionally, when I babysat their little girls, Fraser would visit. He came and went. We didn't date. We "hung out together," our children would call it.

My parents seemed to drive to the Cities more often after the divorce. Were they worried about me? They never said so; they simply dropped off the new clothes Mom had made for me, asked how I was doing and told me to drop them off at a relative's house. I had a car for the weekend. I would inform Fraser I had a car and we would invite Kathy and Bill along for a night out. Suburban roadhouses offered cheap food and drink as Saturday night specials. Lounging in a dark booth, we'd analyze Freeman's progress towards endorsement for governor, discuss past or future party meetings, and recount antics of a particular labor or party leader we disliked or admired. Only after a post-dinner drink or two did the conversation turn personal.

Fraser, like most veterans then, did not want to talk about the war, deflecting questions about it with humorous anecdotes or silence. Their experiences were either too awful for social conversation, or their desire for normal, peacetime life too strong to permit the intrusion of war stories. We knew Fraser had been in the Pacific as a junior naval officer on a destroyer. He did teach me, mock contempt in his voice, that a destroyer was a ship, not a boat. "A boat is something you put on a ship, silly." Driving, he taught me port was left, starboard right. To this day he'll ask, "starboard?" and I'm to report any traffic to our right.

One memorable roadhouse evening, with his sly, shy grin, he told of being confined to quarters for insubordination. His ship was being attacked by Japanese fighter planes. The captain kept yelling down to Fraser, the radar officer, for readings on an approaching plane. Radar, then, was still imprecise. After one too many demands, Fraser reported a reading down to a millimeter. The captain wasn't pleased. Fraser was reprimanded and confined to quarters, though he treated the incident as a great joke.

Somehow this tale lead to a discussion of authority. I asked why ships had only one captain. Why not co-captains? Why did one man have complete authority? There had to be a better way to run a ship, I argued, some limits on authority. He smiled, enjoying the argument. He's never forgotten it. He was testing me. I was still raw from living with a tyrant. The sub-text of this conversation was marriage, but I didn't realize it then.

Down to 104 pounds a month after the divorce—forty less than I had weighed after my first year in college—I was ripe for any bug going around. Food, except sweets, was never high on my priority list. My rooming house didn't include kitchen privileges. I looked good—thin, that is—and kept going, my grandmother's and mother's daughter. Illness was to be borne; you kept working. I lived on nervous energy, milk, cigarettes, and whatever the unappetizing Midland Bank coffee shop offered for breakfast.

In mid-January, 1950, there was another Fraser house party. Fever or no fever, I was not going to miss it, though I ached in every bone. I can sleep all day tomorrow, be fine by Monday morning, I told myself as I dragged myself out of bed. My new, soft beige wool dress will show off my slender self, I mused as I undid the pin curls I'd so carefully put up that morning in preparation for the party. Feeling glamorous but sick, throat sore, I told myself I'd be fine after a few snacks and a beer. Maybe Fraser and I could find a quiet corner and just talk.

There was no quiet corner. The DFL precinct caucuses, only a few weeks away, animated everyone. Who was running for state convention delegate in what counties? What city wards could Freeman count on? What about state party offices? There was no dancing this evening. This was serious, heady, power politics, punctuated by laughter when someone predicted or mimicked a labor or old Farmer-Laborite leader's speech. This University and young professionals crowd was intent on gaining the 60 percent needed at the state convention to endorse Freeman for governor and retain control of the party. But they had a lively sense of humor and delighted in the game of politics. The most intense discussions were in the kitchen where men gathered around the bar set up beside the sink. I didn't join them. I was supposed to be impartial as secretary to the chairman of the party and simply Fraser's date that night. He was deep into politics, not romance.

Around eleven o'clock, aching and burning with fever, I retreated into the empty study, and sank into Fraser's mother's big old wing chair, no longer able to ignore the fact that I was sick. Not long afterward, I was roused by a voice:

"Why are you here alone? You look terrible." Fraser had disengaged himself from the kitchen conversation, come to check on me.

"Thanks," I responded with a sardonic smile. He looked concerned, in no mood for banter. "I feel terrible...my throat's sore and I ache all over. Sorry to be a party-pooper."

"Forget it," he said, frowning as he put a cool, competent hand on my forehead.

"Wow. You have a real fever. You belong in bed. Wait a minute." I expected him to get my coat, ask Tommy to take me home. Instead he conferred with MacIver, probably sent him up to make a bed and stuff dirty clothes in a closet.

"Come on. You're going to bed." A naval officer command. He lead me up the creaking front stairs and opened a door. The street lights outside revealed twin beds. The room smelled like men's dirty underwear, but I was beyond caring about smells or anything else.

"Get in bed. I'm going to take your temperature." Meekly I kicked off my pumps and sank onto the far bed, near the window. It felt good having a heavy but soft quilt gently tucked around me, that cool hand on my head again.

He opened another door, flipped the bathroom light switch and I heard a medicine cabinet open. Next I was being ordered to open my mouth and saw his left hand shaking a thermometer with a nurse's flair.

"Under your tongue, silly. Haven't you ever had your temperature taken?" I was beyond talk, beyond worrying about propriety. Sleep was all I wanted as I felt the thermometer being gently removed, heard his quick intake of breath:

"103. I'm going to call Boyd." Boyd was Dr. Thomes, a Second Ward DFLer we both knew. I dozed off. Sometime later, that soft hand on my forehead again, my shoulder shaken.

"Mmmm." I snuggled deeper into the pillow, resisting.

"Come on. Wake up. Here's a glass of water. I'm going to take you home. Boyd says a few days in bed should cure you."

The house was silent. I reached out for the glass, felt it being put in my hand.

"Quiet! Everybody's asleep." I rose, searched with my toes for my pumps, smoothed my dress, and was steered quietly down the stairs, his arm around my shoulders. Under the dim front hall light, I admired the toile wallpaper as I slipped my arms into the coat he held. He handed me my purse the way men do—as if a purse is a lethal weapon. The heavy front door closed gently behind us.

"How do you feel now?" he asked as he drove down the street. Marvelous would have been partly true, but weak, aching with both illness and desire.

"You can be my nurse anytime."

"Call me Dr. Fraser. Your orders are to get to bed and stay there. Call me when you wake up—but not before noon—and drink plenty of fluids."

We drove through the dark, empty streets in Tommy's little Ford. A familiar, synchronized, unspoken routine. Steering left handed, his other arm around me, my head on his shoulder, I operated the shifting lever. We'd done this many a time. I'd been driving cars and trucks and tractors since I was twelve, could sense when to shift gears. The court house clock showed three.

"What's a girl like you doing out at this hour?"

"Driving around town."

"You're good at it. Never miss a gear." He had complimented me on my driving skills before.

"Trust me."

Ten minutes later we pulled up in front of my rooming house. He turned off the lights and motor. Neither of us moved. Politics was now the last thing on our minds. He murmured into my hair.

"Take care of yourself. Boyd will have some medicine sent over. I'm not going to kiss you goodnight. You're contagious. I don't want what you've got. Now get to bed."

I disengaged myself, gave him a peck on the cheek, fished my key out of my purse, and walked up the sidewalk, knowing he watched and waited until I was safely inside.

I spent a few days in bed, sleeping, trying to read, savoring all I could remember of the evening, wondering where it would lead. I could count on him when I was sick or in trouble, but what did that mean? He was a good soul, the smartest, most quick-witted man I'd ever known. Shy, not too talkative—or demonstrative for that matter. Not demanding. But this was an office romance. Serious necking on weekends was simply a part of dating—or was it mating? Did I want to marry again, so soon? I was going on twenty-five. If I wanted children—and lots of them as I'd always said—I'd better get busy. But I loved my job, tolerated the rooming house. Apartments were scarce and above the means of secretaries.

As the weeks rolled by, the office tempo increased. Preparations for the precinct caucuses, county, district, and state conventions kept Tommy and I working late many evenings, supervising volunteers, putting convention kits together. Fraser often dropped by to go over convention reports, assess which delegates were solidly for Freeman, who could be trusted to keep their word, and what the undecideds and unknowns might do, before dashing off to another meeting. We still had coffee almost every afternoon. The multilith ran smoothly. I was now an expert on it and called on Fraser less frequently.

In fact, I began to feel spurned. Fraser's first love *was* politics. Engrossed in his law practice and the DFL conventions, I felt second, third, or fourth fiddle. I had a new and frequent Saturday night date who was fetching. He paid attention to me, took me to movies, plays, and parties with his wealthy suburban friends, and spent hours talking to me about his dreams for the future. Reluctantly, I gave up on Fraser. I was tired of waiting for him, tired of the rented room, tired, tired, tired. I had to look out for myself. Looking out seemed to mean finding a man who cared about me. Marriage was what women did. But this time I was going to be picky. I was in love with Fraser, but he apparently preferred politics to me.

My new companion, whom I had first met in the Humphrey campaign, seemed smitten. He owned and ran a small-town weekly newspaper almost a hundred miles away and intended to run for office one day. I knew things were turning serious when he asked if I would have dinner with his parents at their Lake Minnetonka home. He warned me the dinner would be rather formal, but not to worry. I got through the evening, thanks to his kindly mother and quiet father who made special efforts to put this DFL girl at ease. They were typical Minnesota liberal Republicans—good people, conservatives with hearts and brains.

Apparently I passed muster for the next Saturday night my friend proposed. I took the path of least resistance. This gentle Yale man was open about his love for me. With unalloyed joy, he talked about the ring he would buy me, the exciting life we would have. Diamonds were not my goal. A good marriage and children were. Our backgrounds were dissimilar but our interests were not. We both liked books, travel, and politics. Very seriously he explained his finances, assuring me I would be well provided for. Complimented and vulnerable, it all sounded and felt right, every young woman's dream. We agreed we would tell no one. The engagement would be formally announced and we would set a wedding date sometime in the future. I told myself I was lucky to find a man who wanted me as a partner, not a subordinate. I could be active in politics in rural Minnesota, build a nice life, come to the Cities anytime I wanted. Fraser could fly his own kite.

Not two weeks later, on a brilliant May Saturday afternoon, Fraser called. Would I go with him and some of his old friends to his family's cottage on the St. Croix River the next day for a picnic and a swim? My heart sank. We hadn't been out together for weeks, even coffee hours had become rarer. He was busy with politics. Why this now?

"I can't," I sighed, treasuring that voice and thinking how wonderful it would be to go swimming again, and with him. My reaction scared me. What had I done? This was crazy. Why couldn't he leave well enough alone?

The phone line hummed. Incredulity can be heard in silences.

"Well, what are you doing tonight? We could go to a movie."

"I can't." My fiancé was not coming to Minneapolis that weekend, but I had enough sense of decorum to know an engaged woman didn't go out with other men. I didn't want this thing with Fraser to start all over again—and yet I did. Quit it, I told myself, waving a red flag in front of my mind's eye.

"Why not? Is something wrong? Are you all right?"

"I'm OK. I just can't go out with you. I can't, that's all."

Another long pause. I could sense his astonishment. Good, I thought. Serves him right. He's not used to women turning him down, doesn't take no for an answer easily. He can stew in his own juice. I was through waiting around, being taken for granted.

"Well, okay," disappointment audible. "I'll see you Monday at the office."

"Yeah."

He hung up slowly. I sat on the steps, drained, staring at the phone in my hand until it began to beep. I was in the now familiar tiny front hall, remembering the many nights Fraser and I had sat entwined on these same steps, me totally in love with the guy, he seeming eager, both of us brimming over with longing but too prim and proper to go up to my bed.

My weekend—maybe my life—was ruined. I was in love with one man and about to marry another. Stupid. Stupid. Stupid. How did I get into this mess? I had to do something. Get out of this place. Go to the corner drugstore, buy the latest *Vogue* magazine, plan a new wardrobe. I picked myself off the steps and walked to the drugstore. Opening the door, the Baby Ruth bars jumped out at me, my old solace when lonely and depressed. I grabbed two, giant sized, paid for them and rushed back out the door, forgetting the magazine. I tore open the candy bar wrapper, salivating at the prospect of that soothing chocolate, sweet caramel and crunchy nuts. A long walk was what I needed. I'd go over to Lake of the Isles, savor the warm day and blue sky, clear my brain. Fraser be damned.

Crossing Hennepin Avenue, I glanced down the hill and saw the old hotel where I had spent my first wedding night. Ironically, last New Year's Eve at midnight Fraser had kissed me, long and hard at a DFL party there when the lights went out. I remembered the cheering and clapping when the lights went on again. Those thoughts did me no good. I walked around the lake and back to my claustrophobic little rented room, despondent. What had I done? How stupid could I be? How stupid could Fraser be?

Sunday was no better. I could be swimming. The day was glorious, blue sky, fluffy white clouds, but in my head dark storm clouds roiled.

I got up Monday morning, hating the prospect of the office for the first time. I wasn't there five minutes when the phone rang.

"Good morning. DFL Office. Mrs. Morgan speaking. Can I help you?"

That familiar voice: "What's the mystery. I want to talk to you. Come down for coffee."

"I don't have time...too much work to do."

We could still be friends, I thought, but not today.

"Well, how about lunch or after work? We need to talk."

I debated. He had to know sometime. Get it over with—but not on the phone. Not this morning.

"OK. OK. Come by when you're through work."

As I put down the phone, Tommy came in the door, a big grin on his face.

"Hey, kiddo. What did you do to Fraser? He pouted all weekend, said you turned him down."

"Fraser can go peddle his precinct. That's all he wants to do anyway."

Raising his black eyebrows, chuckling, he patted me on the shoulder as he passed my desk on the way to his own office. I longed to follow him, plop down in a chair and tell him the mess I was in. I hated to admit it, but I needed a shoulder to cry on. The phone rang again. Not Fraser this time. There was a pile of mail to open, central committee meeting notices to get out. I lost myself in the tasks at hand, skipped coffee and lunch. I didn't want to meet Fraser in the hall or coffee shop. The end of the day would come soon enough.

At five fifteen the office door opened and there he was, rumpled shirt, tie askew as usual and that shy, slightly crooked half-smile that got to me every time.

"I drove today. Are you ready?" I wasn't ready, at least not emotionally, but the summery weather beckoned. I yearned to get outside, get this over with.

Silently we walked down Fourth Street to the parking lot and the old navy blue Chrysler limousine he'd just bought cheap from a rich client. Tommy and I had teased him about it. We knew the client, an obese divorcée from a distinguished industrial family who was a DFL contributor and demanded a lot of attention. Had she taken pity on him, I asked, and given the car to him? He looked at me with that familiar pseudo-contempt.

He drove up Nicollet Avenue, away from downtown, saying nothing.

"How about a drink at the President?" he asked. It was the Minneapolis Millers baseball fans' hangout. There would be no political people around.

"Fine," I answered, angry at myself for enjoying riding along with him again.

We sat at a table, nervously ordered drinks. I lit a cigarette to distract myself and smiled. When you can't do anything else, smile, that's what women do. Smile and wait for what happens next. This man hadn't paid much attention to me for weeks. The county and district conventions couldn't take all his time. I was through waiting around. Time to take charge of my own life, settle down, have children.

We sipped our drinks, made small talk. I played with my cigarettes, smoked one, stubbed it out. He asked for one. Never buying his own, he smoked others' occasionally. "OPs,—other peoples'" we called them. He stared over my shoulder and kept folding and refolding his cocktail napkin, studying it intently. My refusal to go out with him over the weekend yawned in the almost empty cafe.

Finally, straightening up in his chair, as if he were about to address a court room or convention, he reached across the table, covered my hand with his, and quietly asked:

"Will you marry me?"

Would I marry him? I almost laughed. I'd give the world to marry him but....but....but...

That hand felt good. I could trust this man, those soft, sad brown eyes, his slow, deliberative manner—that still occasionally irritates the hell out of me. I felt like standing up and yelling as loud as the most ardent baseball fan: "He asked me to marry him!" But I didn't have the strength. There was nothing to say except: "Yes,......but...," confess the mess I'd gotten myself into, and beg his help one more time.

Six glorious, harried political weeks later, we were married at 9 a.m. on Friday, June 30, just days after expiration of the legal waiting period between divorce and remarriage and two weeks after the DFL state convention. Dad stayed sober. Mom poured all her talents into an elegantly simple blue cotton wedding dress with tiny buttons down the front. The brief ceremony was held in a Methodist chapel because the University's Continuing Education Center wasn't available. Then a brunch/reception in "our house." Fraser had bought it from his parents, totally furnished and on favorable mortgage terms, a week before he proposed. He was ready for marriage too.

His housemates joked about being summarily evicted. No rugs were rolled back this time. The furniture was polished by the bride-to-be. The senior Mrs. Fraser's good china and glassware came out of hiding. Surrounded by more than a hundred DFLers plus a few of my relatives and Don's childhood friends, we sailed through the brunch. The old Chrysler limo—its automatic windows never closed

The old Fraser house

Arvonne as a young bride in 1951

properly—sat in the garage, full of gas, swim suits, and canoeing gear for our Boundary Waters honeymoon, five hundred miles and two tanks of gas away.

The hard part had been the dis-engagement. I hated hurting the dear man I had promised to marry, but made myself call him the day after Fraser proposed to me. A couple of evenings later Fraser drove me down to see him, leaving us to talk alone. Initially shocked, he was grieved, but understanding. There are many forms of love. We all three remained friends, not close but respectful. We were invited to his wedding a few years later. I wore a smashing white hat—hats were *de rigeur* at weddings then—and greeted his friends a bit uneasy, being unsure about which ones knew our story.

During the six weeks from "Will you marry me?" to our "Here's to our eight kids" vow as we cut the wedding cake, Fraser and I lived on ecstatic energy. Evenings and weekends we negotiated a marriage contract, never calling it that. We deferred our euphoria during the day enough to carry out our separate responsibilities for and at the 1950 DFL convention in Duluth. Freeman was endorsed for attorney general, not governor, and Karl Rolvaag was elected party chair.

We agreed we liked the old Fraser house in the city, that we never wanted to live in the suburbs or entertain just to get clients for his law practice. We didn't need a fancy wedding with a photographer. We would remember it. I do now wish we had a picture of his lifting me up and twirling me around the minute we exited the chapel. There would be co-captains on this ship. One now was called Don privately, Fraser publicly. The other—not yet an overt feminist—dropped one married surname for another and only laughed when some colleagues forgot and used her former name.

My continuing to work was assumed. We needed my salary, which was still larger than his. We each had four siblings and were used to extra people living with us. Housing was still in short supply. We had a big house. Of course we'd rent out rooms to university students. He didn't manage money well. He would be the lawyer; I'd be the accountant and business manager.

We had learned a money lesson the week we flew out to California so I could meet his parents, sandwiching this trip between the state convention in early June and our wedding at the end of the month. I feared meeting his parents. Don had written them a glowing letter describing me and our impending, sudden marriage. They responded with an invitation—and airline tickets—to San Francisco. Would they, this feared but respected old law school dean, and his League of Women Voters wife, about whom I'd heard so much, be contemptuous of this divorced farm girl working in politics? I needn't have worried. Instead of the severe giant with flashing brown eyes and elegant wife I expected to meet us at the San Francisco airport, a shy, unassuming couple stepped forward who looked and were old enough to be my grandparents. That soon described our relationship.

Duty week went well. I don't know what they expected but they told Don they were relieved and pleased at his choice. I admired the aplomb with which Mrs. Fraser drove us up and down San Francisco's hills to show us the city. Alone, Don and I swam in the

Pacific, lolled on beaches for hours, got sunburned, and forgot politics. When the four of us drove back to Minneapolis, each evening Dad Fraser calmly marched into a motel office, rented two rooms, one for the men, one for the women, peeled as many twenties as necessary off the roll of bills he carried in his pants pocket and sent Don and me off for the evening, saying, "We've got to get an early start in the morning."

"Does he always carry a wad of bills like that?" I asked, incredulous. "Doesn't he worry about getting robbed?"

"He was a poor boy, paid his own way through college and law school working on a ship in the Atlantic. Having money in his pocket makes him feel good."

We weren't so smart. In Reno we lost our heads and shirts in a casino shell game we should have known better than to try. But we were happy, in love, and out on the town. Later that night, I sat patiently sipping my beer as Don, an undergraduate math major, sat with pencil and paper figuring the odds of winning that game— about one in a million, as I recall. Chagrined, we limited ourselves to one beer each night and vowed never to gamble again. Life and politics were enough of a gamble.

Don's parents

Chapter 6

A Grey Flannel Coat
and the Matriarchy

"Passionate Protestants," Gene McCarthy, Minnesota's Fourth District Catholic congressman, called us one night at a party when I was grossly pregnant for the fourth time in as many years. Our first, Tommy—named after Tommy Hughes, Tom Paine, and Thomas Jefferson—was born in April, 1951, nine and half months after our wedding. I had continued to work at the DFL office until two weeks before the delivery—a rarity, I learned later. But nobody complained about my bulging belly. My colleagues probably knew we needed my salary. Mary Mac, was born in August during the 1952 Stevenson for President campaign. John arrived in October, 1953. I rarely experienced morning sickness, and found babies and politics compatible and challenging. Fraser's "pretty good for seven months' pregnant," when I jumped over the bow of a boat as we came ashore one day on the St. Croix River, I took as a high compliment.

Pregnancy and volunteerism earned women praise in the "lets-get-back-to-normal" 1950s. Summers at the Fraser family cabin only thirty five miles from the city were like summers on the farm with cousins around. His.sisters and parents converged from the east and west coasts. I indulged myself after they arrived, tending almost naked babies on the beach, reading while the children napped. It was my time off. This compensated for the long hours Don and I spent opening up and maintaining this beloved but remote place. He commuted to the city daily. The newcomer in this extended family, I was oblivious at first to its tensions. The daughters were expected to be what later were called Super Moms. They were to have a career, raise polite, well-nourished children; be good cooks; keep the husband they married no matter his faults or indiscretions; and spend two weeks each summer with their parents. Success in a career was the measure of worth; disappointment was veiled, but thinly.

I was exempt. I had married the parents' unplanned but adored last child. Listening to their gossip about university faculty and stories of growing up in Canada, they treated me more like a granddaughter than daughter-in-law. Their idiosyncrasies could be endured for two months each summer. The rest of the year, our old city house continued as a convenient, unofficial party and campaign headquarters. Bigger than most, it was ideal for meetings and informal social/political events. I found volunteering for the DFL Party a nice counterbalance to diapers and dishes. Editing the state party newsletter, serving as Second Ward DFL Club secretary, and supervising production and distribution of the biennial precinct caucus kits could be done as my little ones played or slept. My home office was complete when we installed a large, old, roll-top desk that reputedly once belonged to Governor Floyd B. Olson in our study, which doubled as the children's playroom. When electric typewriters became available, I got one as a Christmas present. When the multilith was rejected by my successor in the DFL office, we brought it home.

One evening shortly after John was born, Bill Kubicek, a university professor, DFL party secretary, and good friend, came over to convince us that Don should run for state senate the next year. Emmet Duempke, the conservative incumbent in our district, was criticizing the university, a cardinal sin in the minds of DFLers. Since Don had been gaining attention as president of our neighborhood association, as an organizer of the new Citizens League and of a group supporting Minneapolis public schools, he would be the ideal candidate to take on Duempke, Kubicek argued. Our district was liberal and the whole university community would support him. But we had all these children and Fraser was building a law practice, I countered, torn between political and family concerns.

Kubicek sympathized but was relentless. Don sat quietly, rocking in his father's old chair. I could tell the idea tempted him.

All three of us understood the campaign would be a difficult. Duempke had deep roots in the northeast community. He owned the area's newspaper, inherited from his father. We would have to aggressively cultivate labor support, wean ordinary union people away from voting for their longtime conservative incumbent, and rely heavily on university faculty and liberals in our neighborhood for votes and money. With Freeman—Don's law partner—running for governor, the election would be old politics vs. new, conservative vs. liberal. It was our—the DFL Party's—opportunity to change the state. Wasn't this what we had all been working for since 1948? Kubicek asked. We had elected Humphrey U.S. senator and half the Minnesota Congressional delegation. Now was the time to take on state government. Although the legislature was officially non-partisan, the Conservatives (Republicans in all but name) would likely retain control of the Senate, but the House might go Liberal (DFL). If Freeman won, we could begin to write into law ideas we had in the party platform—continued strong support for the university, increased support for elementary and secondary schools, and more liberal tax policies. To elect Freeman, the party needed to get every possible DFL vote out of its strongholds, Minneapolis, St. Paul, and the Iron Range. Fraser running in the 49th district would improve Freeman's chances and those of the whole DFL Party.

I gave in. Our family would survive. It might even be fun. Without fully realizing it, we were embarking as co-captains of a new ship that would sail for more than half a century through good winds and storms. Fraser and I were launching two careers that would criss-cross from local to national and international work and back again. Fortunately, we were blessed with supportive families. My brother Ken, a university student, was our early in-house helper. When he was drafted during the Korean War, Mrs. Pesina, a widowed neighbor who needed part-time work, replaced him. My sister Bonnie, who had graduated from Mankato and become a teacher in a nearby suburb, served as my standby mother's assistant, on call when we needed her.

The 1954 campaign ended our somewhat serene family life. Evenings while Fraser rang doorbells, I ran off hundreds of invitations to neighborhood coffee parties in Fraser's handwriting on the multilith. With the aid of volunteers, and with children playing nearby, we clipped the invitations to campaign brochures. Other volunteers distributed the invitations throughout the neighborhood where the coffee party was to be held. Hostesses had visions of hordes arriving, but we assured them we would be lucky if one percent of the invitees came. The idea was to introduce Fraser as the candidate, make people feel he was accessible, and encourage them to at least look at the brochure.

I didn't attend many coffee parties. Being the dutiful, admiring wife was not my forte. Organizing things behind the scenes was. I maintained the card file, wrote the campaign newsletter and fundraising letters, helped design the brochure and signs, typed thank you notes for Fraser to sign, and monitored campaign expenditures.

A good friend, Gerry Dillon, ran a print shop and was campaign treasurer. I found learning about printing, photography and design stimulating. I learned how to crop a picture, lay out a brochure, select type face, plan a print run and what colors were best for lawn signs. Together Gerry, Don, and I wrote the campaign literature. We found Jerry Liebling, a talented young photographer, who was both patient and creative with the kids and Don, all of whom hated being photographed. Liebling understood the ideas we were trying to convey: Fraser as a family man with a variety of interests, a serious, knowledgeable guy who would protect the university and promote the interests of the "working man."

Campaigns are social as well as political affairs. Common interests breed friendships. Few women worked outside the home in 1954. Like me, they found volunteering in a campaign, doing its drudge work, a stimulating break from the isolation of keeping a house and tending small children. Sitting around my dining room table afternoons, stuffing envelopes with newsletters or fundraising appeals, we'd also discuss books we were reading, an issue we cared passionately about, or the latest news. "Pass me some envelopes" or

"I'm out of stamps" or even, "No, Suzie, you can't have another cookie!" to a child, didn't disrupt ongoing conversations. Most of my old Minnesota friends—men and women—I can trace back to some campaign.

Margaret Harding, director of the University Press, was Don's campaign chair. The contemporary of his parents, she knew every current and retired University faculty member in the city, and their spouses. She practically demanded from them a financial contribu-

Arvonne at work

tion for the Friends of Fraser, our campaign committee. Campaign meetings at her house were no-nonsense affairs. Watching her dark eyes flash with delight over an idea, or with contempt at some stupidity, I knew why the University Press was renowned. When the meeting was over and coffee and dessert was served, she'd relax and regale us with stories of university history. I delighted in the one about women faculty having to sit "behind the potted palms" in the Campus Club until she changed that. Tough but never malicious, she was the first female executive I encountered and a great role model. Later I came to appreciate her recounting how, after her children were in school, she became somewhat depressed, until her husband suggested she get a job because "you have to have something to get up for in the morning."

As the campaign progressed, my card file of names, addresses, and phone numbers became tangible evidence of individuals, many of whom I cared deeply about. Mrs. Cram, was one. Whenever I saw her card, I'd recall the gossip about this friendly widow who still washed clothes by hand but contributed substantial amounts of money to Community Chest drives. She endeared herself even more when she donated her husband's blocks—a basketful of large, plain pine blocks polished smooth, that he had played with as a child—to the campaign rummage sale. I bought them, and still think of Mrs. Cram when our grandchildren play with these century-old blocks.

Mrs. Cram's crowning achievement was election eve. Crews were organized to ring doorbells in a last minute get-out-the vote effort. The November night turned bitterly cold and windy. Who in their right mind would go out on a night like this? But Mrs. Cram, then at least seventy, was undeterred. She and her troupe of friends from Prospect Park, the faculty neighborhood, bundled up, tramped through snow and sleet, and did their assigned precinct in a Northeast working class neighborhood. Returning to our house to report, they were elated over their reception. We always felt that stalwart group contributed a great deal to Fraser's winning the election by a tiny margin. I was learning that small actions by courageous, committed women can make a big difference. Alpha Smaby, a younger woman among the group, later ran for state representative. She served with distinction, becoming one of Minnesota's ardent anti-Vietnam war leaders.

While most of our stalwart campaign workers came from Southeast Minneapolis, and were women, we knew we had to win Northeast and win it big. That meant getting labor union endorsements. Don's liberal credentials got him labor support, but grudgingly, because he was identified with "the University crowd" and what labor guys (and I) called "do gooder" community organizations. Knowing politics is about creating impressions, stimulating favorable conversation about the candidate and his campaign (it was almost always *his* campaign in the 1950's) I was ruthless in portraying Fraser as the bright, new light, the good family man, a liberal who cared about everybody—which was true.

But ringing doorbells scared me. Yet I had to be able to say I'd done it if I was going to recruit others to do it. One lovely summer afternoon after naptime, I cleaned and dressed up our three youngsters, put the made-for-twins stroller in the back of our station wagon with plenty of campaign literature on the front seat, and set out for the old Italian neighborhood not far from our house. It voted heavily Democratic in national elections but was used to the conservative incumbent. Parking at the end of a block with the big, homemade Fraser for Senate sign atop the car, I unloaded stroller and kids. Tucking campaign literature and a baby bottle in the stroller, I told myself I could do this. Resplendent in my cotton maternity jumper—number four already on its way—I proceeded to push the stroller up the sidewalk as if I were out for an afternoon walk.

I didn't have to ring a single doorbell. Mid-afternoon, almost every yard was filled with grandmothers sitting on kitchen chairs, aprons across their bulging stomachs, slimmer mothers leaning against fences between the yards chatting with neighbors. Every yard was filled with young children, all enjoying the perfect weather. Approaching the first group, I parked the stroller, pulled out brochures, smiled a greeting and managed to blurt out my rehearsed opening to the friendliest looking grandmother:

"Hi, I'm Mrs. Fraser. My husband is running for state senate in this district. We hope you'll take a look at this booklet and vote for him. He's DFL."

Without waiting for an answer, I handed her a brochure, face up as Don had instructed, so his picture was visible along with the large, stark words "Vote for Fraser for State Senate."

"You get about one minute to get your message across, make an impression," Don had said, frightening me even more at the prospect of calling on strangers.

"Nice family," a matriarch responded in heavily-accented English, pointing to the children and smiling. Then she turned to her friend and spoke rapidly in Italian. I recognized "bambino" and "Fraser." The ice was broken; the matriarch's actions had been a signal. I could see the rest of the group unfolding arms, ready to receive brochures. Another sturdy grandmother moved toward the children, smiling and clucking, asking Tommy his name and how old he was.

I relaxed somewhat. I'd grown up with old women who couldn't speak English and identified with mothers who paused to enjoy their only free hour of the day. The housework done, the children happy after naps and a snack, the men not yet home, they had time to relax. The baby boom hadn't been named yet but I was evidence of it and this was a good Catholic neighborhood.

"Boys or girls?" another woman asked, nodding toward the stroller as she accepted a brochure without looking at it. "How old?" asked another. "Oh, DFL. That's good, " still another said.

Thanking the group, I moved on down the street, repeating my spiel, knowing there would be talk about me and, hopefully, Fraser for the rest of the day. I only did two blocks before the little ones got restless, but the word spread. Fifty years later, at least once a year, somebody comments about my ringing doorbells in that neighborhood. I smile and don't admit I never rang another doorbell for a campaign.

Once was enough. Running campaigns was more to my taste, though sometimes things got out of hand. Our dilapidated old two-story garage, originally a barn for horse and carriage, was where Don and volunteers built campaign lawn and car-top signs. It was also an intriguing playhouse for the children. By 1958 and Don's re-election campaign we had Annie, our devil-may-care child, who drank turpentine left in a pan by volunteers working on the signs. Mary Mac saw Annie, but too late, and came running into the house screaming.

"Mom, come quick. Annie drank something out of a pan." A quick smell and I knew. Scrambling all five children into the car, I rushed to Minneapolis General Hospital's emergency room. After her little stomach was pumped out, the incident had to be recorded. When asked her birth date, I totally blanked, had no idea when that child was born. I did know my name and address. All I could think of was, thank heavens she's all right. As I carried her back to the car, her devilish smile said, "What's the big deal?" That was Annie who was lucky her mother didn't believe in hitting children.

With Freeman as governor and Don in the state Senate, our living room became a place for shadow-cabinet and legislative strategy sessions. I was welcomed as a quiet, if not totally silent, participant. By

1956 I had been elected a state party vice chairwoman and member of the DFL State Executive Committee. These sessions became my graduate seminar in the policy process. University graduate students would have fought to watch Professor Walter Heller, later President Kennedy's Chairman of the Council of Economic Advisers, outline a pay-as-you-go taxation scheme for state income taxes, now called withholding. Or to see how a constitutional amendment changing the governors' term from two to four years got drafted. Don's brilliant suggestion to make the amendment effective four years later—after Freeman would be out of office—brought a laughing cheer. Of course. That would make the amendment innocuous, and might well ensure its passage. It did.

Less fun was a Sunday afternoon session right before the 1958 election when the burgeoning civil rights movement came home to us, literally. A scurrilous sheet had been put on cars parked outside North and Northeast Minneapolis churches. It implied that blacks would be inundating those predominately white lower-income neighborhoods because Senator Fraser and his liberal colleagues had introduced a fair housing bill. The bill hadn't passed but a committee had been formed to study the problem.

Fair housing proponents, including many blacks, joined worried liberal legislators and their campaign managers and party leaders in our living room, decrying the attack and debating what to do. If unanswered, the charge threatened Fraser's re-election and that of other liberals as well. The facts about the bill could not be denied or disowned. But, as was often jestingly said, "To be a statesman, you first have to get elected." The decision was to equivocate, buy time. We decided to blanket the same area with postcards saying only that a committee had been formed to study the issue. Most heartening to me was that a legislator whom our group often disdained was the most outspoken in support of Fraser and the bill.

Fraser's 1958 re-election was graduation from Campaign Management 101 for me. Don was no mean campaign strategist but being candidate and campaign manager simultaneously is no way to win elections. We co-managed his campaigns and had many an argument about strategy, but he relied on me to carry the organization. Building an effective campaign organization is like staging a play around a star. You put him on the stage, tell him what to do and where and when, but what he believes and says are his. You can argue backstage but it's *his* campaign. Campaign contributors are the play's backers, campaign volunteers the stage hands. And as a Fraser staffer said some years later, someone has to be the SOB, the lieutenant who says no to supporters and contributors and allows the candidate or elected official to be Mr. Nice Guy. Being Mrs. SOB was one of my roles.

It wasn't all sweetness and light. The closing night of Fraser's first session of the legislature in 1955, I eagerly awaited his return home. As I put the children to bed I thought about how good it would be to have Don home again and to learn what finally happened in the closing hours of the session. The winter months had been exciting, but lonely. Lois, our fourth child, was born February twelfth on an evening Don was in Duluth speaking to a group. Bonnie, as usual, was on hand and drove me to the hospital. It was a quick and easy birth. A beautiful baby with her grandmother's name, Lois MacKay Fraser, she became "Yoyo" because our John couldn't pronounce his l's. Four were a handful, especially in the dead of winter, but also a joy. Watching them grow and develop, their different personalities, the way they looked and smelled after a bath, compensated for the work involved. Still, the lack of adult company got to me on gray winter days.

I was proud that in his first session Don became a leader of the tiny Liberal Caucus in carrying Governor Freeman's legislative program. I felt part of politics and state government because of my DFL activities and the meetings in our living room. I understood the pressure on Don with two jobs—law and legislature. His firm, now named Larson, Loevinger, Lindquist, Freeman and Fraser, had been decimated by the election of three partners to public office in 1954—Freeman, Fraser and liberal Republican Leonard Lindquist, also elected to the legislature. Elated as we all were about the victories, the reality was hard on everybody.

That final night of the session I got the three oldest children to sleep by eight, then tried to read until Yoyo's ten o'clock feeding, but my mind was at the Capitol. Nursing her, I caught myself dozing off, and decided to go to bed, and wake when Don got home. I wanted all the details. At the two o'clock feeding, he still wasn't home but sleep has never been my problem. The next thing I knew he was climbing into bed. Roused, I mumbled: "What time is it?"

"Four o'clock," a tired, defensive voice answered. "We finished and then went out for a drink." I could tell by the weight of his arm that he was asleep in a minute.

So, his friends were more important than I! Five months I've been alone day and night, and he can go out with the boys! Furious, I rolled to the far side of the bed. Next thing I knew four children were awake, clamoring for attention, baby crying, and my legislator-husband dead to the world. Throwing a robe on, I grabbed Yoyo in one arm, hoisted year-old John onto the other hip, and we all descended the back stairs to the kitchen. Another grey day, another breakfast, the kitchen reeking of soggy diapers. Other mornings I'd laughed at making Malt o'Meal and pouring orange juice with one hand, hungry baby in the crook of my left arm. This morning I slammed the refrigerator door, slopped milk over cereal, and ignored the childish chatter I usually relished. Wallowing in martyrdom, I munched a piece of dry raisin toast, as I nursed Yoyo while watching the others breakfast.

"About his turn," I resolved. "Time he learns what I have to cope with every day, all day." I burped the baby, plopped her in the tiny, downstairs crib, swiped a wet cloth across three faces and thirty fingers, and marched them upstairs again for their morning shower with Mom. The little bodies weren't adorable this morning. I noticed anew that the shower needed cleaning. Teeth clenched, I stepped over wet diapers, pajamas, and towels, and shooed three vigorously dried, naked children toward our bedroom and their sleeping father.

"I'm going out. You can take over." I announced to my own surprise, as I pushed three bare butts up onto the bed, encouraging them to wake Daddy.

"Where're you going?" a shocked voice said over squealing children.

"I don't know. Just out. They're all yours." I opened the closet and pulled my new green wool suit off its hanger.

"They've had breakfast. Yoyo will need a bottle sometime between ten and eleven. Throw the stuff in the bathroom down the clothes chute."

Dressed, I dabbed on lipstick and ran a comb through my hair. Back downstairs, I made a bottle for the baby, careful I didn't spill on my suit, put it in the refrigerator, grabbed my purse and car keys and slammed the door behind me. He could cope, figure out how to get them all dressed and keep them happy, out of mischief. I'd be back before lunch. But where now? The public library? No, Amluxen's, the upscale fabric store women traveled hundreds of miles to patronize. I needed a more tactile lift, and people.

The look and feel of the elegant cottons and wools from Europe temptingly laid out on Amluxen's tables didn't enchant me this morning. Like a tiger out of her cage, I was out for blood. I strode up Nicollet Avenue to Dayton's, the department store known as the refuge for idle women. Ignoring the children's department where I bought T shirts and Stride Rites in bulk during every sale, I took the escalator up to the *haute couture* Oval Room. My good black pumps sinking in the clean, thick carpeting, I feasted my eyes on the suits and coats designed in Paris. A lovely light gray flannel coat—straight, tailored, with striped grey and white taffeta lining—caught my eye. Before I could utter my standard "just looking," to the immaculately dressed saleswoman, she was slipping the coat off its hanger. "It's exactly your style," she said, appraising my suit, giving no indication that she knew it was home-sewn. My spirits soared.

A rare petite size, I could reach the bottom of the pockets without leaning over and the sleeves were almost the right length. I stroked the soft flannel appreciatively, marveled at the buttonholes, admired the perfect roll of the collar, knowing I hadn't the skill to replicate it. Slyly, I glanced at the price tag. $75! I'd never spent that much on a coat before.

"Smashing," the consummate salesclerk said in her most enticing voice, adjusting the hang of the garment ever so slightly by
patting my shoulders. "We shorten the sleeves and hem at no cost.
Come back with me and we'll get it measured. We'll have it delivered it to you in a week."

I followed her like a lamb to slaughter. If he could stay out
half the night with the boys, I could jolly well have this coat. I was
in charge of my own destiny, wasn't I? I pulled out my Dayton's
card and signed the credit slip with a flourish, remembering the
trouble—and satisfaction—I'd had changing that card to my own
name when I got divorced. I felt triumphant and could hardly wait
to get home, see the children, have lunch and get all the news about
the session. I was becoming part of the DFL matriarchy—devoted
mother, party officer, campaign volunteer, and occasional shopper—
but with a mind of my own.

In 1956 Alpha Smaby and Geri Joseph led the Minnesota Volunteers for Stevenson along with Eugenie Anderson of Red Wing, a
Truman-era U.S. Ambassador to Denmark, thanks to her friendship
with Senator Humphrey and leadership in the party. Both the DFL
and the Republican parties at the time had party rules requiring
election of a chairwoman paralleling every chairman. Recognized,
but rarely admitted, was the fact that in many districts the chairwoman was a more powerful political force than the chairman. Alpha Smaby was a tall Scandinavian, an outspoken League of Women
Voters member and, alongside her husband, active in the cooperative
movement. With three tall, blond daughters and energy to burn, Alpha was active in the Second Ward DFL Club.

Geri, a brilliant and extremely good-looking journalist who had
made a name for herself investigating mental health conditions for
the *Minneapolis Tribune*, had married a prominent grain executive,
and was now at home with children. Her joining the DFL Party
was considered a coup and I had given a resounding speech for
her nomination as state DFL chairwoman. Both Geri and Alpha
represented a new generation in DFL politics, a younger breed of

professionals, intellectuals, artists, and housewives who thought of partisan politics as much more stimulating and satisfying than tennis, golf, or watching a Gophers football game.

Volunteers for Stevenson was essentially a women's group that I eagerly joined. Adlai Stevenson, the former governor of Illinois, and second-time presidential candidate, was our kind of liberal. A close friend of Eleanor Roosevelt, he gave women visibility in his campaigns. In our downtown Minneapolis campaign office, we created a play space for the children we brought along as we played our deadly serious game of politics. We organized rallies, peddled our precincts with little ones in tow, solicited contributions, and built card files of supporters. Stevenson lost to Eisenhower but we were undaunted. We had Hubert Humphrey in the Senate, Gene McCarthy in Congress, Orville Freeman as governor, more DFLers in the Minnesota Legislature, and a powerful group of women in our ward clubs and county units. Earlier we had all watched with horror on our new black and white TV sets as Senator Joe McCarthy of Wisconsin held his hearings on the danger of supposed Communists in government and cheered when he was discredited. We were thrilled at the decision of the Supreme Court in *Brown v. Board of Education* that mandated school integration in the South. We called ourselves "liberals" and understood that politics was not just about campaigns but about discussing and promoting the social and economic issues about which we cared strongly.

In Minnesota this meant being active in the DFL Party year around and making ourselves heard. "Tough broads," and "the matriarchy," some men in the party called us, though never to our faces. We knew how to count and court votes. During campaigns we "manned" the phones. At precinct caucuses and local and state conventions we elected our slates of delegates, made speeches, and helped determine who got endorsed for public office. Endorsement meant a place on the party sample ballot distributed to households across the state. It was key to election, although occasionally maverick candidates with good Scandinavian or Irish names got elected in the primary.

At a post-election luncheon in late 1956, hosted by Alpha Smaby in the Minneapolis Athletic Club— treat after countless coffee parties and meetings in our homes—the idea of a Democratic Women's Forum was floated. Soon called simply the DWF, we spent the early part of 1957 getting our new group organized, meeting in each other's homes mid-day when the children were in school, some bringing still-nursing babies along. Others brought knitting, their needles clicking as fast as their thoughts and mouths. Elected in 1956 as a DFL state party vice chairwoman, I became the DWF"s liaison officer, the link to the party. I didn't realize it, but this was the beginning of my overt feminist political activity. Our DWF goal was to attract more women like ourselves to politics, maintain and increase women's influence in the DFL Party and, to get more women in elective offices. We were moving from campaign offices and political backrooms and conventions into the mainstream of politics.

The DWF's first public meeting on October 17, 1957 was called a Coming-Out-Party—a phrase that now has other meanings— which featured Emily Taft Douglas from Illinois, a former congresswoman and wife of U.S. Senator Paul Douglas speaking on "Democratic Women in Politics—A New Look. "The notice we sent out said her speech would be followed by a panel of women discussing their "own feelings about and adventures in political life and whatever joys and satisfactions it has brought." The letter accompanying the invitation to the party also posed the question: "Why is it that public-spirited American women will devote time and energy to such non-partisan organizations as P.T.A, church groups, and the League of Women Voters, but are reluctant to take part in politics? And why don't more women who *are* politically active run for office themselves?" The letter concluded with the new organization's aim: "to attract intelligent, liberal women who are not now active in the DFL...",

The word intelligent now jumps out at me. It wasn't inadvertent. We *were* an elite group, an urban female "smoke-filled room," for many of us smoked and were unapologetic about our intent to capture and exert political power. We were bent on defeating the Republican Party, which had dominated Minnesota politics for decades, but we wanted women to be part of the action. We were not above deception. We conformed to norms as we flaunted them. An internal, membership invitation listed officers by their first and last names only, not a Mrs. among them. A second "Dear Friend" announcement, sent to a much wider list and to the press, identified the officers as Mrs. Bernard Bowron, Mrs. Lee Wattenberg, Mrs. Donald Fraser, etc.—and Mrs. Douglas as "her husband's 'right hand man' in Washington."

One hundred twenty eager women showed up at the venerable Leamington Hotel at 10:30 a.m. that morning, paying $2.50 for registration and brunch, assured of being home by 3:30 when children returned from school. The extensive newspaper publicity the event attracted sent the DWF on its way to becoming a political force. The following June, Lucy Bowron made her fashionable Lowry Hill house available for a Saturday night Art Bazaar. Local artists contributed serious works for an auction to raise DWF campaign funds. Senator Humphrey was one of the auctioneers. Over $2000 in cash was collected that evening plus hundreds more in checks. The treasurer didn't sleep all weekend. She'd never had one-tenth that much cash in her purse and had to guard it until she could get to the bank Monday morning. (ATM's with deposit slots were non-existent in 1956.)

The 1958 campaign put DWF on the political radar with strong signals. Selected candidates received substantial DWF contributions, as did the DFL Sample Ballot Fund. Carefully worded cover letters to the candidates promised DWF women as campaign workers. In 1960 Lucy Bowron and her friends again recruited the aspiring artists from her Art Bazaar to design and contribute colorful political signs with clever slogans, garnering attention for both the artists and the Kennedy for President campaign. When Jack Kennedy came to Minnesota for a rally, my two oldest children held up a "Kids for Caroline" sign at the huge evening rally and were delighted when TV cameras were directed their way. When Fraser ran for Congress in 1962, the DWF and the artists were among his strong supporters. Selling the signs to supporters brought our campaign substantial funds and provided it with humor and panache.

During its short life, the DWF proved that the DFL was not simply a merger of two staid old parties but a new party attracting a post-war generation of voters, especially women and professional and businessmen—a group that had traditionally been Republican. While our children watched *I Love Lucy* and *Leave It to Beaver* on TV, DWF women were quietly deciding there was more to life than being mothers. Bit by bit and one by one, they began going back to school or seeking paid employment. Just as many of us had been mothers of the baby boom—having as many or more children than our mothers—we also became part of the massive re-entry of women into the paid labor force during the 1960s and 70s. I just took longer than most to find a paid job. I was enjoying my political career.

Chapter 7

Off to Washington

A sk not what your country can do for you. Ask what you can do for your country." That challenge in President John F. Kennedy's inaugural address stirred the nation. The first Catholic to be elected president, his campaign theme, "Get America moving again," ushered in a new era. President Dwight Eisenhower, Kennedy's predecessor, had commanded Allied Forces in Europe during World War II. Kennedy came to the presidency as an injured young Navy veteran and as a U.S. senator from Massachusetts.

Don and I broke ranks with the DFL establishment by supporting Kennedy early. Usually we waited until we got "the word"—instructions—from Humphrey or Freeman as to whom to support. But by 1960 their firm grip on the DFL Party was weakening. At the Democratic national convention in Los Angeles that year, the Minnesota delegation was split. Our other DFL senator, Gene McCarthy, gave a nomination speech for Adlai Stevenson; Freeman spoke for Kennedy; and everybody hoped Humphrey would be chosen for Vice President by whoever got the nomination. Instead, Kennedy chose Senator Lyndon B. Johnson of Texas because he thought that state was crucial in a close election. We were disappointed, but Kennedy was right. His speech in Texas to a Protestant ministers association helped allay fears about electing a Catholic president. Barriers were being broken.

Don became chairman of the Kennedy campaign in Minnesota and brought our usual Fraser campaign pattern to presidential politics, driving the male campaign manager crazy until he realized there was nothing he could do to change it. While the older children were in school I went to the Kennedy campaign office, with Annie and

Yoyo and gear to amuse them. I also brought campaign plans and directives Fraser and I had talked about over and after dinner, and again at breakfast, between conversations with and about the kids. It was how we had jointly run his campaigns for state senate and it worked well. We didn't plan this; didn't proclaim it. Like water seeking its level, the pattern emerged. Don had his law practice to tend, a living to make. Politics was our avocation. I was co-strategist and de facto campaign manager, not a wife, delivering his instructions. To make things worse for the poor campaign manager, I was an acknowledged politician, a state DFL vice-chairwoman and a leader in the Democratic Women's Forum. Impossible to ignore, but only part-time, I was too busy and too focused on winning a campaign to feel or do anything about the tensions that ensued—or even to wonder myself about this anomalous role.

The DFL party and campaigns were all headed by men in the 1950s and 60s, but women undergirded these entities. Their volunteer help and fundraising capacities were essential, although this was rarely acknowledged. We didn't expect praise; we had power, and used it. We endured the sexism, but the Democratic Women's Forum was a signal that we didn't take it lightly. We took great satisfaction in overhearing male colleagues make derisive comments about "the 2nd ward matriarchy," though only some of us lived in the Second Ward. It was verbal shorthand for the University crowd.

We weren't originals. Strong women preceded us, and the men knew it and accepted it. Our group of younger women would never have acknowledged that Blanche McIntosh was our role model, but she was a foremother. A formidable politician despite—or maybe because of—her lustrous white hair, Blanche had little time for the DFL's younger group. She coined the term "diaper brigade," and later, after Freeman was elected governor, called us—men and women included—"the palace guard." Revered by some, heard by all because of her oratorical and organizational abilities, she was feared by our younger group at district and Hennepin County conventions because she wielded power. She was our symbol of strong old ladies in politics. I laugh at my white-haired self now. Am I a latter day

Blanche McIntosh, a thing of the past young people listen to while going on their merry way? Probably.

Anne Vetter and her 12th ward, labor-oriented and American Legion auxiliary friends could always be counted on to come in and stuff literature. But when it came time for precinct caucuses and party conventions, Anne and her group were to be watched and feared. Freeman courted them in his macho way but they followed labor leaders more than Freeman. Though she and her friends looked like ladies who lunched, Anne's slate usually got elected in her ward and Freeman, Humphrey, and other candidates relied on Anne to introduce them around American Legion or Catholic gatherings during and between campaigns.

I hate to admit it, but I now believe there was a great deal of both classism and racism in the Democratic-Farmer-Labor Party in those years. This may have been because we were trying to lure professional people and executives away from the dominant liberal Republican Party. League of Women Voters activists, who might look like nice ladies but were tough politicians—some going back to suffrage days and the origins of the League—were courted by Freeman and Humphrey. Emily Knuebuhl from the right side of the tracks in the 7th ward was one, with her young friend, Sally Luther. With her own election to the legislature, Sally carried on that ward's tradition, begun with the election of Mabeth Hurd Paige in 1922 when women were first allowed to be candidates. Myrtle Cain, another of the four women elected in 1922, was too often overlooked, even disdained by some in her later years. She was from Northeast, a blue collar neighborhood. Nellie Stone Johnson and Cecil Newman, black activists, were forces in the DFL, devoted to Humphrey, but there were few other blacks in prominent positions. Politics is complex and democracy imperfect but, as Winston Churchill famously said, it's the best we've got.

With Kennedy's election, Freeman went off to Washington as Secretary of Agriculture, taking Tommy Hughes, Dorothy Jacobson, and a number of our other DFL colleagues as assistants.

Dorothy had been Freeman's policy assistant in the governor's office. Don's law partner, Lee Loevinger, became an assistant attorney general under Bobby Kennedy. The firm's senior partner, Earl Larson, was appointed a federal judge. The public service credo of that firm reaped rewards. Walter Heller and Joe Robertson, Don's allies in the Freeman "shadow cabinet," also joined the Kennedy administration. Don's and my focus turned from the state to the federal level with Kennedy's victory. In 1962 Don ran for Congress.

The pattern of my being de facto campaign manager continued. I wasn't happy when Don hired a man with little political experience as campaign manager. He wanted a man's name on the campaign literature. I felt sorry for the poor guy who was left hanging out in proverbial left field. His ego was more bruised than mine. Though he got paid in dollars; I got the kudos, which are satisfying. We bought groceries and paid the mortgage on Don's income, a possibility then.

Our Fraser for Congress campaign slogan, "A Strong America Begins at Home," coined after weeks of brainstorming, was a winner. We used it relentlessly. Anybody vaguely interested in politics had it ingrained in their minds before the campaign was over. We think it's the best campaign slogan we ever used. In 2004, John Kerry used it in his presidential campaign for awhile. Hindsight tells me he should have kept it. Good political slogans are double-edged. They have a positive slant while obliquely criticizing the opponent. Congressman Walter Judd, the man Don ran against, had twenty years of congressional service, had been a medical missionary in China, and was revered for his experience in foreign policy. Cold War tensions ran high in 1962. Fraser's strengths and experience were on domestic economic and social issues. The 1961 state legislature redrew Congressional district lines because Minnesota lost a congressional seat after the 1960 census. Judd's safe south Minneapolis district was expanded to encompass all of Minneapolis plus a small Northeast suburb, St. Anthony Village. Now a much more liberal district, it was winnable.

Our slogan had a third implication. Although the baby boom was nearing its end in 1962, large families and extended families were still admired. Our campaign brochure included pictures of all our children, Don's father, his brother, and me. Cut lines under the pictures reinforced the strong family message. Even my sixth pregnancy was mentioned in one newspaper ad that featured the oft-used family picture on the front steps of our house. What later came to be called "family values" by conservatives was then liberal orthodoxy, assumed, implied but never named. Political contexts change and campaign managers bend with it. Gradually our campaign literature focused less on our large family, a subtle, unacknowledged—even by us—response to growing concerns about population growth.

We rented our St. Croix summer house to friends and concentrated on the campaign. It was a family affair. Pregnant again, I strode around the campaign office in maternity outfits. The kids tagged along to the office and campaign events. They ate more sweets than they should have but the older ones proudly displayed their expertise at stuffing envelopes and in peddling precincts on lovely fall Saturday afternoons. Dale MacIver, ever our friend and helpmate, wandered into the house at breakfast with the morning paper. Many evenings, campaign meetings were held in our living room. The kids enjoyed the excitement and the attention they got from adults and young campaign workers. They were bug-eyed watching the parade when President Kennedy came to town to campaign for Don. Gerry Elliott, a tireless staffer, took Annie, aged 5, along campaigning one day on Washington Avenue, then a rather squalid commercial area. Her comment, on hearing they were on Washington, was that she didn't think she'd like to live there. That made the rounds of the campaign office, evoking smiles. Our opponent's wife was never seen in public, and his official biography lists neither wife nor children.

Organizing and managing things is in my blood. As our number six child, Jean, once said, exasperation in her voice, when I expressed amazement that she got high marks on the in-and-out-box section of the Foreign Service exam: "Mom, I hung around offices all my life!" I hung around farm men and women in my childhood. You don't survive in farming unless you are a good manager, making sure everything is done right and on time, watching every expenditure.

I thrived on making the campaign run smoothly, walking around the headquarters checking every detail, cajoling and sometimes exasperating volunteers and staff. Deadlines, people, and controversy energize me. The diversity of tasks—from designing and getting out mailings to critiquing ads to fundraising—means you deal with a diversity of people. In one day I might go from picking up a large contribution from an executive to helping the ex-convict who volunteered to clean the office. Campaigns attract all kinds of people. That ex-con forged a check on his lover's account after the campaign and went back to jail, we heard later. He never stole a penny from us.

Fraser never left major decisions to his staff. We made them, after advice from many. We argued often, laughed oftener and kept the days we were scared silly about the outcome to ourselves. In many ways, a campaign is like a pregnancy. You know it will end and your control of the outcome is never assured. Jean Skelton, our sixth, was born December 8, a month after the election, as I was cleaning out our house for renters. We departed for Washington two weeks later in a two-car caravan. Behind our little blue Nash, Don and the boys had a U-Haul trailer packed with household goods and clothes. My sister Bonnie and I shared driving our 1957 red and white Chevy station wagon packed with baby bassinet, toys, games and three excited girls. Santa found us in a motel room somewhere in Indiana. The reek of smelly diapers—in a pre-Pampers era—driving along freeways with all the car windows rolled up, was more memorable.

"YUK, roll down the window," a child would yell. Then "Roll it back up, it's too cold!" another would shout as we barreled sixty-five miles an hour or crawled over icy turnpikes at twenty-five, trying to keep the other vehicle in sight. By Illinois I was expert at changing and nursing the baby while playing Twenty Questions, and deft at rinsing out dirty diapers in rest stop toilets. After one chaotic stop, waiting for food orders with restless kids pushing and shoving each other or playing with napkins and salt and pepper shakers, we developed a plan. Fifteen miles before reaching our previously designated rest stop was car-cleanup time. A smaller child held the trash bag, the older ones cleaned up the back of the station wagon, the playroom for the kids in this pre-seat belt era. Then it was time to don boots and coats, older kids helping younger. Bonnie and Don led the troupe to the toilets. I took charge of the baby. Eleven-year-old Tom was sent into the café to commandeer a large enough table or booth and order "twelve hamburgers and sixteen milks." Incredulous waitresses wondered what was going on until our horde emerge from the rest rooms.

Joy over Don's election victory and the adventure of moving to Washington buoyed us throughout the trip. On our arrival, Annie wondered if President Kennedy had shoveled the snowy walk for us. But three weeks later, in suburban Chevy Chase, in a rented-furnished diplomat's house ten miles from the Capitol, six of the eight Frasers were in a funk. Don was on a high and baby Jean was oblivious to everything but me.

I had become a non-entity, Mrs. Congressman. The frequent "Is it Indianapolis or Minneapolis you're from?" question grated on my nerves. No longer the victorious campaign manager, Minneapolis Board of Public Welfare and DFL State Executive Committee member, my ego hit bottom. Managing four disillusioned school children who entered classes mid-year knowing no one, and who had to be careful at home with someone else's good furniture and carpets, was my new career. While Don was feted on Capitol Hill, interviewed by newspapers, radio, and TV for having defeated the venerable Dr. Judd, I was supposed to feel soooo lucky that my wonderful husband had found us a good house. Dutifully posing for news photos in an apron, serving breakfast to my crew with a happy smile in our new Washington house, I pretended delight. Inwardly, I seethed. How could I have been so dumb? Why hadn't I considered what it would be like if he won?

With children, we had been told, families had to live in the suburbs, not the District as Washington, D.C. is called by insiders. White liberals never said outright that one couldn't have one's children going to the virtually all black District schools, but that was implicit. *Brown v. Board of Education* was six years old. Black children integrated white schools, not vice versa. *How racist can one get?* I said to myself, but never publicly. The notion of political correctness hadn't been named yet but it was observed. Back home my friends were deeply involved in the election recount to determine whether our friend, Karl Rolvaag, or Governor Elmer Andersen won their achingly-close election. They were also preparing for the off-year conventions I had helped write into the DFL Party constitution. Reading Minneapolis papers two days late, I wanted to be part of the telephoning, caucusing, rumor gathering, and socializing that had been my life beyond children for the last twelve years. Instead, by mid-January I had rented an electric typewriter, obtained library cards for myself and the kids, and was learning sixth grade math as taught in Maryland's suburban schools.

Crying is not my style. Mom—and even Grandma Skelton— didn't tolerate tears. You bit your lip and moved on. While the older children were in school I poured out letters of complaint to Caroline Rose, Marilyn Gorlin, and other close political women friends. You didn't call long distance just to chat. I pleaded with party colleagues for the latest insider political gossip, and wrote upbeat accounts to both sets of parents about the Kennedy administration's doings. I wasn't going to admit to our parents my disappointment. Watching Don put on his new tux and go off to parties in Georgetown or on the Hill—as I learned the Capitol area was called—I reveled in martyrdom. My excuse for not attending Don's swearing-in ceremony was that I had to drive Annie to afternoon kindergarten. In truth, I never have liked ceremonies much. Election night parties were more my style. I was not to be mollified, but I did appreciate comic relief. One cold afternoon with baby Jean in my arm, I went out the backdoor to drive Annie to kindergarten. Slipping on the icy steps, the baby popped out of my arms and glided smoothly down the icy sidewalk. Swaddled in soft wool blankets, she let out not a peep. Even I had to laugh after I found I hadn't killed her. It made a great story for my interminable letters.

My funk deepened when Don came home from a party at Vice President Lyndon Johnson's house to report that Senator Humphrey had told him that it had taken Muriel, his wife, two years to begin to like Washington.

My introduction to diplomatic circles didn't help. Don achieved his goal of membership on the Foreign Affairs Committee and was being honored at a dinner. U.S. Foreign Service officers, all freshly showered white males in navy blue suits, white shirts, and conservative red ties, interrupted their conversations long enough to acknowledge wives with a nod, a word and a glassy-eyed smile. Their well-trained wives smiled more broadly and murmured congratulations. In the car going home after the third of such dinners, I threatened to wear a street vendors' signboard saying "congressional wife, six kids, living in Chevy Chase." It would go nicely with my little black dress, I added sarcastically. Hearing wives talk about overseas assignments and treasures acquired abroad while men had brandy and discussed affairs of state was not my idea of an evening that merited feeding kids early, getting gussied up, and finding and paying a sitter. I got really good at making myself and my husband miserable.

Even being invited to speak to the prestigious Women's National Democratic Club didn't improve my morale. Jane Freeman, wife of now-Secretary of Agriculture Orville Freeman, picked me up in her husband's chauffeur-driven limo. On the drive to the club, she bubbled about how wonderful Washington was. I nervously puffed on my cigarette, observing too late that my smoke burned her eyes.

"Is that navy blue or black?" a *Women's Wear Daily* reporter asked, leaning over two other attendees to stroke my thigh to assess the quality of wool in my skirt. Flattered yet offended, I was in no mood to be patronized. The event honored us wives of the 1963 class of Democratic Members of Congress. I was asked to give a five-minute talk on how I'd helped my husband get elected. Jane Freeman considered this a real coup; I was too deep into post-partum and post-election depression to appreciate anything.

I perked up a bit when Mrs. Hill of Alabama spoke for I had heard of the Hill-Burton legislation. She described how even in the South campaigns were changing. She was now expected to attend coffee parties with voters. Another senior woman noted that the practice of leaving calling cards at the White House was becoming extinct. She assured us we needn't worry about that rule in the Washington protocol book we were all given. This was the farthest thing from my mind. I was worrying about whether Jane Freeman would call the limo in time to get me home before the kids returned from school.

Lindy Boggs was a breath of fresh air. The very proper but intelligent wife of the well-known New Orleans congressman, Hale Boggs, she later became a member of Congress herself. At this meeting, she told us that she was her husband's congressional administrative assistant, adding with a laugh, that she knew more about his district than he did. She didn't mention she was on his payroll. I discovered that later when Don proudly authored legislation to outlaw such nepotism. To get his bill passed he had to "grandfather in" relatives on congressional payrolls—the sexist language surprising no one. I was learning the ways of Washington but nothing improved my disposition.

Our gregarious, sharp-witted, long-time friend Norman Sherman, became my savior. Having been in our campaign he understood Fraser needed my help in the congressional office. He found Rosetta McDonald, a big, genial woman from North Carolina. who was related to Humphrey's driver and looking for work. She talked to me, not much at first, as she bustled about the house, washing everything in sight—including wool sweaters—in hot water. Sweaters were expendable; Rosetta was not. She cuddled Jeannie and cleaned the house as if both were her own. To those who looked a bit askance at my hiring household help, I joked that Rosetta was much cheaper and more useful than a psychiatrist. The children responded to her presence too. Daily it was "Hi, Rosetta...Bye, Rosetta," or, with dismay, "Didn't Rosetta come?" as they took one look at the house and me.

With Rosetta's help, by late spring 1963 I was commuting to Don's office three mornings a week, driving in with him and taking the bus home in time for the kids' arrival from school. An office atmosphere, complete with like-minded adults to talk to and work with, improved my spirits. Fraser's new congressional staff—some of them old Washington hands—evinced no worries about the boss' wife being in the office. Lindy Boggs and others had paved my way. I could type a hundred words a minute, compose letters Don signed on first draft, and called the congressman Fraser, not honey or dear. Don or Norman's emergence from the inner office to ask my advice about a constituent or a Minneapolis institution conveyed a clear message. The Frasers were a political team, and both, at last, were content.

I knew nothing about congressional protocol or even how to get around the Cannon House Office Building or the Capitol. Pearl, our very formal black receptionist who had worked for the Army, became my willing guide and compatriot. Soon she was almost pestering me for extra things to do, confessing that at her previous job she had few responsibilities.

"There's no harder work than putting in eight hours a day with almost nothing to do," she confessed one day." *This woman has spunk,*

I said to myself. When I discovered she, a single mother, sent her daughter to a private school, I was incredulous:

"On your salary you send your child to private school?" I blurted out.

With fire in her deep brown eyes, she looked straight at me, saying: "There's nothing more important for my daughter than a good education. I went to segregated schools in this city." The naïve lily-white Minnesotan who took access to good public schools for granted was face to face with segregation, its remnants all around me. Between phone calls and typing, Pearl continued my tutorial, telling me what she knew about Washington and urging me to read the book, *Secret City*, which in horrific detail taught me its history as a segregated city.

At home Rosetta contributed to the education of our whole family. Seven-year-old Annie divulged her secret one afternoon. I was back from work and we were all in the kitchen. John asked Rosetta to help him with a word in his schoolbook.

"Don't you know Rosetta can't read!" she spit out accusingly, her blue eyes flashing with anger. Rosetta's dark face blanched. I'll never know how Annie learned that. She probably asked Rosetta to read her a story once.

"I had to work in the fields. I couldn't go to school," Rosetta said in a quiet voice, almost apologetically.

Our normally noisy house turned deathly silent. Not one of us had ever met an adult who couldn't read. How could she get to Washington from North Carolina? How did she know what bus to take to get to our house? She had handed me her Social Security card promptly when I asked for it. How did she know what was on the slips of paper she took out of her huge purse? Those questions and more went through my mind. Our respect and admiration for her grew in this radicalizing moment.

In the Cannon Building on Capitol Hill, next door to our office, was Rosetta's opposite number. There Harlem's congressman, Adam Clayton Powell, held forth as the powerful chairman of the House Education and Labor Committee. Tall and

Shoes for everyone. Annie, John, Arvonne (holding Jean), Mary Mac, Yoyo, and Tom in the foreground

urbane, his starched white shirts, elegant silk ties, and beauti-fully tailored suits set off his handsome brown face and perfectly clipped moustache. He was as brilliant and sophisticated as he looked. His panache and sense of himself was something Fraser would never achieve—or want to. At the peak of his power, Pow-ell used it effectively. His legislative legacy ranges from minimum wage increases to education improvements and civil rights guar-antees. He was fascinating to watch as he strolled down the hall or popped in with a greeting or bit of information. Awesome, my kids would say.

It took some trials and errors before we assembled an effec-tive staff in both our Washington and Minneapolis offices. In late 1963, we turned to our old friend, Dale MacIver, a Duluth lawyer, Minnesota Commissioner of Aeronautics under Governor Free-man, and Don's former housemate. When he became aeronautics commissioner he had moved to a Minneapolis apartment around the corner from us. Rather than "Mother MacIver," he became the children's extra father, wandering in to soothe baby Annie who resisted sleep, taking the boys out to run errands or simply to get them off my hands for a weekend afternoon.

Dale understood legislative process, bureaucracy, and the Frasers. We became a political ménage a trois, two quiet, decent men who cared passionately about government and a woman who thrived on organizing, office work, and politics. Dale added Elsie Wonneberger, a returning-to-work Virginia housewife, to our team. Earlier, she had worked for the Army and Department of State. Senior staff and even Members of Congress did not overly impress her. Her system of four carbons for every letter we typed—with pink, green, and yellow for the subject, chronological, and alphabetical files—brought complaints but proved its worth many times. She and I soon became known as the people whose muster one had to pass if they wanted an appointment with the congressman.

"Can't you guys talk without food?" she once asked a senior staffer who always wanted to schedule Fraser for luncheon meetings. When Fraser's middle-aged eyesight became a problem and she saw him stretch out his arm to read his daily appointments card she suggested:

"If you put the card on the desk and backed up maybe you could read it. Or you could buy yourself a pair of glasses."

Men who couldn't tolerate strong women didn't last long in our office. Val Fleischhacker, an acerbic-tongued single mother from Minnesota, handled the Washington end of the case work. Meek-looking, compassionate, but tough-minded Georgia O'Brien handled it in our Minneapolis office. I didn't know what case work was at first. I soon learned that many constituents ask their congressional representative to help them when they have a problem with government. Meeting constituents' needs was good politics. Once helped, they tell their friends about it. That counts in future elections.

Both Val and Georgia enjoyed taking on the bureaucracy when they thought a constituent's cause was just. Georgia's favorites were Social Security problems, getting birth records from old family Bibles and even from foreign countries, and finding obscure provisions in the often-amended law that covered unique situations. Val spent an inordinate amount of time on one case involving the mysterious death of a Minnesota woman in Mexico. After helping get the body home, she and staff members from the Center for Disease Control in Atlanta puzzled long and hard to find the cause of the woman's mysterious death. Years later we learned the woman had died from the after-effects of a botched abortion, which was not legal in the U.S. in those days.

After Norman Sherman left our staff as press aide, I encountered Mercer Cross, a Minneapolis newspaper reporter, on an airplane. Sitting beside him on a trip back from Minneapolis with baby Jean on my lap, I decided this man knew the issues and the politics of our district almost as well as Norman. "What have you done for me lately?" is what voters want to know. Mercer could help us explain to constituents what Fraser did besides serve on the Foreign Affairs Committee.

Helping to train and orient young interns and staff became part of my job. (Did I say I was never on the payroll?) Young people, eager to make policy, first needed to understand and be able to articulate issues effectively. They were often disappointed to learn they could develop that skill by answering constituent mail. In the 1960s, pre-computers, men thought they were above typing; women did that. I decided that since they had typed papers for college classes, they could jolly well type letters to constituents. I hadn't become a full-fledged feminist yet, but I was on my way. What saved me was that I like eager young people. I answered their questions, gave them advice and am rewarded now by an occasional public accolade: "Arvonne taught me…" or "Arvonne showed me how…" from a state legislator or distinguished writer who once was an intern in our office.

Don and Dale assigned me to screen applicants for the Army and Naval academy appointments, a laborious task that involved checking test scores, assessing recommendations, and occasionally fighting with the academies which had their own candidates for the limited admissions slots. The job bored me until one day, tired of my complaining, Don said:

"Think of this as civilian control of the military, an important democratic theory. You are selecting future generals and admirals. Pick the kind of men you think would make good ones." Women weren't yet admitted to the military academies. I was delighted when a few years later they were.

My favorite task was monitoring what was happening back in Minneapolis and reporting to constituents on Don's activities via newsletters and other mailings. We had a loyal constituency, but Washington is over a thousand miles from Minneapolis. Email and the Internet were far in the future. The telephone was our instant communication medium; mailings a bit slower but essential. When one of our best supporters, a distinguished university professor, wrote: "If you can't keep your records straight and spell my name right..." after he'd received three copies of a mailing, I winced. I learned in a hurry that details matter. We engaged Winnie Leonard, a former campaign worker, to handle our lists. She shared my view that her addressograph plates represented live bodies, often people she knew. She tracked deaths, moves, marriages, and divorces as if they had occurred in her own family. As I had in the campaign, I either wrote or helped draft mailings about legislation that Fraser was proposing or co-sponsoring.

Lois Binder, our deeply-committed but irreverent Minneapolis office director, called every morning to report what was in the paper and who was mad, concerned, happy, or gossiping about what. Our Washington staff reported to her on pending legislation and Fraser's activities. A bright League of Women Voters member and campaign volunteer turned congressional employee, Lois made everyone—from bank president to housewife to homeless veteran—feel good about the attention they were getting from Congressman Fraser's office, even when she had bad news to convey. She could tell the hangers-on that all political offices attract to stop wasting her time without letting them know that's what she was doing. She even kept her cool when an angry, mentally-disturbed constituent picked up and overturned her desk one day. After that the usually-invisible security personnel in the Federal

© Star/Tribute Mpls. St. Paul

Arvonne, Mary Mac, Don, and Tom at 1962 victory party

Office Building installed a buzzer beneath her desk to summon them when needed. She used it rarely.

Listening to Val, Georgia, Lois, and our legislative aides, I became more knowledgeable about policy matters. In the 1960s, who wouldn't? Kennedy brought a bevy of bright thinkers into his administration. Lyndon Johnson followed with his Great Society proposals and War on Poverty. Martin Luther King, Jr. came to Washington and, although I didn't attend the massive March on the Mall, Rosetta and I watched it on TV. Sometime later Rosetta told me of her daughter's worries about sending her children to integrated schools in North Carolina. Would there be trouble, she asked.

"I know it's going to be hard, but in the long run it's the right thing to do. I don't think they will get hurt," I said, hoping I was right. I understood then the security in segregation, of old ways, and how harrowing it must be to send little children into a hostile, even dangerous, world. School integration was easy only in theory.

The Equal Pay Act of 1963 prohibited discrimination on the basis of race and sex. The 1964 Civil Rights Act was only for discrimination in employment on the basis of race, age, or national origin until the old Southern committee chairman, Howard Smith of Virginia, inserted a little three letter word: "sex." This was seen as an effort to defeat the bill. Congressmen laughed, but Congresswoman Martha Griffiths didn't. She strongly supported the amendment and the bill passed. In 1965 President Johnson signed the Voting Rights Act. Civil rights became the mantra of liberals and the focus of media attention.

Meanwhile I was reading Betty Friedan's *Feminine Mystique*, and recognized the "problem that had no name" as my own. A whole generation of women, especially those who were college-educated, was searching for an identity beyond home and children. We wanted to be individuals, not adjuncts. The divorce rate was rising; we were entering the era of the displaced homemaker. Many women who had worked a few years before marriage, helped put their husbands through college or start a business, and then left the paid workforce to become dependent homemakers, were left in severe financial straits when the husband walked off twenty years later, usually to marry a younger woman. The 1950s white picket fence mentality was becoming history.

Summers the children and I returned to our beloved summer place on the St. Croix River. Don could enjoy it too, between meetings on weekends and during congressional recesses. I stayed in touch with the office by phone. We had overpopulated the original Fraser family cabin, creating tension between generations. A six-bedroom Arts-and-Crafts era "cottage" no other buyer seemed to want became available in 1956, so we mortgaged our future and bought it furnished, including boat and motor. Reachable only by water or on foot through woods, but only thirty-five miles from Minneapolis, it was a convenient and ideal retreat, the one place where family superseded politics, most of the time. Each June, the day after school was out, the children and I took an early morning flight home. Shepherding six children and mounds of baggage out of

Washington, I tried the patience of some business men at the check-in lines and amused others. Don commuted weekends, looking out of place as he arrived by boat in suit and tie.

Election years, I commuted to our Minneapolis campaign headquarters weekdays. My sister Bonnie, an elementary school teacher who never married, spent her summers as our children's extra mother. We never discussed our relationship; it simply evolved. I needed her; she enjoyed the kids and the St. Croix. I gladly gave up cooking, which she enjoyed. She thought I wasted money but never said so. I never could have had a career without her. Now she enjoys "our" grandchildren almost, but not quite, as much as I do.

With Bonnie in charge summers, I savored my solitary commuting hour. Time to think and muse. Driving, I mulled over Fraser's schedule, reassessed our opposition candidate or simply enjoyed the scenic final miles. As I headed downhill the last mile to the marina, my thoughts shifted to the children and food. How had their day been? Were there groceries I was supposed to pick up?

By mid-August of election years, tanned and sated with swimming and extended family—Don's parents continued to come to their place annually almost until their deaths—we moved back to Minneapolis to temporary living quarters. The first re-election campaign year we shared our old house—rented furnished between elections—with my brother, Ken, his five children and pregnant wife, Murphy, a nurse. (Nurses then were known by their last names; with us, that surname stuck.) While Ken studied for his PhD at the university, genial, patient Murphy served as housemother for the crew. I escaped the chaos, going to campaign headquarters and evening meetings with no worries. We installed sets of bunk beds and cribs and each couple had a room of their own. The cousins had a ball; the milkman delivered a restaurant-sized milk dispenser, refilling it every other day. Mornings were wild until we got the eight older children out the door, ours to public school, theirs to parochial. Luckily we all had a sense of humor, enjoyed and respected each other, and knew it was temporary.

I never looked forward to returning to Chevy Chase. Though I had found a soul mate in a neighbor, Jean Tolbert, Chevy Chase was too far from the Hill. Taking the bus home each day took an hour and a half. My most memorable bus ride was on November 22, 1963, after Congressman Powell's assistant rushed into our office, ashen faced, exclaiming: "The President has been shot." All work stopped. Incredulous. Our young, dashing, liberal President Kennedy. Everyone was glued to the radio. The nation was in shock, but I had to get home. The kids would be coming home from school. Rosetta left at three. Boarding the Friendship Heights bus, I found it deathly quiet, full of mournful faces, black and white. As the bus turned to pass the White House, a collective gasp escaped from every mouth. The flag was at half mast. The President was dead. We didn't realize this was the first of the political and family deaths we would have to endure in the next few years.

By early 1966 I drove in six carpools—to school, dance classes, and music lessons. Every weekend I drove to National Airport to drop off or pick up Don, station wagon full of children. I was sick of driving and riding the bus. When Dale came to Washington he had moved into a new urban renewal area in the shadow of the Capitol in Southwest Washington. Tucked between the Potomac and Anacostia Rivers with Ft. McNair at the rivers' intersection and bounded on the north by the Mall, it had been one of Washington's worst slums. Leveled, it was rebuilt gradually with upscale condos, high rise apartment buildings, and public housing. The area intrigued me. We could live by a river again. Don and I could walk to work. The kids would be near the office and could attend what were considered good integrated schools. National Airport would be only a few miles away. Free at last, it said to me—from carpools, long bus rides, and long drives to the airport.

One lovely spring Saturday, Annie and Jean in tow, I went to look at the Tiber Island development, a city block with townhouses around its perimeter flanking four high rise apartment buildings at the points of the compass—north, south, east and west—on the banks of the Potomac. A four story brick townhouse that reminded me of four railroad box cars stacked atop each other, though much more elegant, beckoned to me. It had no windows. Glass walls with sliding doors led to small balconies that overlooked 4th Street S.W. and an inner courtyard. With tiny private patios front and back, it was a far cry from our Victorian in Minneapolis and colonial in Chevy Chase but the four stories could accommodate all of us easily. The Capitol dome was visible from the living room balcony. I was ready to move.

Then our Annie was killed. She never did look carefully enough before crossing streets. Always in a hurry coming home from school, getting there was a different story. She'd sit halfway down the staircase, one shoe on, the other beside her on the stairs, her blond curls in snarls, freckled nose in a book.

"Annie, time for school. Put your shoes on. Get a brush and I'll do your hair."

"Annie, move. I can't get by you."

"Annie, come on, we'll be late."

And then one terrible morning she wasn't there anymore.

The Montgomery County death certificate says it all. Date of death: May 24, 1966...Suburban Hospital...Age: 8 years, 10 mos, 28 days... Cause of death: laceration and contusion of brain due to multiple injuries from coliding (sic) with auto. Interval between onset and death: 4 days...Struck by auto when crossing street. Time of injury: 3 p.m."

I knew I was late that day. I'd been at the office but we needed groceries and I'd run up to Magruders, our local grocery. It was busy. Too many mothers were picking up a few things for dinner before the children came home from school. At the checkout counter as I was paying my bill, Yoyo appeared, breathless, her beautiful brown eyes stark with fear.

"Mom, something happened to Annie."

I'll never know how I got the groceries and Jeannie out of the cart and the three of us in the car, or how I drove the few blocks home. Seeing Jean Tolbert standing on the sidewalk in the front of our house, I knew instantly the news was going to be terrible.

"Don's on his way." Neighbor Jean's blunt declaration and demeanor as she opened my car door told me she had things in hand. Jeannie and Yoyo would be provided for, but what about Mary Mac, John, and Tom, who were still at their junior high school?

"Send somebody to Jefferson. Get the other kids home," I ordered as I was guided into Jean's waiting car. Annie might be hurt but Yoyo was in shock. She hadn't said a word on the way home from the store. I hadn't asked. She had to have the other children with her in this strange place that was still not home. They needed each other.

What I didn't know then was that Don had been told Annie was already dead.

"Let me see her. Let me see her," I screamed as Jean and hospital staff ushered me into a tiny empty waiting room, sat me down in a hard chair against a wall.

"Here, take this. It will calm you." A nurse pushed pills at me, paper cup with water in her other hand. I recoiled.

"What are they?"

"Valium. They will help you."

Annie was the one needing help. I pictured our five at home sitting around the dining room table, bereft. In their rooms, quietly crying. I couldn't cop out.

"No." I yelled at the nurse. "I want to know what's going on. I don't want to be drugged."

Then out of the corner of my eye I saw her, flat on a gurney, wrapped in sparkling white sheets, being rushed down a hall by running doctors and nurses, blond curls askew, face distorted. I wasn't intended to see. I heard Jean gasp.

"They're doing all they can for her. They're doing all they can for her." This constant refrain from hospital staff over the next hours was ominous. Meant to console Don and me, after he arrived with Dale as driver, both ashen, struggling to hold back tears, the refrain conveyed how serious her injuries were. Gradually I learned she'd dashed across the street in front of cars waiting at a light, apparently not seeing or obeying the don't walk sign. A green left turn arrow allowed one lane of cars to move. Ordinarily she came home with Yoyo.

Our little Annie, the most gregarious of our bunch, had friends among neighbors I hardly knew. When she wasn't reading or playing with Yo, she was out and about as children of that era were allowed to do. I recalled spanking her once, desperate with anger and fright. I'd seen her dash across the street in the middle of our block.

"Annie. You can't do that! You might get hurt. Now just sit here on this sofa and think about that. Don't you ever, ever do that again," I remembered scolding her. Irrepressible, she was always in a hurry to get where she wanted to go.

The four days she lived are a black hole. Don and I arrived home late that first night, going from bed to bed stroking each figure huddled under covers, asleep or not, telling them to cry as much as they wanted. Crying was good. Annie was badly hurt but she wasn't hurting. She was unconscious. She didn't know what had happened. The doctors were doing everything they could for her. We would just have to hope she would all right. Don and I repeated that litany at each bed and for days after. We all moved like robots. Clumsy, quiet, doing only what was necessary, biding time.

Machines kept her alive. We lived the four suspenseful, agonizing days in and out of the hospital, wandering around the house, hearing the doorbell as people brought food. Condolences and telegrams flowed in. Bonnie flew in from Minnesota. Dale, almost as stricken as we, drove us to and from the hospital. Sitting with the children at meals or in the living room, Annie's absence was the terrible presence. We didn't blame the driver. We didn't blame Annie. It had happened. Nights Don and I held each other, sobbing. One afternoon I lost control, screaming "Why doesn't she die? Why doesn't she die?" and pounding the car seat as Dale bought gas for the car.

Vacillating between hope and utter despair, I sometimes envisioned her home, slowly recovering, swathed in bandages, me tending that precious little body. Yet she had no brain left. Another day, I was furious at a nurse when she said, with a happy smile, "She urinated today." Urinating! Our precious Annie, face distorted, front teeth missing, unconscious amidst tubes and wires, green blips pulsating on screens above the machines. Her heart pumped, she breathed, but what is alive? Is being unconscious, without a functioning brain, living? Leaving the hospital one day, I resisted the urge to pull the huge plug out of the wall that fed electricity to all those machines. I'd end up in jail. The other kids would have no mother.

Yoyo was the child we worried about most. We'll never know if she actually saw Annie being hit or carried off in the ambulance. She told us over and over again that she and Annie had an agreement to meet outside the school and walk home together. Annie didn't show up that day and Yo started home alone. She must have seen the accident. Why else would she have run the six blocks to the grocery store? How did she know I was at the store? Far more questions than answers.

We had called Don's sister Elaine, a psychologist, that first night. Please come down and stay with Yoyo, sleep in her room, console her, get her to talk. Neither Elaine nor any of the rest of us ever got a coherent story about what Yo had seen. She was traumatized. We thought it unfair to ask her for details. The fact was Annie was killed. We didn't need to know the gory details. Neither Yo nor the rest of us—Don, I and the other children—have ever quite recovered.

At a congressional dinner sometime after Annie died a man said it all. "Losing a child is the worst thing that can happen to anyone. You can lose a spouse, that's normal…but losing a child…" His voice tapered off, the sentence unfinished. He was right. Nothing is worse.

On the third day of waiting, my friend, Ruth Loevinger, and I watched Don at the dining table, poring over letters of condolence. Shoulders drooped, head in his hands, the picture of grief. The messages of condolence helped. Others who had lost a child shared their stories and grief, offered advice. A psychiatrist in California, having read about Annie's death, sent us a letter and a paper he had written saying, essentially, don't forget the siblings. Too often only the parents are consoled, but for children it is a life-changing experience. They will never be the same as others. It was the best advice we got. The grief came in waves—and to this day pops up unexpectedly at odd times and places.

Having the other children around, things to do, helped. We even laughed the time John answered the door, brought in one more chocolate cake and, with a disgusted look on his twelve-year-old face, said:

"Another chocolate cake? I'm sick of them. Why don't we get more cookies?"

Our refrigerator, freezer, and kitchen counters overflowed. Ruth Loevinger, Jean Tolbert, and Bonnie kept the household functioning. Morbid humor surfaced as we pondered proper attire for the boys for Annie's memorial service. Non-church-goers, our boys had no formal attire. Jean Tolbert, the ultimate pragmatist, took Tom and John to the local Junior League used clothing store and came home with handsome, barely used suit coats, shirts, and ties. We speculated about at what rare events other boys had worn those garments. We laughed again when Stokes Tolbert half-joked that it would take two Valiums to get him through his eulogy. It took me two Kleenex to hear it.

Children shouldn't have to deal with death. Out our dining room window I saw our neighbor boy sitting on his back step, elbows on knees, head between his hands, staring at our house. And the empty lot next door, the neighborhood playground, was just that—empty. A neighborhood mother and friends suggested a children's wake the Friday afternoon after Annie's memorial service. Some thirty children, clean faces and clothes, arrived at our house with home made or purchased sympathy cards or flowers. They shyly handed their schoolmate or me their offering and then with relief headed for the cookies and punch. The silence was broken. I understood then the function of wakes. Another neighbor organized a tree-planting ceremony on the schoolyard but I could not bring myself to attend. Just last year that school was expanded and the tree had to go. The mother of one of Annie's schoolmates called me. Her son, Annie's long ago schoolmate, insisted they were going to plant another tree in her memory. The woman wondered what we wanted on the plaque. It all came washing back—almost four decades later—and I had trouble finishing the conversation.

Two weeks after Annie's death, a campaign year, we went off to the St. Croix. I spent June alternately pacing the floor and huddled on the porch chaise lounge with a blanket covering my body and head, dozing. At dusk I'd walk out to the very end of the sand point that stretched out into the river and stare at the sky and water, seeking solace, I suppose, in that wide arc of nothingness. I left everything, including the children, to Bonnie. My friend and neighbor said later she watched, fearful one night that I might just walk off into the river. I never considered it.

We buried our grief in work but it remained just below the surface and popped up at odd times and places. For years I couldn't bring myself to enter the children's room at the downtown public library. Annie, the reader, now with only a memorial fund at that library. I'd taken the children weekly to the library, cardboard box in hand for all the books they wanted, when we lived in Minnesota. The California psychiatrist was right. Our children are different, closer because we endured Annie's death, and later another. Mary Mac told me recently that we never talked enough about death or about Annie. She's right. Don and I retreated inward. Tom remembers her birthday every year with a contribution to the memorial fund and reminds me how old she would be. Jeannie named her first child Anne and calls her Annie. She warned us when she knew it would be a girl. I found the prospect difficult at first but by the time she was born, I was pleased. The new Annie is another reader, a charming reminder of her predecessor. And all the grandchildren know the source of Annie's name. Once grandson Jack asked: "Which Annie do you mean, the dead one or the one in San Francisco?" when he overheard his father and me talking about Annie. Unto the second generation.

I got up from the chaise lounge in mid-July, 1966, moved our crew into town, and went to work managing that year's campaign.

But the prospect of returning to live in Chevy Chase was too hard. We bought the Tiber Island townhouse that summer. The kids attended Minneapolis schools that fall and we returned to the Chevy Chase house just long enough to pack up and move. On Thanksgiving Day we had the Tolbert family to dinner in our new townhouse with rugs still unrolled and some boxes still unpacked. For this new beginning we needed friends around.

Chapter 8

The Nameless Sisterhood and WEAL

Friends in both Washington and Minneapolis thought we were urban pioneers or just plain crazy, moving into the District to a townhouse two blocks from public housing and sending the children off to public schools. I thought of it as a fresh start, coping with life without Annie and living what we professed to believe. Don represented a city. We ought to live in one. We believed in public education and integrated schools. As I had told Rosetta when she asked me about her grandchildren going to a new integrated school, I knew it would be hard but it was the right thing to do. Could I do less with my own children?

It wasn't that simple or high minded. Escape was also a factor. I didn't realize then another pull for me was the deep desire to live beside water. Son Tom identified this when he later asked: "Why do we always live by water?" I hadn't been conscious of this need. Born and raised on the banks of the Cottonwood, living near and always intrigued by the Mississippi in Minneapolis, the prospect of living on the shores of the Potomac, I realized later, was a factor in my ardent desire to move to Tiber Island.

Our development took its name from Tiber Creek, a stream that once divided Southwest Washington from the rest of the city. It had been a slum of poor blacks and whites until it became the site of one of the nation's first large urban renewal projects. Its reputation as a hidden, dangerous place lived on. Few Washingtonians or tourists ever entered Southwest unless they were going to Arena Stage theater, then sitting starkly amid blocks of empty land just across M Street from us. Our junior high students said they walked across "fields" to Jefferson Junior High. A chance airplane seatmate who had grown up in Southwest told me our house on Fourth Street was on the site of one of the most notorious bars in the city.

The whole family had much to learn—and experience. The neighborhood had three elementary schools, remnants of a formerly dense population and segregated school system. Invited by Martha Lewis, another liberal Midwestern wife who had followed her husband to Washington, I joined WISE, Washington Integrated Secondary Education, a biracial group concerned with the schools. Two junior highs—one now closed—sat within four blocks of each other. Jefferson, the former white school, was considered one of the best in the city. Uniforms were mandated—white blouses and shirts, dark pants and skirts—to blur the lines between rich and poor. Jefferson's principal earned my undying respect one day when he admonished a small, handsome young lad misbehaving in the hallway with:

"How do you expect to be the best lawyer in Southwest someday if you keep acting like that?" The young man straightened up and smiled. Not too many white men of that era expected a black kid to become a lawyer. Together that principal and I organized a PTA with the support of black and white parents. I felt part of a community again.

New activities kept me from sinking back into depression over Annie's death. Keeping busy was my instinctive antidote, inherited from my mother. "Don't just stand there, do something," had been one of her favorite admonitions. I couldn't do anything about Annie's death. I turned my anger over death that is a part of grieving onto the wider world. There was plenty to be angry about, and I was not alone.

Our 1966 campaign had shown me that people were dividing into camps. Tensions between formerly compatible groups were exacerbated by the Vietnam War. Women and college students—important factors in our campaigns—were increasingly vociferous in opposition to the war. I shared their views but had a campaign to win, so I was careful what I said where. It wasn't just the war. Baby boomers, now in their teens and early twenties, were questioning

Arvonne at a campaign meeting with Audrey Larson and Garrison Keillor (lower left)

and rejecting the values of their parents' generation. Hippie clothes and communes, men and boys with long hair, the protest songs of Bob Dylan and others were manifestations of this rejection.

At a grocery store near the university I overheard one male worker say to another that it just wasn't fair that young working men like themselves were drafted and "these college guys" get defer-ments. Antagonism to college men touched our campaign. I took a rather shy university student named Garrison Keillor, a steady vol-unteer, along to our ad agency to help me decide on a campaign ad. On the way out of the agency's office an employee made a snide remark, assuming Garrison knew nothing about the contemporary music that would accompany the radio ad. Garrison endeared him-self to me when he quietly responded that he knew every song in the top 40. Another afternoon as volunteers discussed the differences between white and blue-collar voters over the war and the draft, a union retiree said, somewhat maliciously:

"I'll bet Garrison couldn't get two lawn sign locations in North-east." The tension was palpable. Called "a workingman's district," we all knew that long-haired or bearded college students, civil rights ad-vocates, and hippies were not admired in Northeast. Getting Fraser for Congress lawn sign locations there was a campaign imperative.

Without telling anyone, Garrison went door-to-door and se-cured thirty-some lawn sign locations along Johnson Street, the main artery in Northeast. Born and raised in blue collar neighbor-hoods, he knew he should emphasize Fraser's liberal voting record on Medicare and Social Security and his labor union endorsements when ringing doorbells to request permission for those signs. We won that election rather handily, and I still think Garrison should run for office some day.

On Thursday evening, April 4, 1968, Martin Luther King Jr. was shot in Memphis, Tennessee. The next morning, driving to the of-fice, some young boys threw small stones at my car. I thought this was just boys behaving badly enroute to school, one more random incident in a difficult time. When, around noon, our office began hearing rumors of unrest in the city, I understood the significance of the stone-throwing. As usual, when the world seemed threatening, I headed home.

By three o'clock the sidewalks outside our living room win-dows were jammed. The city was shutting down. Looking up the street toward Ft. McNair, two blocks away, I gasped. Its windows were boarded up. I'd walked freely through its gate and grounds. Now it was really a fort, fortified. I instinctively held four-year-old Jeannie at my side. Rosetta had been relieved to see me home early and had left on a bus. Now, jeeps full of soldiers began emerging from Ft. McNair, moving toward downtown or the Capitol. I was nervous. Where were the other kids? What was happening?

The phone rang. Breathlessly, Yoyo reported she was at a friend's house, a few blocks away. School was out, but she was afraid to come home. She'd seen boys throwing bottles and fighting in the streets. In my calmest voice I told her not to worry, just stay there. Soon John burst in, equally breathless, with Paul, his tall black friend and Jefferson schoolmate, who was afraid to take the bus home. Could he stay with us?

"Of course. Call your parents."

I assured them he was more than welcome, that we were safe. Paul could stay overnight, until the city settled down. Projecting a calm I did not feel, I told the boys to make themselves and Jeannie a snack. I stayed glued to the window. It was like watching the sky when one feels a storm approaching. I was watching eagerly for Tom and Mary Mac who had to come across town on the city bus from their high school. An hour or so later, I breathed a sigh of relief when I heard the front door open. They were home. Pale with concern, they reported their bus had inched through the jammed streets downtown.

A few moments later Yo called again, saying it looked okay outside and she wanted to come home. She could run the two and a half blocks between her friend's house and ours. I reluctantly agreed. I heard the refrigerator door slam as I waited anxiously at the front door for her. Teenagers and food, I thought. Luckily, we always had plenty on hand. I relaxed as I saw Yoyo open the patio door. Everyone was home.

Don was in Minneapolis. It would be a long night. Time to get dinner, find things to occupy the kids, turn on the TV and see what was happening beyond our street. Looking back, I'm amazed at how we all took this in stride. Had Annie's accident and death inured us? Was my brain and body telling me again to stay calm, keep everyone calm until this is over and then you can fall apart? About ten o'clock that night Don called, deeply concerned. Were we all right? He had heard about the rioting in the poor black neighborhood, seen the news reports on TV. I assured him we were fine, there were soldiers on patrol in our area. Vice-President Humphrey lived in the next block, I reminded him. I didn't tell him we could smell the smoke from the fires across town, or that I was much more worried about Rosetta, who lived on R Street in the heart of the ghetto where most of the disturbances were occurring.

The weekend curfew was hardest. Used to roaming the Mall, Capitol Hill, and the waterfront, the kids now felt imprisoned. They kept assuring me they wouldn't get into or cause any trouble if they went outside. I kept emphasizing I wasn't worried about them, but that the police and military had their hands full. They didn't need kids running around the neighborhood, extra people to watch. From our windows we could see soldiers, rifles at the ready, on our street corners and in front of the small shopping center at the end of our street. When Mary Mac and I went over to buy milk—essential trips were allowed—there were soldiers in front of the shuttered liquor store and the Safeway. Paul's parents, Jamaican diplomats, were deeply concerned about their only son staying in what they perceived as dangerous Southwest. They came to pick him up on Saturday mid-morning, defying the mayor's admonitions and interrupting the boys' interminable chess games. Their visit was a welcome break, but I was somewhat shocked and irritated when his father said they had decided to drive around the city on their way home, see what was happening. The TV and radio were full of warnings to stay away from the troubled areas.

By late Sunday the city had grown quiet and the curfew was lifted. Monday morning the children went back to school and I went to the office, but tension was in the air. Relations among schoolmates deteriorated. John reported later he was scared every time he went into the men's toilet at school. Mary Mac reported being accosted by groups of teenaged girls on the street, epithets thrown at her. I tried to explain to the children how many blacks felt, asking them to imagine what it was like being black and poor in a city where the white minority had power and privileges. I may sound like a cruel mother but I believe children need to learn how to cope in the world and understand its hazards and imperfections. Our older four again roamed Capitol Hill, biking or walking up to their father's office after school, occasionally accompanying him to the floor of the House when he walked over to vote. The boys rode the subway cars between the House and Senate and haunted the Space Museum. Mary Mac and Yo liked the small arboretum below the Rayburn Building and later, to my dismay, I learned they sometimes skipped school and rode the tour buses half the day. They did report frequent visits to the Smithsonian.

I never felt threatened. My graying hair and increased weight, now that I had stopped smoking, protected me, according to my Minneapolis friend, Caroline Rose, a sociologist with expertise on race relations. White women who look like grandmothers usually have no trouble in black neighborhoods—or any other for that matter, she had once said. I continued to walk or bike to Don's office frequently, especially in nice weather, through the poor and public housing sections of Southwest. I'll never forget the cute little black girl I passed one day who gleefully commented to the adult with her: "Look at that grandma riding a bike!" I laughed but was a bit irked. I was fat and gray-haired, but I didn't like being thought of as a grandmother yet.

With Don traveling a great deal, I missed my old Minnesota confidants. After Arnold Rose died in 1968, I urged Caroline to come to Washington and live in the apartment building next door to us. She and Arnold, both distinguished sociologists and Minnesota DFL activists, had earlier worked with Gunnar Myrdahl on his famous study of race in America, although she never got adequate credit for her share of the work. She yielded to my pleas and quickly found a job teaching at Washington's new Federal City College through her friend Jesse Bernard, another eminent sociologist who had written widely on women and marriage.

Caroline fed my burgeoning interest in the emerging women's movement. Together we investigated the new organization called NOW, the National Organization for Women, an outgrowth of President Kennedy's—later President Johnson's—Status of Women Commission. Locating a Washington chapter, we attended one meeting. The women seemed politically naïve, more interested in complaining about women's situation than doing anything about it. Caroline only stayed in Washington a year but over countless cups of coffee she continued to mentor me.

Son Tom still teases me about my favorite word being "organize," as in "next week we're going to get organized" or "OK, kids, let's get organized." One afternoon he brought home a copy of *Off Our Backs,* a tiny free newspaper. It reported on the women's consciousness-raising groups that were examining women's subordinate status in American society. Seeing how avidly I read that paper, he bought me a subscription and I passed my copies on to my other

friend and confidante, Ruth Loevinger. Ruth was another somewhat disgruntled Minnesota spouse in suburban Washington with
young children and a busy husband. In Minnesota she had been a
leader organizing the Minnesota Nurses Association. We often talked
about meeting interesting women at dinner and cocktail parties but
the men's conversations dominated these events. How and where
could we get to know these women better? The Women's National
Democratic Club, despite its suffragette history, featured white male
speakers we read about in the newspapers and sometimes met at
parties. We didn't need to hire sitters to hear these guys again, we
told each other.

We decided to organize a non-traditional luncheon group. This
would be no ladies with white gloves affair, we told our invitees,
nor would it be a consciousness raising or "women's lib" group. Everyone simply could bring her own brown bag lunch; we'd provide
coffee. We wanted to get to know each other better, we explained,
never admitting—even to ourselves—that we were doing exactly
what the young "women's libbers" were doing—creating an informal women's support group.

More than twenty women showed up at my Tiber Island townhouse one lovely spring day in 1969. Ranging in age from early
thirties to seventies, many were wives of elected or appointed officials, diplomats or newspaper reporters. A sense of pent-up energy
and excitement pervaded my living room. Washington formality and
rank were out the window. We asked each woman to introduce herself and tell what she was doing, thinking, or wanted to talk or hear
about. When a few forgot and reverted to the typical Washington
"my husband is…" one woman piped up:

"Let's not introduce ourselves by our relationship to any man. In
this town we're always Mrs. Somebody or Other. I'm tired of that."
Cheers and smiles greeted her outburst. Two women described lobbying the Civil Service Commission to count significant volunteer
work as productive employment and to offer more part-time jobs.
They argued that an officer of a large organization, who chaired a
board or mounted large, successful fund raisers, even if unpaid, was

doing managerial and executive work that should be recognized by potential employers. I shared that view, having managed several campaigns and a congressional office without salary.

My Washington school group friend, Martha Lewis, reported on our work with the public schools and on her French, raised-bed, backyard vegetable garden. Barbara Hughes, a feisty soul and former secretary in Governor Freeman's office, brought up the question of legalization of abortion, describing a friend's search for other than back-alley alternatives. All this led to spirited questions and comments. We had hit a chord. The time went fast. Many rushed out to pick up children at school, a few hurried back to work. A distinguished older woman hung back. Shaking our hands heartily, she said: "This is the first time in my twenty years in Washington that anybody has ever asked me *who I am*."

We met monthly. Personal anecdotes and frustrations poured out at each meeting. Some spoke with tears in their voice or eyes. Others concealed their deep anger with sardonic humor. I surprised myself by telling a story I'd never told anyone before. Immediately after the birth of our sixth child, lying in the recovery room with my husband and doctor standing on either side of the bed, I said I wanted my tubes tied. I was thirty-seven years old, too old for more children, as we believed then. The obstetrician who had seen me through sixth births and two miscarriages—a man I considered a friend—talked not to me, but to Don. He described the then-necessary procedure requiring the doctor's appearance before a review board that would okay or veto the procedure. My age and number of children made approval likely. But, he added, he was sure Don, as a newly elected congressman, wouldn't want that kind of publicity even within the medical community. They spoke as if I wasn't there.

Word about our group began circulating, prompting questions. We weren't a conscious-raising group, we insisted. Yet after each meeting, I was on a high, savoring the intelligence, passion, and humor of the event. Soon we had fifty names on our membership list, which I maintained, with twenty to thirty women attending each time. We rotated houses and responsibilities, with a different chair and lead discussant every month, but never named the group.

When a Washington reporter for the *Minneapolis Tribune*, also a personal friend, called on me at Don's office to inquire about the group, one of his first questions implied, "who are these women's husbands?" He put it more delicately than that but we both knew that was what he wanted. I parried, explaining our early decision not to introduce ourselves as related to any man. To illustrate our discussions, I laughingly told the reporter a story of my own. Some years earlier in Minneapolis a Midland Bank officer had refused to return to me a stock certificate in my name that Don and I put up as collateral for a car loan. After the loan was paid off, with baby in arm and toddler by the hand, I went into the familiar bank to retrieve the certificate.

Without blinking an eye, the bank officer said:

"Oh, I can't give that to you. Your husband has to come in and pick it up."

"But I co-signed the note. I bought that stock with my own money."

"Sorry. That's our policy," he said, his voice implying who was I—a mere woman—questioning his authority.

I walked off fuming. I'd been doing business with banks since I was a teenager, had deposited my paychecks in that bank and handled all our family finances.

Within days of the reporter's story appearing in the Minneapolis paper, I received a call in Don's office from the bank's senior vice president.

"Mrs. Fraser, we saw the story in the paper and want you to know that old man retired from the bank some time ago. He certainly wasn't reflecting bank policy," a chagrined voice said. "We value your business and certainly don't treat women customers that way anymore. If there's anything we can ever do for you, don't hesitate to give me a call." He gave me his phone number and apologized again.

Disguising the triumph I felt, I thanked him politely, and then couldn't resist exulting before the whole office staff. When I gleefully reported the incident at the next meeting of our group, adding that I hadn't given the reporter the name of anyone who attended, a woman called out: "Hey, we're the Nameless Sisterhood." The house rang with laughter and applause. The name fit. It became our badge of honor.

The world was changing, albeit slowly. Women's anger at discrimination was being voiced. Along with the civil rights movement, the new women's movement was drawing media attention and some things began to change. The *Washington Post's* women's section was renamed Style. It might as well have been called Power or the Who's Who in Washington section. (Blacks, the majority of the population, got little newspaper attention except on sports or crime pages.) Read over breakfast by every political person in the city, this section reported who attended what important dinner party or charitable event and what powerful individuals had revealed in conversation. [Arvonne, is this what you mean by 'revealed'?] The custom at dinner parties of women retiring to another room while the men had brandy and cigars was also dying out. Still, while the civil rights movement was treated with respect, at least by liberals, the new women's movement was the butt of jokes.

At one evening gathering around a sparkling white tablecloth with silver candelabra, dinner guests lingered over coffee and cigarettes. The host, in an attempt to be amusing, made a derisive comment about this new women's movement he'd read about in the *Post*. I can't remember exactly what he said, but it made me furious. Though I was below the salt, I couldn't contain my wrath. I objected to his remark, mentioned the Sisterhood, and said he'd be surprised who attended. Conversation stopped. Eyes dropped, coffee was sipped until Abigail McCarthy, the very proper and erudite wife of our Minnesota Senator Gene McCarthy, seated on the host's right, came to my rescue.

"I think this new movement is rather interesting," she said in her soft voice. "I'm surprised at how many of my friends are talking about it."

The host, without missing a beat, rose and said: "Maybe we should adjourn to the living room." This incident didn't make the *Post's* Style section but I was delighted when I heard it was telephone gossip for days.

The Nameless Sisterhood gave me and many of its other members a new sense of identity and confidence. Sisterhood success stories abound. At one meeting a young mother confessed that she was investigating law schools but didn't know if she could go. Her children were young, her husband so busy…Her voice trailed off. She got more encouragement than she needed and was urged to take the LSAT. After finishing law school she became an officer in the National Women's Political Caucus and subsequently, when Republicans came to power, was appointed to the Federal Trade Commission. Unlike today, in the 1960s and 70s Republicans and Democrats were often friends. They shared an interest in government, respected it and each other, and could laugh, work, and relax together despite their differences.

Sala Burton, another Sisterhood member, was an attractive statuesque blond. Always immaculately dressed, she was one of my many friends who had emigrated with her parents to escape Hitler and the Nazis. Now a California Democratic Party leader, Sala also assisted her husband in his congressional career. Even I was impressed when I overheard her, during a party at their house, giving instructions to a San Francisco political colleague. Her voice exuded authority. When her husband died, Sala was elected to succeed him. Sometime later another Sisterhood member, then living in San Francisco, heard Sala tell a large audience how the Sisterhood had given her the confidence to run for office. I was astounded. I thought of Sala as the last person in the world needing her confidence shored up.

During our first year of Sisterhood meetings, the *Post* carried a story about Bernice Sandler, a Michigan woman who was filing discrimination complaints against universities based on President Johnson's executive order prohibiting discrimination on the basis of sex in any institution receiving funds from the federal government. This was a dire threat. Almost every educational institution in the country, public and private, received federal funds. Sandler, the story said, was working with a group called WEAL, Women's Equity Action League, in filing complaints. The story said WEAL concentrated on discrimination in education and employment. I was intrigued and invited Sandler to speak to a Sisterhood meeting. She was our first outside speaker.

Sandler inspired me and numerous other Sisterhood members to join WEAL. Soon I was asked to form a DC chapter. Within a year, I was elected national vice president and, with WEAL members recruited from Sisterhood ranks, established a legislative office. Envisioning what can be and setting out to make it happen, I discovered, was as exhilarating for me as downhill skiing is for son Tom. But this was uphill, so perhaps the analogy should be to mountain climbing. During the 1968 campaign I suffered a more serious bout of depression over Annie's death, possibly exacerbated by all the political and personal tumult of the '60s. Our oldest children were teenagers, Don's campaigns were still fun but becoming too easy, and underneath everything was this gnawing feeling that I had to decide what I was going to do with the rest of my life. Don was so concerned about my mental health that he got me an appointment with a psychiatrist whose sage advice was that somehow physical activity and having something to get up in the morning for helped. He prescribed an anti-depressant, which I took for almost eight years, but my three WWW's—WEAL, walking, and the women's movement—also helped me scale my personal mountain.

Organizing the DC chapter of WEAL was my first step, although I now realize everything I learned raising children, managing campaigns and offices, and organizing Sisterhood paved the way. Raising children—"rearing" children I consider an offensive term—taught me to take the long view. Managing campaigns and offices means you don't do anything alone. You take people as they are and build on their talents. The Sisterhood and my friend, Caroline Rose, taught me to build on positive momentum. I was ready for the women's movement, and it was ready for me. (I wish, as I write, I knew where to find positive momentum today. There are so many things that need attention.)

I didn't realize that organizing the Washington WEAL chapter was the start of my new life. "Bunny" Sandler brought a Georgetown University law student, a single mother with a young child, who was helping her with EEOC complaints, to our first meeting. Betty Boyer, the Cleveland woman who started WEAL, sent us a list of WEAL members living in Washington. Her current effort was to stop newspapers from running separate Help Wanted employment ads for men and women. Val Fleischhacker, Don's aide, and I found interested Capitol Hill staff members. Everyone had a Rolodex full of names and phone numbers of friends and colleagues who might be interested. We were on a roll.

Soon we had an energetic cross section of committed women with experience and contacts in government. We built on the work of consciousness-raising groups across the country and writers who were analyzing, satirizing, and publicizing the plight of women. All this activity had created a new, charged atmosphere. Later Sara Evans, a feminist historian, identified me and our WEAL group as the "legalists," bent on changing laws and policies. Compared with the others who were taunted as "women's libbers," we were considered semi-respectable.

Nationwide, WEAL was a small group. I soon realized that allying with the traditional women's organizations—the League of Women Voters, American Association of University Women, Council of Jewish Women, and League of Catholic Women and others—on legislation gave us needed and additional political clout. Women's liberationists tended to look down their noses at these old organizations. But it didn't take the old organizations long to realize their membership was interested in this new women's movement. They had astute lobbyists who responded to this interest, the best of whom was Olya Margolin of the Council of Jewish Women.

A craggy, grey-haired, serious woman who wore plain black dresses, Olya didn't look like the force she was. Born in Lithuania, she came to the U.S. as a child and joined the council in 1944. By the early 1970s, when I knew her, she had helped form civil rights coalitions and moved from working for equal opportunities for blacks to promoting them for women. Anytime WEAL needed to get the traditional organizations to sign a joint letter to members of Congress, I'd call Olya. She usually got all the other groups to sign. Congressional offices paid attention. These groups represented millions of voters. WEAL's alliance with them was a marriage of convenience.

One spring afternoon in 1971, Mary Gerault, a National Education Association lobbyist, called on me in Don's office with an idea. An active member of the old National Women's Party—founded during the women's suffrage era—Mary was deeply interested in women's issues. Like Olya, she knew Capitol Hill well. She suggested WEAL publish a periodic report on issues before Congress of interest to women, and offered to gather material for it. She was certain other women lobbyists would do the same. What a great deal, I thought. The information was all public record. All WEAL had to do was package what our volunteer lobbyists fed us. Another marriage of convenience.

Carol Foreman, a savvy, red-headed Sisterhood member who worked on abortion and family planning issues, volunteered to edit it. My secretarial skills were tested typing the mimeograph stencils but it was worth it. Named the WEAL Washington Report, it listed legislation introduced or in committee with provisions affecting women, the bill's authors or co-authors, and, if a committee vote had been taken, who voted aye or nay. This pioneering effort, after a few issues, brought us the offer of a tiny office in the National Press Building by a publisher who wanted to distribute our report with his *Women Today* newsletter. With this alliance, we went from bigamy to tri-gamy with no compunctions.

The office had no windows, but beggars can't be choosers. We scrounged donations of office furniture and supplies. A Sisterhood member volunteered to staff the office part-time. We were on a roll. "Big Sister is watching you" was the unspoken message to Congress, not only from WEAL, but also from NOW, a new Women's

Lobby, and the older organizations. Soon Marguerite Rawalt and her friends who monitored court decisions affecting women were contributing to our report. One section of *WEAL Washington Report* urged readers to contact their congressperson and instructed them on effective lobbying from wherever they lived.

After Jeannie, our youngest, entered first grade I spent mornings in Don's office and afternoons at the WEAL office. I had two unpaid but satisfying jobs—three if you counted raising children. As a result of media attention, a woman buried in the National Institutes of Health bureaucracy called me to say there was a bill that, with only a few words added, could affect thousands of women. I went to Dale MacIver, always my friend in need, for advice.

An invitation to a WEAL fund-raiser honoring Arvonne (1977)

"Well, we find the subcommittee that's handling the bill, find a sympathetic member, give him the language, and a story about who, how, and why it will help, then show that it won't cost any or much money…"

It was that simple—and that hard—but it worked. We got the few little words added. I have forgotten the woman's name and the needed words but not what the experience taught me. Words count, if you know where to put them. And when you need advice, ask. The victory was sweet. I had been organizing and managing. Now I was diving into the legislative process.

Richard Nixon was president but the Congress was Democratic and the women's movement kept gaining momentum. As Caroline Rose had said, "a movement is like a snowball rolling down hill. It grows and gains momentum." By September, 1973, when I was WEAL's national president, my report to the membership astonished even me. It proved what a small group can do if it focuses and finds friends. I still smile to myself when I read about Title IX of the Education Amendments in 1972 as "women in sports" legislation. That wasn't our goal. We wanted to get more women into law, medicine, engineering, architecture, and other professional schools that limited or denied women enrollment. Bunny Sandler's filing of more than three hundred discrimination charges against academic institutions resulted in millions of dollars of salary raises for university women faculty. But filing discrimination charges after the fact could go on forever. We needed legislation to deter discrimination against women and girls in all educational institutions. Working with sympathetic members of Congress we got Title IX.

Recently over a dinner, Bunny Sandler and I laughed over how worried and scared we were in those early days, never anticipating that in thirty years women would be half the students in medicine and law *and* that American young women would be winning Olympic medals in sports. This time the theory of unintended consequences worked in women's favor.

Caroline Rose was right. The women's movement snowballed because one idea led to another. Adoption of Title IX gave Arlene Horowitz, a young secretary in Congresswoman Patsy Mink's office, the idea for what became the Women's Educational Equity Act. She came to see me one day in Don's office to say she believed elementary and second schools would remove sex-stereotyping faster if there were federal funds to do so. NOW and WEAL both had committees studying sex-stereotyping (gender came later) in elementary school textbooks, most notably the Dick and Jane books I had read in kindergarten. They were still being used. In them, Mom was a housewife, Dad the breadwinner, and Dick and Jane had typical boy and girl roles. I was delighted by Arlene and her idea. I've always had a soft spot for secretaries. Too many people think they don't think. I encouraged Arlene to pursue her idea and she drafted a bill.

Bunny and I and our women lobbyist friends didn't think the bill had a chance for passage but if hearings could be held on it, the issue would be highlighted. Testimony at congressional hearings is printed for public distribution. We could circulate copies around the country. Because we would get women's organizations to testify, all our research on discriminatory curricula would be publicized with the imprimatur, if not the support, of Congress. Meeting one evening to fine tune Arlene's bill, which her boss, Congresswoman Mink, had agreed to introduce, we came to the "authorization of funds" section. (Bills that will cost money require this section.) With great hilarity we put in thirty million dollars. What the heck, why not ask for what would really make a difference since all we expected was hearings?

By this time Bella Abzug of New York had been elected to Congress. A short, chubby woman who always wore a large hat, Bella came to symbolize the modern women's movement for the American public. She and Representatives Shirley Chisholm of New York, Pat Schroeder of Colorado, Martha Griffiths of Michigan, and Edith Green of Oregon co-sponsored our bill. They and many congressmen had women on their staffs. A kind of feminist underground passed information around and helped on women-oriented legislation. Even male aides in many offices who cared about and worked on social and economic issues became part of our network. Ellen Hoffman, Senator Mondale's aide, convinced him to introduce our bill and hold Senate hearings on it.

Ellen got Senator Mondale to invite the former U.S. Commissioner of Education, Harold Howe, then with the Ford Foundation, as lead witness. His appearance and statement would set the whole education establishment on its ear. Because of his reputation and position, his testimony would be a warning to educational institutions across the country that they better pay attention to sex equity in the curriculum and the way they treated female students from kindergarten through college. Congresswoman Mink more than did her part on the House side, and the bill was adopted in August, 1974, with the thirty million authorization intact. That taught me it never hurts to ask for what you need or want. You just might get it. Asking for what you think you can get usually means you get even less.

Marguerite Rawalt, by then WEAL's in-house pro bono lawyer, already knew this. She was an old hand, and rarely tentative. She thought if WEAL publicized her cases, it would inspire other to sue or take cases on behalf of women. She wrote WEAL's amicus brief in the Pittsburgh Press case. Newspapers quit running employment ads as "Help Wanted: Male" and "Help Wanted: Female." Then Marguerite suggested establishing a WEAL educational and legal defense fund to support landmark legal cases, and research and education on discrimination against women issues. Among the cases the fund supported was that of a University of Minnesota chemistry professor named Rajender. The university fought the case in court and lost. Over a decade later, when I was back home and at the university, my paycheck was one among hundreds of female faculty that included "Rajender money" as part of the university's settlement agreement.

Another WEAL employment effort involved the prestigious fellowship and scholarship programs men listed on their resumes. Men in business and government often answered the charge that they weren't giving women more than menial or traditional jobs by arguing they couldn't find qualified women for executive positions. This angered Judy Nieman, now known as Judith Nies. No woman could put on her resume that she had been a Rhodes Scholar, a White House or Nieman (no relation to Judy) Fellow. Women were denied admission to these and many other prized programs. Together we started WEAL's Fellowship Project.

We picked the most prestigious programs to challenge. If we could embarrass the men in charge of them with adverse publicity and make them change, the less prestigious would (and did) follow. On WEAL letterhead we fired off complaints to the executives and boards of these programs and issued press releases, pointing out the obvious, but now newsworthy point. The Men Only sign on these programs was unconscionable, we said. They had to change. The Rhodes program was the toughest. With the help of sympathetic and angry women journalists, the Nieman and White House Fellows' boards caved under the pressure of adverse publicity. The American officers of the Rhodes Trust responded that they were powerless to change. Eligibility conditions were in Cecil Rhodes' will, incorporated in an Act of the British Parliament.

When Linda Kamm, a WEAL and Sisterhood member and Capitol Hill legislative assistant, decided to accompany her husband on a sabbatical year to London in 1972, she offered to see what she could do about the Rhodes. Using her legislative skills—one parliament is like another—she found a sympathetic male British MP. Working with him and buttressed by the publicity about the problem on both sides of the Atlantic, the restrictive conditions were finally changed in 1975. I was delighted to learn that Minnesota's first female Rhodes Scholar, Lois Quam, was from Marshall. Today she's a high ranking health care executive.

Successes were wonderful, but there was always more to do. Much as I loved politics, the Democratic Party was no paragon of virtue. My Washington neighbor, Phyllis Segal, a young mother and law student, wrote a paper on women's unequal representation in national Democratic conventions for one of her classes. Congresswoman Griffiths inserted it in the *Congressional Record*. Sissy Farenthold, Gloria Steinem, and I—all good Democrats—used Segal's data in a challenge to the party. Eventually, equal participation was mandated.

Women were also tired of being the party workers while men predominated as elected officials. In 1971, Representatives Abzug in Mink and Chisholm, called a meeting in the Rayburn House Office Building to discuss the situation of women in politics and public office. With phone calls stimulating word-of-mouth, more than a hundred women jammed the meeting room including Liz Carpenter, Lady Bird Johnson's White House press secretary, and Johnnie Tilman, a nationally known black activist. The idea for a bipartisan National Women's Political Caucus was floated. An organizing committee was set up.

That summer, back in Minneapolis, I helped organize a Minnesota Women's Political Caucus. Then in 1972, I was asked to chair the constitution committee at a meeting in Houston, Texas, called to formalize the national organization in a somewhat decrepit old hotel. Every wing of the U.S. women's movement from practically every state was enthusiastically, and often raucously, represented. Staid League of Women Voters or American Association of University Women types sat alongside radical women's liberationists. The division within the movement was vividly displayed in my committee. There was agreement on ends but not on means. Passion became the order of the day. To most women's liberationists, leadership was a dirty word. Leadership was something men exerted, they argued. Women should be collaborators, make decisions by consensus. Their segment of the women's movement was characterized by small groups in which consensus was rather easily obtained. Among them were brilliant and notable theoreticians, writers, and spokeswomen. Their goal was to change culture—the way people thought, acted and looked at the world—and they were, to a great extent, successful. Without them, the "legalist" arm of the movement to which I belonged could not have achieved what it did. Together, we created a revolution.

But no revolution is peaceful, as the meeting to organize a National Women's Political Caucus confirmed. What can be said is that in our women's revolution no one was killed in armed conflict, although many were psychologically wounded and retreated from action.

Chairing the constitution committee was a grueling and yet fascinating experience. I let everyone talk, but made them take turns. We were in an era in which mass participation and grass roots politics were venerated. I tried to bring order out of the chaos, to get agreement on a governance and membership structure for the new organization, but failed. All I could get was agreement on a steering committee to continue the work. That bought time. The organization is alive and well—and democratic—in the twenty-first century.

That experience caused me to think seriously about the difference between leaders and leadership. Consensus is fine, especially in small groups. It doesn't promote leadership and often squelches it. Large groups, with a defined purpose or need, work best if they have a representative structure for selecting leaders. If they don't, the leaders are either self-appointed, and represent only the dominant group, or are anointed by outside forces, usually the media. That is undemocratic.

The idea that women should be active in and trained for political life took on a life of its own. In 1974, a young southern woman named Sandra Kramer, body and accent every bit the Southern
Belle stereotype, came to me with an idea. She thought a bipartisan
fund to support women candidates for Congress was needed. She
understood the difference between leadership and leaders. Though
I would call her a leader, society hadn't yet. She certainly exercised
leadership not only by coming up with the idea but also by doing
much of the organizing work. Sandra convinced Elise du Pont, wife
of a liberal Republican congressman, to co-chair the new Women's
Campaign Fund with me. With Sandra, we recruited a politically
savvy and well-connected board.

One humid summer day with the temperature hovering in the
90's, I found myself walking up New York's Park Avenue to ask a
liberal philanthropist for ten thousand dollars for a direct mail campaign to raise money for our new fund. He refused, but said he would
lend us money. We took the challenge. The mailing worked, and we
paid him back. Another then-Republican congressional wife, Teresa
Heinz, now Teresa Heinz Kerry, became one of our good supporters. Bipartisan, socially visible fundraisers in Washington and around
the country made it possible for us to hire a staff and provide money
and technical assistance to women candidates. (Lack of recognition
for women with ideas still bugs me. At an early Women's Campaign
Fund brunch, Don was introduced as my husband, which shocked
some of the distinguished men in attendance.)

A critical mass of women was learning and copying the ways of
the male world even as we denigrated it. Marguerite Rawalt and I
founded the WEAL Educational and Legal Defense Fund in the mid-
70s to use tax-deductible contributions to finance our non-legisla-
tive activities, especially court cases. We were following the example
of the NAACP, the National Association for the Advancement of
Colored People, and its fund. Although we found pro bono lawyers,
filing lawsuits still cost money. Rajender's was just one of numerous
cases we helped fund across the country. Later I devised an intern
program for our WEAL Fund. Under a Ford Foundation grant, we

brought young women interested in public policy into WEAL and gave them a chance to learn as they worked. I convinced Ford to let us support one paid intern so that the program would not be limited to those with affluent parents. Occasionally my day is made when a well-placed woman calls me about some matter and tells me, with pride in her voice: "I was a WEAL intern."

At about the same time, Ellen Sudow and Margot Polivy, Capitol Hill veterans still in their early thirties, presented me with an idea for a tax-deductible education fund as an adjunct to the National Women's Political Caucus. They believed women candidates would benefit from needed education and training in campaigns and for public policy careers. Some Caucus members viewed the fund as competition for scarce dollars, but Betsy Wright, an astute liberal Democratic politico, who became executive director of the National Women's Education Fund, allayed those fears. She designed a very effective manual which she used to trained candidates across the country. A few years later those of us on the NWEF board were nonplussed when Betsy announced she was moving to Arkansas to help a young governor named Bill Clinton. By 1992 she had helped him become President.

Relating that this woman came to me and that woman phoned me—most of them young—gets repetitious, I know. But it makes an important point about synergy's role in creating social and political change. One idea lead to another. One human connection leads to many others. Washington and Capitol Hill were—and I hope still are—attractive places to creative young minds. I happened to be in an advantageous position—visible, accessible, and eager to give encouragement and help, a kind of big sister with a "sure, why not… let's try it," attitude. I was easy to find—either in Don's office or at WEAL—was married, had children, a threat to nobody and full of enthusiasm about the new women's movement. I also don't subscribe to the idea that the pie—whatever pie we're talking about—is finite, that one person's power or accomplishment diminishes when new folks come along. I just think you make or bake a bigger pie. Every woman who came to me with a new idea had thought it through carefully, and was willing to do the work. I was simply a sounding board with a "what the heck, nothing ventured, nothing gained" view of the Washington world. The civil rights movement had broken the path. The idea of equal opportunity was abroad. Why not for women too?

This era of optimism and the ideas of a women's movement expanded beyond national interests. Republican and Democratic women interested in foreign affairs collaborated in developing and passing the Percy Amendment to the Foreign Assistance Act. It mandated integrating women into U.S. foreign aid programs. It also illustrated how women's networks functioned, and how handy husbands can sometimes be. I had met Irene Tinker, a feminist research scholar, early in my Washington life and worked with her in numerous women's groups. She, and Mildred Marcy of the League of Women Voters and later the U.S. Information Agency, called on me to urge Don to hold hearings on the situation of women in developing countries. Ordinarily I didn't involve myself in anything Don did in the Foreign Affairs Committee except to help him pick good staff. This time I did.

Irene and Mildred, in collaboration with Virginia Allen, a Republican appointee as a deputy assistant secretary of state and then the highest ranking woman in the State Department, and others were looking toward the 1975 United Nation's International Women's Year and its world conference on women. They decided an amendment to the Foreign Assistance Act was needed if women were to get any benefit from U.S. foreign aid dollars. Don held the hearings and Mildred drafted the amendment. She got her husband, chief staffer on the Senate Foreign Relations Committee, to convince Senator Percy to introduce the amendment. Engrossed in domestic legislation concerning women, I was paying no attention to the amendment until one morning I got a call from New York. A woman at the YWCA headquarters told me the amendment was in trouble. It was being laughed about in the House committee. This was news to me but I was fed up with laughter about women and feminism.

Furious, I sat down and typed individual letters on my most elegant personal stationery to every member of the committee, except, of course, Don. I could make sure he voted right on this. My letter to the other members, most of whom I knew, said I had learned about the amendment from a colleague in New York and the laughter it provoked. I assured each that I knew he wasn't the one laughing (when he probably was) and asked him to support the amendment. I was not the only one who wrote or called. Interested women deluged the committee members' offices with calls and letters. The amendment, in essence, simply said the Agency for International Development (AID) should pay attention to women in the developing countries to which the U.S. gave foreign aid. What could be more innocuous? It passed. (I didn't realize then that a few years later this amendment would not only have a profound impact in other parts of the world, but change my life and solve my problem of how to help fund our children's college tuition and our retirement.)

We, in the legalist branch of the women's movement, didn't limit ourselves to legislation, court cases, and getting women elected to public office. We took on discrimination whenever it was brought to our attention. One day Alice Rivlin, a distinguished economist then at the Brookings Institution and a candidate for appointment to head the Congressional Budget Office, telephoned me. She was concerned that her sex was a factor in competition for the appointment. She was on the short list for the job, but nothing was happening. Again, my ire rose. I called Sissy Farenthold, then chair of the National Women's Political Caucus, who became equally incensed. We fired off a joint letter on NWPC letterhead to Senator Muskie, chair of the selection committee for the position, expressing our concern that Rivlin's sex might be her limitation. I signed as WEAL president. The implication in our letter was that Congress certainly shouldn't be guilty of discrimination against women. Rivlin got the job and did brilliantly.

Five marvelous years—from 1969-74—changed my life and the lives of thousands, probably millions, of others. During that time women began to look at themselves and the world with new eyes.

We no longer identified ourselves as related to someone else—wife, mother, daughter. We developed our own significance. Or, as I would call it later, we became human, like everybody else, persons in our own right with our own ideas and agendas. We didn't leave home, we simply added another dimension to our multi-faceted, multi-tasking lives. At the most elementary level, I no longer tolerated being called Mrs. Donald Fraser. I was Arvonne Fraser. The term Ms. was coined. Others, especially younger women, kept their own names upon marriage—never mind that the surname they kept was their father's. This preoccupation with names was as significant for us as it would be for my husband if he were to be called Mr. Arvonne Skelton. This is what the liberation feminists meant when they said, "The personal is political."

One Sunday morning in Washington a friend of mine, a leader in the Women's Campaign Fund, hosted a brunch for friends at her Capitol Hill house. It was a purely social event and husbands were invited. Some were congressmen, some journalists, but they came— perhaps with a bit of reluctance. Women hosting social events with men included was a new phenomena in Washington. As a group of us chatted in front of the fireplace, enjoying our Bloody Marys, a new couple came in. Without thinking, the hostess introduced Don by simply saying, "this is Arvonne's husband." Dead silence, then surprised, slightly embarrassed male laughter. In an instant, women laughed too. It was one of those clicks Gloria Steinem had written about when people realized things were different. Even in Washington Congressmen could be introduced simply as husbands.

To many, the changes among and about women were unsettling and bred insecurity and fear. But the germ spread, infecting the country. I wasn't the only activist woman who had others come up to her and whisper a variation of: "I can't support you publicly, but keep doing what you're doing." And I smiled when reading letters to the editor that said, "I'm no feminist but…" and then proceed to argue in support of equal pay, better and less-expensive child care, or some other feminist issue.

A CODEL in Europe. Arvonne is in the checked suit.

Chapter 9

From Domestic to International

B efore working on the Percy Amendment on integrating women in U.S. foreign aid programs, I considered Don's foreign affairs committee work his bailiwick. I concentrated on domestic issues— both political and personal. But we were sounding boards for each other, trying out our ideas, asking for advice, and listening to each other's problems. He indulged, encouraged, and seemed proud of my feminist activities and the resulting publicity. I was consulted on his hires of committee staff and hosted—catered and bar-tended might be better words—impromptu and casual meetings of his foreign policy colleagues. Gradually I was drawn into the foreign affairs world. Recently Don said it was I who suggested he get involved with international human rights issues. I don't recall that, but it sounds plausible.

About once a year, after Jeannie was a toddler, I joined CODELS—congressional delegations traveling overseas. Seeing new places and learning the problems and politics of other countries was stimulating, but I disliked "the wives" programs. Congress and the Foreign Service were male-dominated in the 1960s. The lunches, shopping, and teas that the wives of U.S. Foreign Service officers posted overseas were required to put on for the traveling congressional wives were not my idea of fun—or theirs either. These wives were precluded from paid employment and required to carry out, unpaid, the entertainment role then thought necessary for good foreign policy work. Failure to fulfill this role could jeopardize a husband's career. I felt sorry for them—especially for the younger wives with small children—having this entertainment function thrust on them. In many ways we represented two different cultures—the very formal, hierarchical diplomatic world vs. the much freer and informal world of politics.

I did enjoy the sight-seeing but it was occasionally obvious that the diplomats' wives had given these tours too often. The evening receptions and dinners made the trips worthwhile. Who wouldn't be impressed to hear and see a head of state speak on current foreign policy issues in a magnificent, often historical, setting. Often I was the lone woman at the post-dinner informal conversations between congressmen and parliamentarians. I was welcomed because Don introduced me as his campaign manager as well as his wife. Comparing ideas and experiences and hearing entertaining stories about European politics—the laughter and informality increasing in proportion to the brandy consumed—fascinated me. European politicians were full of questions about American campaigns. Comparing the real and subtle distinctions between parliamentary systems and our own tripartite division of powers system taught me much. Don and I were both interested in the then-new European Union, a vision that was gradually becoming a reality.

Meeting with European activists and, occasionally, political dissidents were the highlights of these trips. Politically I have always been somewhat to the left of Don, my heritage from my Farmer-Laborite father. Late one night in Madrid, I accompanied Don and his committee staffers, Cliff Hackett and Bob Boettcher, to a small café. There we met clandestinely with opponents of Franco, many of them young students, who told us of their underground activities and aspirations. Spain's notorious dictator was then in his last days of power. We could sense the political winds were shifting.

Hackett and Boettcher had both been in the Foreign Service but resigned in favor of more direct action as legislative staffers. Cliff Hackett was, and remains, especially interested in the European Union. Boettcher focused on the United Nations. I liked and respected both of them, having worked with them in Don's office. Even then congressional overseas trips were often looked at askance, as boondoggles. There was often a member just along for the ride, wanting to see and shop the world. Still, I share Don's view that these trips are worth what they cost the taxpayer. Even that disinterested member learns that Ghanian farmers and German workers don't wake up each morning and bow to Washington. I couldn't argue that spouses should go along on congressional overseas trips at taxpayer expenses. And I certainly am glad that the rules for Foreign Services wives have changed. But these trips taught me a lot. Bob Boettcher understood my ambivalence about these trips for he too was a bit of an outsider. Don and I were supportive when he came out as a gay man, a difficult decision then. I believe that made him more sympathetic to my feminist activities. When Don became subcommittee chairman, Boettcher asked what I'd like for the wives' program on a projected trip to NATO in Brussels. Without thinking about the interests of the other wives, I responded:

"I'd love to meet with representatives of women's organizations in Europe."

I can only imagine the consternation that request caused in the Brussels embassy. But what a subcommittee chairman and his wife wanted, they got. Seated around a highly polished embassy conference table over coffee one morning, I was introduced to a group of European women. The diplomats had done an excellent job of assembling a representative sample of female activists for me. One, active in the underground during World War II and now a distinguished lawyer, said she thought the new feminist movement silly. A queen bee, I thought, which is what we then called successful U.S. women who thought anybody could do what they did. Alongside her were young feminist activists and older leaders of traditional women's groups such as the YWCA, the International Alliance of Women, and European social welfare organizations. This session was probably the beginning of my international career, but I didn't know it yet.

My international education continued. Africa came alive for me at conferences sponsored by the Carnegie Foundation, although again I was a tag-along. I learned more about the Middle East and Asian politics at a meeting arranged by the Stanley Foundation of Iowa. Max Stanley, a successful Iowa businessman, was a passionate advocate of the United Nations and world peace as was his wife. Early in the 1970s they invited the leaders of Pakistan and India— arch enemies—to meet with parliamentary leaders from America and the Scandinavian countries, the major foreign aid donors at the time. The Stanleys believed that global security and international organizations could be promoted if leaders of nations could meet, talk over problems, and get to know each other. They understood that Pakistan and India depended on foreign aid and probably couldn't resist meeting leading representatives of donor nations. The fact that the meeting was held at an elegant resort high in the Swiss Alps didn't hurt either.

I watched with awe as these well known enemies—Bhutto and Nehru—their elegantly suited legs crossed above expensive Italian leather shoes, sat face to face in a relaxed after-dinner conversation discussing world politics and world leaders they had known. We all laughed over their comments on the idiosyncrasies of other world leaders, as they skirted around their own differences. None of us approved of Pakistani strongman Zulfikar Ali Bhutto's autocratic leadership but he was a charming, extremely intelligent man who spoke eloquently about his student years at the University of California/Berkeley. Using his oratorical skills to gain power as a populist, he didn't practice democracy in Pakistan although he seemed to venerate America. Overthrown by a coup a few years later, jailed and about to be hanged, Don and I joined an international campaign to prevent his being executed without a trial. The campaign failed to save his life but I'm glad we joined. Even autocrats deserve a trial.

Bob Boettcher observed and encouraged my growing interest in international affairs. In 1974 he maneuvered my appointment as a member of the U.S. delegation to the United Nations Commission on the Status of Women. Every U.S. delegation usually has one member not of the president's party and by then even Republican politics demanded a women's movement representative. As president of WEAL and a Democrat I was a "twofer"—a somewhat derogatory term used in civil rights circles to mean two qualifications were met in hiring or appointing one person, as in black woman or Democratic feminist.

Although many Americans find the UN slow and confusing, I found it engrossing. Formed in 1945 when I was at the university, I shared the great hopes for this new international institution whose charter proclaimed that it was "to save succeeding generations from the scourge of war...reaffirm faith in fundamental human rights...(and) in the equal rights of men and women." Entering the impressive UN building at 44th Street in New York, I felt humble and scared. The farm girl from Minnesota in this great place? And meeting to prepare for the first UN world conference on women to be held the next year? It seemed inconceivable. Yet here I was.

Shirley Hendsch, the State Department official who staffed the US delegation, took me under her wing, explaining the unfamiliar procedures and introducing me to Commission members from around the world. I soon discovered they were much like me, active in women's organizations and in the governments of their countries. Gradually I relaxed, telling myself this was simply a new kind of politics. I knew the substance, women's issues. I could learn the procedures. Listening to Aziza Hussein of Egypt, later president of

International Planned Parenthood Federation, and others during the proceedings, I was pleased to discover many delegates shared my interest in women's organizations as the means for improving the status of women. I decided a resolution to that effect would be useful. Shirley introduced me to Aziza who taught me how to write a resolution in UN language. Our resolution ran into opposition from the Soviet and Cuban delegations. They feared non-governmental organizations. Let people organize and they might get out of hand, overthrow their leaders. That was their worry, but they put their opposition more obliquely.

I was also astounded to learn, in promoting the resolution, that many governments would not allow any new organizations to be formed without government approval. This was a real shock for an American who thought if there was a problem, you organized a group to solve it. A few years later I discovered a group called Isis, based in Rome, that communicated with the women's underground—women who organized small feminist groups despite government regulations. Later, dealing with some of these groups directly, my staff and I were careful not to blow their cover. Doing so could put them in real jeopardy—in jail, or worse.

In 1975 Boettcher again was responsible for my appointment as a member of the US delegation to the 1975 UN world conference on women held in Mexico City. By this time I was as passionate about the interests of women abroad as at home. At the conference, I did not buy the argument made by many developing country governments—and some women—that economic development automatically improved women's status. Look at us in the U.S., I wanted to say. Despite our advances, women are still considered wives and mothers first, not active contributors to the social and political development of our communities and our nation.

But UN proceedings don't allow individual interventions. Delegates speak for their governments. Aziza and I had to get our governments' approval for our resolution, making it a U.S. and Egypt cosponsored resolution. Getting additional governments as co-sponsors and trying to insert feminist language—without ever using the word feminist—in the documents we worked on was like working with Congress as WEAL president. I felt just as triumphant whenever a few words I proposed got accepted. The issues were much the same—education, employment, legal rights, and health—but the dimensions were very different, especially in the developing world where many women were illiterate, self-employed, in poor health, and had little or no legal standing.

I understood that we were not writing legislation at the world conference. We were drafting global policy statements and providing the rationale for them. The document the conference would adopt was guidance and recommendations to the member governments of the United Nations and to all UN agencies, the World Health Organization, UNESCO, the Food and Agriculture Organization, the International Labour Organization, and many others that dealt with world problems.

I resonated to the introduction in the World Plan just as I do to the opening statements in the U.S. Declaration of Independence and Constitution. Noting the "differences in the status of women in different countries and regions of the world, rooted in the political, economic and social" structures and the level of development in a country, the Plan went on to say that "basic similarities unite women…" Its prediction in 1975 that "in our times, women's role will increasingly emerge as a powerful revolutionary social force" was daring and intellectually stimulating. Thinking about that last phrase—powerful revolutionary social force—over the years, I have decided it was accurate. Attitudes and practices have changed, though not nearly enough. As one of my international colleagues said not too long ago, "In terms of women, the world is still developing."

Fine-tuning the draft of the World Plan of Action was a huge challenge. Rarely vocalized, but understood, was that everywhere women cooked, sewed, married, had babies, and took care of homes and children. We wore different clothes and spoke different languages but in every culture and legal system we were recognized primarily as wives and mothers—or potential wives and mothers—and never as equal citizens. Commission and conference delegates understood that both laws and cultures had to be changed in every country, industrialized and developing alike, if women were to be the equals of males as guaranteed in the UN Charter. It seemed to me sadly ironic that women everywhere were assigned the job of maintaining and transmitting their culture to the young, the very culture that gave women second place.

The fact that we were drafting this Plan of Action was revolutionary. Such a thing had never been done before. The minimum objectives set out to be achieved within five years—from 1975 to 1980—were unrealistic. It would take far more time than that to achieve a "marked increase in literacy and civic education of women, especially in rural areas;" or to guarantee "equal access at every level of education." We hadn't achieved the latter in the U.S. Despite my concerns about the time frame for achieving these objectives, I was delighted that education was the first on the list but I found my American background was occasionally a limitation.

Because attendance at the conference was higher than expected, there weren't enough rooms to hold sub-committee sessions. The education subcommittee I attended met informally one afternoon on the conference center lawn. It was a beautiful day—warm and sunny—and just being outside made the atmosphere more collegial. I was a bit chagrined that in discussing the education objectives, it was a Greek woman who suggested we insert the word "co-educational" in the phrase on compulsory primary school education. Why hadn't I thought of that? As an American I assumed primary school education meant for boys and girls. I had a lot to learn. We didn't get co-education in. Too many countries objected, but that one incident taught me how careful one had to be in thinking globally. What Americans take for granted, others don't.

The other minimum objectives concerned employment opportunities and eliminating discrimination in employment; equal opportunity to vote and stand for election; equal pay and equal legal capacity; increased provision of health education and services, family planning and other welfare services; and equal rights in "marriage, citizenship and commerce." The last five objectives started with what

I believed was the crux of the problem of women's status. Boldly stated, it was: "Recognition of the economic value of women's work in the home, in domestic food production and marketing and voluntary activities not remunerated." I resonated with that. This work undergirded every society, but everywhere "women's work" was denigrated. Paid work is doubly valued—in salary and the status it confers. Families and countries depend on women's work but make jokes about it.

My favorite—"the promotion of women's organizations"—was on the list. Without that provision I didn't think any of these minimum objectives could be accomplished. Who would really push for achieving these objectives if women didn't organize to do it? I thought this more important than the final objective that called for the establishment of governmental women's bureaus or commissions. Important as these were, I believed they would only be as good or as powerful as women's organizations made them. Somebody had to be pushing governments to pay attention to women and usually that push has to come from outside government, by women. The balance of the Plan—pages and pages—spelled out why these objectives were important and how they could be achieved. An American writer looking for maximum readership might well have titled the whole document: "All You Ever Wanted to Know About Women Worldwide and How to Make Her an Equal Citizen," or, perhaps, "Women for Dummies."

The themes of the 1975 Mexico City world conference—equality, development and peace—satisfied the three big factions in the UN. The industrialized countries argued for equality for women, the developing countries argued for development, and the Soviet bloc talked about peace. I didn't concern myself much with the sections on women's health, housing, population, social welfare questions, or data collection about women, although the discussions about these educated me. My interest was structural and institutional change. In 1975 many anthropologists and others were still arguing that cultures should not be disturbed. I thought that silly nonsense. Slavery had once been a part of every culture. Did we not want to abolish that? My view about culture was that you got rid of the bad and kept the good.

I had learned from my own experience how deep, almost inherent, cultural norms are. Despite all my work in the women's movement, centuries of culture reared its ugly head unexpectedly, even in me. One night I was talking on the phone to son Tom, away at law school, when he said:

"Just a minute, Mom, I have to stir my spaghetti." Stir his spaghetti, I thought, why isn't Karla—his wife—making the spaghetti? I caught myself before uttering what I'd thought. I had taught my boys to cook and bake, saying, "If you can read, you can cook. Either read what's on the box or get a recipe book." But there I was, a preaching feminist, and my subconscious still thought wives did the cooking.

Another time I wasn't so smart or quick. The basement door at our summer place needed fixing. On the phone with Mary Mac, our daughter who was working part-time fixing up old houses, I mentioned that door, and said I should have John fix it.

"John?" she exclaimed. "I'm the one making my living with hammer and nails! And you're the one who calls herself a feminist." I'd goofed royally. I was proud of Mary Mac working part-time with a non-profit group renovating houses while attending the university, but somehow my mind still associated fixing my house as a male's job. It will take generations for all of us to get over the worst of our cultural heritage and not automatically assign tasks based on gender.

I also had questions about the whole population movement—and still do. Earlier in the 1970s I had been recruited by a Sisterhood member to join the board of a population and family planning group. We both thought the group needed more feminists. She and I believed that most male population experts, no matter how well educated, still looked at women as people who had babies and needed to be prevented from having too many. Once, at a conference, I asked a distinguished male demographer a question I'd pondered for years: "Why did we have the baby boom?"

"Contraceptive failure," was his dismissive response. Every woman in the room was offended. We knew that wasn't true. The reasons were much more complex and are still not well studied or understood. Our mothers and grandmothers had fought for and began using birth control. The post-war baby boom was a psychological event, not technological failure. I'm still waiting for an adequate answer to that question. At Mexico City and since, I have strongly supported access to safe and effective birth control and women's reproductive rights. I believe reproduction must be viewed in human, not technological, terms.

Over seven thousand men and women from 125 nations descended on Mexico City in late June, 1975. Most of them—including me—had never attended a world conference before. I did know there would be two simultaneous meetings, the UN conference composed of government delegations and a non-governmental (NGO) forum, called the Tribune in Mexico City. The NGO meeting is more of a free-for-all, a you-all-come-if-interested affair with seminars and workshops on the subject of the UN conference. Patterned after the 1972 environment conference in Stockholm and the 1974 population conference in Bucharest, these NGO forums allowed interested groups and individuals to exchange information and develop collegial international relationships while helping to heighten world awareness of the issue being discussed at the UN conference. The UN agreed to these parallel non-governmental conferences in an effort to divert interested people from demanding to observe and even participate in the official UN/government meetings. NGO forums came to be essential. No conference or convention center in the world can hold all the people wanting to attend a UN world conference.

The Mexico City Tribune was planned for three thousand participants. Six thousand registered. Meetings overflowed into halls. Bulletin boards announced impromptu extra sessions. These had standing room only crowds. Overcrowding and the diversity of expectations, experience and outlook meant feelings became intense. Women from developing and industrialized countries argued amongst themselves and with each other. They hadn't spent their hard earned money to come to Mexico City for the scenery.

I got my own taste of the intense and diverse feelings manifested at the Tribune when I appeared on a panel before several hundred tired, impatient women. When I casually remarked I had to leave the conference early to be home in Minneapolis for my twenty-fifth wedding anniversary party, I was roundly booed. Another morning our regular U.S. delegation meeting was broken up by a noisy anti-U.S. government group demanding to be heard. Its spokesman—and he was a man—charged that our U.S. delegation was illegal and immoral, composed only of elite women who couldn't possibly understand or represent the millions of U.S. women it purported to represent. This infuriated me. I never have liked protestors who break up meetings although I realize protests can be effective. I was also tired of men being spokespersons, and especially at women's conferences.

Virtually every government delegation in Mexico City was headed by a man, including our U.S. delegation. And I was really tired of the code words "elite" and "grass roots," elite being automatically bad; grass roots, meaning ordinary or poor people, automatically good. That seemed to me stereotyping at its worst. Our U.S. Ambassador Hova, a superb diplomat, asked me to respond, perhaps because he thought I was closer, politically, than the Republican delegates. From their clothes and accents, we knew the protestors were Americans. Speaking to the group, I played my own grass roots to the hilt, surprising them with the fact that I was the daughter of farmers. I suspected that most of the demonstrators had never seen a farm except from an airplane. Both the media and the protestors lost interest and departed.

Despite the chaos and the politics, the World Plan was adopted and a semblance of international sisterhood developed. I flew home to Minnesota an ardent internationalist, excited that the same basic goals I had worked toward in WEAL were ensconced in that Plan, albeit in formal, wordy UN language. The wordiness was necessary to clarify meanings because UN documents are translated into the many official languages of the UN. On the porch and beach of our

St. Croix house that summer, I studied the plan, word for word, trying to figure out how to popularize this historic document.

That fall Don was appointed as congressional representative to
the UN General Assembly. Who could turn down an opportunity
to live in New York, rent free, for four months? We moved to a furnished apartment in the Beekman Towers just up the street from the
UN headquarters for the session. Don commuted between New
York, Washington, and Minneapolis. Once I had Jean in school and
got Yoyo a piano and part-time job, I turned to seeing what I could
do to follow up on the world conference. Joan Dunlop, a colleague
from my days on that population board and who had also been in
Mexico City, convinced her employer, John D. Rockefeller, to fund
my publishing a condensed, popular version of the World Plan. under WEAL auspices. We felt the essence of the Plan needed much
wider readership, that it should not be buried in government offices
and industrialized country libraries.

Back in Washington after Christmas, with the help of WEAL
volunteers, we mailed my popular version of the Plan around the
world using lists we obtained from every source we could find. I was
shocked when one friend thought she was only doing me a favor
by stuffing envelopes. I thought of this task as spreading the word
about a document that was the first of its kind, considering it a gift
to women. Stuffing the envelopes was like wrapping a Christmas
package. I thought about how pleased the recipient would be. Later,
I convinced USAID and the US Information Agency to translate
this gift into French and Spanish and distribute it even more widely.
To me, the printed word is precious and these words for and about
women even more so.

I also came home from Mexico City with a new American
friend, Mary King, who like me was both a feminist and a politician. A colleague and friend of Jimmy Carter, the Georgia governor
then campaigning for the Democratic Party nomination, Mary had
heard I supported Carter, a man then given little chance of success,
and sought me out at the conference. She and I believed a Southern
governor who talked openly in support of civil rights and women's

rights would make the best Democratic candidate for president. I read and watched TV coverage of his campaigning in Iowa and went home to Minnesota to meet Rosalyn, his wife, on her campaign visit to our state. Wherever I went, when the presidential election was discussed, I argued with anyone willing to listen that Carter was the best presidential candidate. In 1976 Don and I attended the Democratic convention in New York where Carter became the party nominee and picked Fritz Mondale, Don's one-time roommate and our friend, as his running mate.

Shortly thereafter, Dick Moe, Mondale's senior assistant, called me. He had helped in Don's campaigns, attended law school, and served as DFL party chairman before joining Senator Mondale's staff in Washington. Dick said Carter wanted women to be an integral part of his campaigns and that Mary King and he had decided I'd make a good regional director. Would I consider it? Highly complimented, but knowing this would mean leaving WEAL, Washington and my family for an intense three months, I demurred. The next weekend, speaking at a Minnesota women's political caucus meeting, I explained my dilemma, saying our Jeannie was only thirteen years old and I wasn't sure I could leave her with Don and Yo to take the job. A woman in the audience whom I didn't know well piped up with:

"You've got to do this. You've been talking about women in politics for years. If you're worried your husband can't take care of her, I will. When she's a little older, she will be proud to have a mother who worked for the president."

Chastened, and made to understand that when push comes to shove you have to do what you urge others to do, I accepted the job. Don and the girls said they could cope. They were proud that I'd been asked. Soon I was off to Plains, Georgia, for training along with the legions of other regional and state directors and senior campaign staff. Turning fifty-one that fall, I was proud and relieved to finally be back in paid, full-time, albeit short-term, employment. More senior than most of the staff, my reputation as a campaign manager made me acceptable among the men, and the women were delighted to have a well-known feminist on board.

Arvonne and Don with President Carter

Starting any new campaign creates a special kind of euphoria among the staff. Who doesn't like the prospect of winning? Multiply that by 10 or 100 for a presidential campaign. And this one was unique with so many women in top positions. Being trained in the South added another new dimension, for a Midwesterner like me and for Northerners generally. Northern Democrats are a bit chauvinistic. We think we own liberalism. Yet here we were in peanut country with a farmer, a southern governor, as our leader. I felt a bit of added pride because Mondale was the vice-presidential candidate. He, Don, and I had all started out together in politics as college students and graduates of Humphrey's 1948 campaign for U.S. senator. Now, not quite thirty years later, we had a chance to elect a president with Mondale as vice-president.

My political instincts dominant, I put my international activities on hold. The women's revolution would take a lifetime. Electing Carter president would only take three months or so. Having a president who supported equal rights for women would contribute to that revolution. After the Georgia training, with a stopover in

Washington to check on how Don and the girls were doing, I flew to Minnesota as Upper Midwest director of the Carter-Mondale campaign. Minnesota always went Democratic. We had a good state director—Mike Freeman, Governor Orville Freeman's son—so I concentrated on Wisconsin and Iowa.

A dear Fraser campaign colleague and family friend, Richard Larson, took a leave from his New York law job to be my volunteer assistant. I was honored and delighted. He had worked for me in Don's campaigns—even once building me, with hammer and saw, a private office. Devotion like that is hard to find. His innovation in the Carter campaign doubled my effectiveness. As I drove hundreds of miles daily through Wisconsin and Iowa, checking on state and local headquarters and attending events, Richard sat on the phone in Minneapolis scheduling interviews for me on small radio stations. Disk jockeys sitting in remote radio stations in northern Wisconsin forests, with only sophisticated technology for company, were delighted to have a live body visit, if only for fifteen minutes. It made a nice break for me as well. Driving down country roads or freeways, slightly over the speed limit, I often heard myself on the car radio. With one eye on the road and another on the scenery, I'd criticize what I'd said at the last radio station and figure out how to do better at the next. Then I'd worry if I would make the meeting I was headed for on time. How was I going to find the damn place? Would I have time enough to call Washington to check in with Don and the girls?

Those calls always cheered me. "Dad isn't doing his share," was one complaint. Especially satisfying was the time they admitted they didn't realize keeping house, doing laundry, and making meals was so much work. I didn't get back to Washington more than one or two weekends a month but I could occasionally see Don when we were both in Minneapolis. He was often back there campaigning and sons John and Tom, now living in Minneapolis, were equally interested in my new adventure.

In an era before cell phones, I used my motel room phone and always kept plenty of change so I could use gas station pay phones to check in with Richard, the girls, or Don. Richard would brief me on the crucial labor or political leader I had to congratulate, cajole, or admonish at my next campaign meeting. The Wisconsin state director didn't much like taking orders or even advice from a woman, but he had no choice. The worst meal I ever had in my life was at a college cafeteria in Iowa. The meat, vegetables, and mashed potatoes tasted like they'd sat in steamers for a week but a campaigner has to express appreciation for food, even if she gags later.

We lost Iowa by 1 percent but carried Minnesota and Wisconsin. I was reminded again that women did most of the nitty-gritty campaign work, keeping the headquarters "manned" and somewhat clean, organizing volunteers, and doing most of the phoning. By mid-November I was back in Washington, ecstatic over Carter's election and worried about what to do now. Midway through the campaign, when Don and I were together back in Washington on a rare evening, he had said:

"If Carter wins, have you figured out what job you want?"

"The thought never occurred to me. I'm too busy trying to win an election."

"Well, you better start thinking about it."

It sounded like an order, but I knew him better than that. He'd never ordered me to do anything, except to be careful when handling electric wires when I helped him on one of his projects. His question and comment were simply sound advice. He knew I was ready to move on. If Carter won, there would be hundreds of appointive positions—patronage jobs in political terms—to be filled. Campaign staff got consideration, if not a job. But I had to know what I wanted. I gave his advice no thought until after the election. Then I got serious.

I didn't want to be one of those hangers-on who showed up post-election to tell you how hard they had worked and how much they had contributed to the victory. I had been around politics long enough to dislike people who thought because they worked in a campaign they deserved a paid job. I could picture the hordes of job seekers in the transition office established for every president-elect and couldn't bring myself to be one of them.

By mid-November the *Washington Post* was filled with stories about the scramble for top positions in the new administration. I agonized and procrastinated, hoping someone in the transition office would remember me and call me to come in and help. I was naive. They were overwhelmed. Running a campaign is one thing. Putting together a national administration in terms of both people and policy in two short months is daunting even for people who know Washington. Carter had only been a governor of a southern state.

I did decide on the job I wanted: director of the Women's Bureau in the Department of Labor. It had an international section. I had known the previous directors and felt qualified. But how could I make attractive the resume of a woman who had been a campaign manager, a landlord, a feminist advocate, an occasional writer and speaker, and an unpaid assistant in her husband's offices? I swallowed my pride and wrote a letter to the president-elect reminding him I'd been his Upper Midwest director and stating my qualifications for the Women's Bureau job. Actually, I didn't sit down and write a letter. I pondered and slaved for days over my red Selectric typewriter, searching for exactly the right tone, the right words, how to make my case succinctly but powerfully. I obsessed over that letter while doing laundry, going to and from the WEAL office, and made myself increasingly depressed. I had never in my life sought a job. In the labor shortage years following World War II, employers sought you. I knew times had changed, but I hadn't. I wasn't shy about telling everybody, when asked, what I wanted, but I simply could not bring myself to go down to that transition office and be seen as one of the job seekers hanging around.

I knew the Washington rumor mill well enough to know that spreading the word didn't hurt. I learned that Carter did read my letter. At a post-election event, Mondale said he had asked about me. That made me feel better, but I didn't get the job. The labor movement, according to the political grapevine, thought I was too liberal and too feminist. I did get called by the new secretary of labor and was interviewed for the position as legislative liaison but both Don and I thought that job might pose a conflict of interest.

Around home I despaired, waiting for the phone to ring, to be asked to interview for another position. To pass the time and keep myself sane, I helped out in Don's office, got a Ford Foundation grant to fund a WEAL intern program, kept sending out the World Plan, and pretended to the greater world that I was content. One afternoon, at my wit's end, I pounded the kitchen counter in frustration and broke into tears. I felt ashamed when I noticed Yo looking ruefully at me. I only cried when someone died. I almost felt like this was my death or at least the end of a career that had barely got started.

The old girls' network saved me. In early January, 1977, a campaign colleague in the White House Office of Personnel called to ask if I would come and help recruit and screen women appointees for the Carter administration. I practically jumped through the phone in anticipation. By mid-January I was walking—read that dancing—the two miles from home to the Old Executive Office Building next door to the White House each morning. A few years earlier I'd written a book for teenaged readers about getting a job in government so I was ready for all the FBI and other forms I had to fill out. Our WEAL work on women and employment was also good background for arguing with male Carter appointees on behalf of female candidates. During my years in the women's movement I had developed good sources for potential appointees. My appointment drew media attention—no previous president had had a women's appointments person—so each day's mail brought a stack of resumes. My phone rang incessantly—at the office and home. But my appointment was temporary. Once most of the positions listed in the "plum book"—the book listing presidential appointments—were filled, I still had to find a job for myself. This time my political networks saved me.

One April morning Governor Jack Gilligan of Ohio, the newly appointed head of the U.S. Agency for International Development (USAID), called and asked if I'd consider heading its Office of Women in Development. He thought my work on Capitol Hill and in the women's movement made me a good fit for the job. I suspect Bob Boettcher and some of his other colleagues on Don's foreign affairs committee had mentioned me to Gilligan. It amazes me still—and bothers me a bit—that none of us who had fought hard for the Percy amendment which led to the establishment of this office had come forth with a candidate. The feminist movement, especially the National Women's Political Caucus, was concentrating on higher level jobs and the more internationally-minded were not yet politically sophisticated enough to be pushing a candidate.

Governor Gilligan said he needed someone to give substance and visibility to this new women's program. The previous administration had put responsibility for implementing the Percy amendment in AID's equal opportunity office, confusing the issue. The Percy amendment was not about employing U.S. women. It was about improving the status of women and including aid to women in the developing countries that received foreign aid. Governor Gilligan thought I could change the perception within the agency about the objectives of the amendment. I was overjoyed. I called Don and the girls, then the boys. Everyone in our family breathed a sigh of relief. They had had enough of a worried, crabby, and depressed mother.

When a young male friend congratulated me on my new position by saying, "back to your roots, Arvonne," I was taken aback, until I realized my farm experience would be an asset. I soon discovered that, although I had no experience in international development, my whole life experience—being the mother of six, an educated woman who liked to learn and do new things, a politician and a feminist, even my gray hair—were assets in my new job. As my friend Bunny Sandler once said about me: "She looks like everybody's grandmother and smiles. It takes the edge off what she says." And unlike the perception of feminists of my time, I didn't view individual men as the enemy. I had many good male friends and colleagues and had learned a lot from them. (I can take advice as well as give it.) I believed men as a group had to learn that women were needed as equal partners in the development of any country, as the World Plan of Action adopted at Mexico City said.

Arvonne being sworn in as AID's Women in Development director, with Governor Gilligan, Don Fraser, and Dick Moe in the background.

Chapter 10

The Politics of Development

In mid-April, 1977, acting as if I belonged there, I strode purpose-fully into the imposing block-long State Department building, flashed my temporary pass, and took the elevator up to the third floor—the Agency for International Development (AID). *Go right down the red-striped hall and turn right into the blue*, I had been re-minded during orientation. I felt like a rat in a maze in this labyrinth of windowless halls with waist-high colored stripes. The heavy dark doors, all closed, added to my unease. The first day on my new job and I'm trying to find Suite 3243, my office. The sound of my heels clicking down the hall resonated as I scanned door numbers to make sure I was heading in the right direction. Working in White House

Personnel had been an extension of Carter's campaign. There I was among friends. Here I knew hardly anyone.

Civil servants don't welcome political appointees with open arms. They see too many come and go. No expert on foreign aid or economic development, I had listened with only half an ear when Don talked about these subjects. Now my job was to convince people behind these dark doors to implement the mandates of the Percy amendment and the Mexico City Plan of Action. A formidable task, but at least I would be paid well. The idea of paying my kids' college tuition by working for women—my passion and unpaid job for years—made me smile. And I would get to travel the world besides! I might be fat, over fifty and still on anti-depressants, but I had run and won campaigns, managed offices, and survived Annie's death. I told myself I could do this, and with pleasure, once I learned the ropes. My courage screwed up, my prospects assessed, I opened the door marked 3243. At least I had found the place.

The deputy in charge was cordial but I sensed her contempt for my lack of development experience. She had been a candidate for my position. She will have to go, I decided. This job will be hard enough without being undermined from within. Much more welcoming were two other civil servants, Faye Thompson, a program officer, and Mary Herbert, the secretary assigned to me. They knew the agency procedures and, as Faye said later, "where all the bodies are buried." I breathed a silent sigh of relief. Politics taught me that people with imposing titles are not always the real powers in an organization. I had to gain the respect of the informal leaders in this place. My instincts told me Faye and Mary would be allies in this effort.

I recruited Elsa Chaney, a Ph.D. with Latin American experience, as my new deputy. I needed her intellectual credibility and overseas experience. She had taught at Fordham University and looked like the stereotypical single faculty member, but didn't act like one. "This office is about subversion," Elsa later quoted me as saying when I interviewed her. I don't remember that, but I needed her badly. I knew she was worried about "joining the enemy," the government against which she had protested so vehemently during the Vietnam War. I didn't advertise around the agency that Elsa was also an active feminist, had worked both on Capitol Hill and in the McCarthy for President campaign. Some might call that subversion but I didn't. By subversion I meant that our objective was to upset the traditional operating assumptions of the agency and the foreign governments it dealt with. I had to make them see and assist the women, not just the men, in the developing countries to which this agency gave millions of foreign aid dollars.

There was no way our small office staff of two political appointees and five civil servants with a $300,000 budget could do much alone. We had to educate the place about the situation of women in the developing world and show them how to design programs and projects that would "integrate women into the national economies of foreign countries, thus improving their status and assisting the total development effort," as the Percy amendment said. Improving the status of women was Elsa's and my ultimate goal, but we couldn't say that. It would sound too feminist and I was already branded as one. Simply haranguing agency workers about women would be counter-productive. We had to show how paying attention to developing country women contributed to the development effort, making the country more prosperous and less dependent on foreign aid. We had to make them understand and appreciate what women already contributed in these poor countries and how they could be made more productive. Too often aid donors depicted women in developing countries as barefoot, pregnant, and working in the fields with sticks for hoes and a baby on their back. That image didn't convey the fact that these women raised much of the food eaten in those countries, pounded grain into flour, walked miles to gather wood and water, and cooked food over open fires. Their unpaid labor was a major, albeit unmeasured, part of the economies of developing countries. With better tools, better health, and more and better education, we could improve their lives and their countries' economies. Ignoring them, as most foreign aid donors did, was both a mistake and immoral, I believed.

The most important thing Faye and Mary taught Elsa and me was that it was fairly easy to issue contracts for outside assistance if we kept them under ten thousand dollars. They also taught us how those contracts should be written. I suspect Faye also put in a good word for us with the somewhat crotchety bureaucrat who had to approve them. Ten thousand dollars bought a great deal of time and effort on the part of researchers, consultants, and women's development groups in 1977. I became expert at writing these contracts and eventually gained the respect of the crotchety bureaucrat. He and I became telephone friends. I never met him in person.

As women colleagues often do, Faye and I exchanged bits about our personal lives as we worked together. She, like I, had moved from a small rural high school to a city to make her way. To save money—and perhaps the indignity of having to sit in the back of the bus—she walked to work for years, three miles each way. Intelligent and determined, she gradually worked her way up the bureaucratic ladder. Like most women of our generation, Faye, Elsa, and I had all started at the bottom of office totem poles and experienced discrimination. As black women, Faye and Mary got a double dose. I decided that as a "women in development" office we could do a bit right in our own office. I started the process of moving Mary from secretary to program officer, not an easy task given civil service rules. I'm secretly glad that wasn't accomplished while I was at AID because Mary was so good for our office. I do take pride in that it finally happened and that she will retire one of these days with a good federal pension.

Flaunting convention, stereotypes, and agency regulations became a kind of game for the four of us. We needed a counterbalance to the derisive comments we got from many men in the agency. One day, on a crowded elevator, a man jestingly said in a voice everyone could hear:

"What are you women in development ladies worrying about? We'll take care of you."

I couldn't resist. The door was opening for my floor.

"Yes, but what if you died?"

As the door closed, I heard him say to the others, "You know, that happened to our minister's wife." *Ah*, I thought. *Point made.*

Feminists, in this pre-computer age, were thought to abhor typewriters as the symbol of women's degradation and to demand all the perks and privileges of executives when they became one. Mary looked somewhat askance when I asked for my own typewriter and a chair that fit my five foot frame but she enjoyed the challenge. Executives had secretaries and man-sized upholstered leather executive chairs. When new Danish-modern furniture for my office arrived unannounced, I could sense Faye and Mary's amusement when I refused it. I preferred the old walnut desk, the round-backed visitors' chairs and leather sofa. Shaking their heads, the workmen took the furniture back, and grudgingly brought me a secretaries' chair so my feet touched the floor. My typewriter arrived soon thereafter. Laughing, but with pride in her voice, Faye predicted the word on the agency grapevine would be:

"That WID office is full of tough women. They know how to get what they want." To insiders the women in development office was WID, the Agency for International Development AID. I soon learned that if you didn't know the acronyms and pronounce them right you didn't count in the agency.

Without Faye and Mary, Elsa and I would have come and gone without leaving much trace. Together, and with two other young academics with overseas experience that Elsa found and recruited as management interns, we became in-house examples of women in development. What kept us going was a sense of humor. Hanging in my house today is a colorful poster Faye and her husband, an advertising artist, did for my retirement party four years later. Beneath a cartoon of me—gray hair, big head and glasses, carrying suitcases with Capitol Hill, the Eiffel Tower and an airplane in the background—is a five-stanza poem that begins:

Excuse me, my friends, a quick farewell I bid
I'm off to the Third World to integrate WID
My intentions are pure, my consciousness raised
I've read all the dogma until I'm half crazed...

What others called dogma, we labeled data and information. We converted a room in our office suite into a resource center open to anyone in the agency. Using the small contracts mechanism, we soon had so many resource materials and were distributing them so widely that we had to hire a publications and communications staffer. We were bent on educating the agency about what "women in development" and WID meant and what they should do about it.

Some looked for easy ways to meet the terms of the Percy amendment. Elsa called this the "walking on roads syndrome." Women walked on roads, therefore a road project could be called a women in development project. Another day, shaking with fury and brandishing an AID population division report, she emerged from her office saying:

"These people can't write the word women without putting 'pregnant' or 'lactating' as its modifier. They think that because they deliver contraceptives to women they are the ultimate women in development project." Another thing that bugged us was characterizing women as "targets and beneficiaries" of foreign aid. Was foreign aid a magic bullet you shot at people?

There was no way we were going to change this agency quickly. We had to think long term, and take advantage of every opportunity. Women were half the people in developing countries, a majority of them lived in rural areas and far too many were illiterate. One of AID's priorities was agriculture and rural development. Title XII of the foreign assistance act gave U.S. land grant universities and their agriculture schools special consideration on AID contracts. They implemented—and often helped design—massive projects in developing countries. Dominated by men who used American farming methods as the model, Title XII contractors assumed the world was made up of male farmers who supported their families. They often complained, "You feminists are upsetting the culture of these countries, importing Western ideas." We wanted to say, "No, that's exactly what you're doing," but were still too new and defensive. Besides, collaboration gets one farther than confrontation.

When Vice President Mondale could not carry out a promise to speak before a national Title XII meeting in Minneapolis, the White House asked me to substitute for him. I gloated around the office saying this invitation will convey a message "to these Title XII guys." The Carter administration means what it says about women. I played my farm and university background to the hilt in my speech, and included an anecdote a sympathetic agency bureaucrat had given me. It involved an ad for a farm sale that listed the machinery and livestock for sale. At the bottom of the ad was the punch line: "Reason for Sale. Wife died." That made my point in terms these Americans would understand. Women were an essential factor in farming.

In many parts of the developing world women, alone, produced much of the food eaten by families. Everybody knew hunger was a momentous Third World problem, so paying attention to women farmers, I argued, was vital. Following up on my speech, Elsa used her academic contacts, and those of the management interns she had recruited for our office, to build a Title XII network of women faculty and researchers who could be consultants on rural development projects.

The prevalent idea that all women were housewives supported by men and that young women's goal in life was to find a man to support them always provoked me, in the U.S. and abroad. Implicitly it said women didn't count, that children were their responsibility, and, in poor countries, they had to be prevented from having too many. Portraying women as barefoot, pregnant, and with a child on their back brought needed contributions to international aid organizations. But many women around the world supported families by themselves, especially as men migrated to cities for work. In an attempt to dispel the universal housewife myth, I contracted with Nadia Youseff, a brilliant Egyptian researcher then working in Washington, to do a study on female-headed households in developing countries. Her finding that about one third of households were female-headed astounded even me, and was an important contribution to the WID movement. We distributed Youseff's study widely. In 1980, it resulted in a provision in the Programme of Action issued by the second world conference on

Arvonne in WID office resource center with Haspida N'Guariera of Chad

women titled: "Women who alone are responsible for families." Numerous countries objected to the term "female-headed households." They argued that, legally no female could head a household, therefore such entities didn't exist. As I think about it now, "women who alone are responsible for families" may be more powerful than "female-headed household," but we got our point across.

Women's legal rights, I soon discovered, were equally, if not more, important in the developing world. When Silu Singh of Nepal, the first woman lawyer in that country, came to see me in Washington, I was enthralled by her stories of using street theatre to teach illiterate women their rights. She understood that knowing your rights is not enough. They must be claimed. She also represented women in court. Land and family law problems were the majority of her cases. Many U.S. feminists criticized anyone talking about inheritance as being elitist, but I knew women farmers or farmers' wives left without land or houses could not support themselves or their children. Male preference in inheritance, especially of land, was a universal problem. (My own father, in his will, left a higher percentage of the farm to my brothers.) I decided that if I could find more women like Silu Singh and get them financial support, I would earn my pay and more. Our office needed help finding pioneers like Silu, and we also needed practical ideas for helping women, especially rural women.

Martha Lewis, my good friend from my early Washington days, was an inveterate gardener and interested in nutrition. Always full of energy and ideas, she came to see me with a very practical proposal. She suggested adapting World War II-era and earlier U.S. Department of Agriculture materials on food production through gardening, saying the gap in development made them relevant for use in our work. I wrote another contract. Based on the materials Martha found and adapted plus her additional research on nutrition, AID's Jamaica mission commissioned her to assist on a soil erosion control and rural development project.

In the Caribbean, many younger women were migrating to nearby cities or the U.S. for work, leaving older women responsible for grandchildren. Martha discovered AID and local extension agents had little respect for these older women and their traditional gardening. Instead, they encouraged importation of food. She thought this plain stupid in a poor, tropical country. Working with a few grandmothers on model gardens, she was delighted when the women suggested improvements that would keep moisture near the plants but let the heavy rains drain slowly down the hillsides, thus preventing the erosion problems plaguing many Caribbean nations. Soon the women were selling their extra production commercially.

When Martha reported this to our office, I crowed with pleasure. She'd been denigrated as "just a housewife," by some of my feminist colleagues and the contracts office fussed about her lack of recent paid employment. That was like waving a red flag in front of me. Martha had a college degree and had organized both material and people. She, like me, was one of the horde of intelligent, mature women who had raised families, aided their husbands' careers, and were now returning to the paid labor force. We had slim resumes by official standards. I believed contracting with Martha was well worth the investment of a bit of taxpayer money. That investment paid good dividends. A year or so later, a Dominican Republic project proudly displayed 5,000 "Martha Lewis vegetable gardens." Excess produce was sold to a local hotel. Later Martha was delighted when she was served kale in a hotel salad. She had introduced it in a project because of its nutritional value. At still another rural development project that ultimately failed, the only thing that remained were the women's gardens that Martha had helped establish.

Another of my small contract "gambles" was with an anthropologist who had accompanied her husband to South Asia and French West Africa. Hampered by Foreign Service rules that denied spouses paid employment, but ever the observer/investigator, Marilyn Hoskins became interested in forestry. Her pioneering study showed how conventional forestry projects undertaken by foreign aid donors shortchanged women who depended on trees and forests for foods and medicines. Her work in this field later resulted in Marilyn Hoskins becoming director of the community forestry unit at FAO, the UN's Food and Agriculture Organization in Rome.

Gradually, and somewhat grudgingly, our office gained a measure of respect and attention inside and outside the agency. A young man returning from Africa came to tell me I had to meet this sensational American woman he had met in Liberia. He had told her to get in touch with me when she returned to the U.S. The result is a treasured friendship and another success story. Vivian Derryck, a young black woman from Cleveland, was married to the Liberian Peace Corps director. She shared my passion about education as both a personal and an economic development necessity. In Liberia and elsewhere in Africa, she had seen how illiteracy hampered rural women and doomed their daughters to the same fate—endless, grueling work for survival and too many pregnancies. Her excellent paper for our office advocating formal education for girls and training for women, if countries were to develop economically and socially, was a pioneering effort but it didn't produce immediate results.

Building dams across rivers is a concrete example—pardon the pun—of what foreign aid money can accomplish fairly quickly and show evaluators. Education takes much longer and is harder to display. But times, and ideas about development, change. Vivian and I feel vindicated now as we read in AID's publications about schools for girls being built with U.S. funds. What saddened me was a senior civil servant telling of his work building schools for girls in Afghanistan in the 1960's. Then education fell out of favor in development circles. Now it's back in vogue. I think of this man when I read about Afghan women leaders defying the Taliban and wonder if they were educated in the schools Americans helped build the 1960s.

Vivian's career and our friendship flourished. She was a determined soul whose deep chuckle and broad smile, even in adversity, added to her effectiveness. We worked together and separately on our common interests: education, women's leadership, and the plight of poor African women. Her education paper demonstrated her abilities. She went on to direct U.S. participation in the 1980 world women's conference and later directed the National Council of Negro Women's international division. When the National Democratic Institute for International Affairs was created, and I was on its board, I suggested her as vice president. There we promoted women's political participation worldwide. Recently her Harvard-educated Liberian friend, Ellen Johnson-Sirleaf, a 1970s WID activist, was elected president of that country, becoming the first female head of state in Africa. We consider that a women in development coup.

Finding good colleagues, forming deep friendships, and finally having a full-time job, were my antidote to tragedy and depression. Early in my AID career, I went off my anti-depressant pills. Still, there were days when I despaired. Charlie Paolillo, deputy director of AID's policy division, became my one-man support person. I hadn't known Charlie well when he worked for the House Foreign Affairs Committee. At AID, his breadth of knowledge, commitment, patience, and good humor endeared him to many, including me. At the end of a frustrating day or week, I often wandered into his office, ostensibly asking for advice. Airing my frustrations, he would urge me to "simmer down," offer sage advice, and we would usually end up laughing or talk about our families. I'd emerge ready to do battle another day.

With Charlie's help, our office struck a blow for farm women at the 1979 World Conference on Agrarian Reform and Rural Development held in Rome. When we heard Charlie would head the U.S. delegation to the conference, we got busy. With Kathy Staudt, our hard working management intern whose PhD thesis had been on African rural women, Elsa put together an impressive collection of background papers for the conference. It included the research and field experience of our Title XII university women's network. Then we drafted language we wanted in the conference report. Charlie took our suggestions and got a whole section in the document. It dealt with property and inheritance rights; equitable access to land, livestock, and other productive assets; equal voting rights in farm or rural organizations; access to rural extension services, and our old standbys, the importance of women's organization and educational and employment opportunities. I thought this a real triumph.

Cynics often ask: what are mere words worth? Why did we work so hard to get words in UN documents? Simple. Words on paper don't go away. They make people think. All laws, policies, and regulations are mere words. Government officials take them into account. Developing countries depend heavily on UN support and funds. Getting our words into a United Nations world conference document meant we were making a dent in international policy, and, eventually, practice.

Inevitable, then, was my preoccupation with the second world conference scheduled to be held in Copenhagen, Denmark in July, 1980. By 1977, Canada and a number of European countries also had women in development offices as part of their foreign aid pro-grams. After I visited the Canadian office to compare notes, AID's representative to OECD/DAC, Lloyd Jonnes, came to see me and suggested we organize an international WID subcommittee. I didn't know what OECD/DAC was, but I was all ears. An international WID subcommittee would impress AID doubters and would help in organizing for Copenhagen. I thought this second world conference could bring women from industrialized and developing countries into greater harmony with one another.

Jonnes explained the OECD/DAC was the acronym for the Organization for Economic and Community Development/ Development Assistant Committee. OECD was outgrowth of the post-World War II Marshall Plan to reconstruct Europe. Its Development

Assistance Committee was formed when many countries became independent and sought foreign aid. Now Jonnes offered to visit "the capitols," meaning, I quickly learned, the heads of other countries' donor agencies, to promote the formation of a WID subcommittee. I jumped at this good man's offer. I assumed Jonnes wouldn't be interested in the world conference. He envisioned our WID group preparing guidelines for integrating women into foreign aid programs. I figured the proposed subcommittee could do that and organize for Copenhagen.

Because this subcommittee was a U.S. initiative, I became its first chair. "Sisterhood is Powerful" was a favorite phrase of 1970s women's liberationists. Our Paris group proved it. WID officers from Canada, Australia, Britain, and the Nordic and western European countries joined me at OECD/DAC's Paris headquarters in March, 1978. Some of us were political appointees, others civil servants. Many of us had been together in Mexico City three years earlier. During our formal sessions we compared our various programs and priorities, discussed the proposed guidelines and exchanged information about projects—what worked and what didn't. When we got to know each other better, during informal sessions, when the microphones were off, we exchanged stories and laughed about everything from our own experiences with discrimination to gossip about our agencies, overseas missions, and the UN. All our WID offices and numerous new international women's organizations had been established after the Mexico City conference. Most of the new organizations depended on us for funds. Over coffee and informal dinners in Paris bistros, the conversations continued. We were all looking forward to Copenhagen.

We would all be delegates from our respective countries to the 1980 conference. I didn't worry about getting the language we wanted in the conference's Programme of Action. We were building on the Mexico City Plan, an excellent document. At Copenhagen I wanted to strengthen language on education and, along with the Nordic countries, promote legal literacy. Everyone in Paris agreed that Youseff's study on female-headed households made new language on that issue mandatory for inclusion. Making the non-governmental meeting, the NGO Forum, a success was my over-riding concern. Effective implementation of the Mexico City Plan and the projected Programme depended on women pressuring at national levels. Even autocratic governments responded to pressure. We could help create it by promoting and funding a well-planned forum in Copenhagen. It would cost millions. Funding a week's program of seminars and workshops on every topic covered by the Mexico City Plan, paying travel costs for participants from developing countries, and providing materials and information that participants could take home wasn't small change. But foreign aid money was rather plentiful in the late 1970s, and women were becoming less shy about asking for it. Nations have egos and our Paris group played on that. AID put in almost a million, of which only half came from my office budget—by1980 I had gotten it up to about three million.

Over 8000 people, 98% women, of every size, shape, color, and age—some dressed conservatively, some in the most exotic costumes imaginable—attended the more than a thousand workshops conducted at the forum. Led by international leaders, experts, and activists, the workshops discussed every issue in the 1975 Plan of Action and new ones. It was truly a melting pot, as women whose homes were separated by thousands of miles found common ground and interests. It was truly, as I often said of women's world conferences, a cross between a county or state fair and a university seminar. Some booths sold crafts, others sold posters, and donors—including my own office—offered attendees more printed materials than they could ever carry home. Almost every participant also returned home with a list of new friends from across borders who were interested in or worked on similar issues.

The media and pessimists the world over focused on the disagreements among women and governments at Mexico City. Controversy makes news. I was confident the great majority of women would leave Copenhagen encouraged in their activism—even if it had to be underground—and that there would be much more international collaboration among women's groups. A backhanded sign of our progress was that the PLO sent Leila Khaled, who today would be labeled a "terrorist." She had been part of an internationally publicized hijacking operation, and was there to condemn Israel in the NGO Forum and tantalize the media. She was photogenic and good copy. Iran maintained a booth with a display defending the Islamic revolution that included a poster of a chador-clad woman with a machine gun. Most of the media coverage concentrated on the Israeli–PLO conflicts and the occasionally flamboyant or contentious events that took place inside and outside the Forum, but it also told the world that an international women's conference was being held. It was an exciting and sometimes wild two weeks but beneath the tumult, as the *Christian Science Monitor* headlined on July 21, 1980: "UN conference shows how women's movement has gained global stature."

Today, as I read news stories about women in Africa, Asia, and the Middle East learning to read in women's literacy courses, or banding together to form cooperatives, change laws, or protest restrictions, I am cheered. (Before Copenhagen, few newspapers carried stories about women's issues or concerns unless it was food or clothes.) As Maryam Rajavi, an Iranian, was quoted last year in the *New York Times* as saying: "I'm optimistic. It may not happen in my generation, but eventually the mullahs will go." I'm optimistic too, most days. But then I read stories of girls leaving their families in some South Asian country to go work in brothels, or of all the women infected by HIV/AIDs, the homeless children, and women killed by brothers or even fathers because they refuse to marry the man chosen for them. There is still a tremendous amount to do.

During the 1980 Copenhagen conference I had one worry. It was Yoyo, our rather lost middle child, by then twenty-five years old with an MA in English Literature. She had concerned Don and me for years. Now, as she was trying to find a decent job and build a satisfying life, without much luck, our worries increased. Our beautiful, seemingly docile child, was brilliant intellectually. She had cajoled us into letting her enter kindergarten at age 4 and college at 16. "But no common sense," her practical sister Mary Mac said once when exasperated with Yo. My mother called her "at loose ends;" others said "a child of the '60s." I once confided to a friend that Yo never seemed to see any good happening.

"Well, in her young life nothing has," my friend replied. "She's lived through Kennedy's assassination and Martin Luther King and Bobby Kennedy, all the controversy over Vietnam and the Washington riots. The only good thing for her is her family and even that...Annie died."

We knew Annie's death had been traumatic for her. In addition she had a bad leg, an ongoing problem, the result of a childhood accident while playing with older children. Three operations and months on crutches didn't solve the problem and she resisted physical therapy. Music lessons and playing her precious Steinway, bought with her own money, were solace for her and for us, but the deep sadness reflected in her soulful brown eyes was immutable. Nothing seemed to work for or with her. Supporting herself with odd jobs, she lived frugally in a small apartment across town but came home often in her beat-up old car, ostensibly to do laundry. Usually she stayed through the evening, talking about everything except what was really bothering her. I, a mother who prided herself on not intruding on my adult children's lives—in this case mistakenly—didn't ask her enough of the right questions.

Her latest interest was photography and filmmaking. Her plans for seeking work in film seemed unrealistic, but I found her a part-time internship with a women's film-making crew going to the conference. She and Jeannie flew to Copenhagen commercially as I accompanied the U.S. delegation on an Air Force jet. Jeannie stayed in my hotel room, Yo in a hostel not far away. The girls toured the city, attended a few Forum workshops and took a train on Yo's days off to Denmark's North Sea beaches, returning titillated over the nude beaches. I didn't worry about them when they were together. Both were experienced, responsible travelers and good friends despite the seven-year difference in their ages.

I hoped this working vacation would put some sparkle in Yo's eyes, teach her a bit more about film-making, and maybe get her some contacts in the film industry. I also had a selfish interest. Jean was too young to stay home or tour Denmark by herself. Life with children, even adult children, is one big balancing act. Yo's life was off balance, but I didn't know what to do. Besides, I write guiltily, I had work to do—fascinating work that kept me from identifying just how serious Yo's problems were.

During the opening ceremonies in Copenhagen I was thrilled watching our U.S. representative step forward to add the United States as a signatory to the Convention on the Elimination of All Forms of Discrimination Against Women (CEDAW). President Carter, true to his campaign promises of equal rights for women, had authorized the U.S. signing of this document. He designated White House women's affairs officer Sara Weddington, the young Texas lawyer who had argued *Roe v. Wade*, the landmark 1973 U.S. Supreme Court abortion decision, to be the signer. I had no inkling in Copenhagen that this convention would become central to my work after I left AID.

My focus as a delegation member was on the Programme of Action. Because governments don't give high priority to women's issues, women's conferences are prone to being testing grounds for international political maneuvers. Our delegation's most firm instructions from the State Department were to be wary of the Soviet Union, the Palestinians, and the question of apartheid in South Africa, the three big U.S. foreign policy concerns in 1980.

Being wary meant being prepared to yield the seat behind the U.S. nameplate to a diplomat, always a man. It was the same with every delegation until one memorable occasion. That day the spectacle of a horde of men in dark blue suits, white shirts, and conservative ties emerging en masse from the hallway was just too obvious. I don't recall the issue but it wasn't a major one. Tittering began in the back rows among the most lowly delegation members. It grew louder as everyone watched women relinquish the country chairs to the suits. Soon, through every headset, compatible chuckles from female interpreters could be heard. Even Tatiana, the sober and unfriendly Soviet representative, turned around and smiled.

The unspoken message was: Men don't trust mere women with the interests of their country. They don't care about women's concerns; they stand in the hallway chatting until a foreign policy issue comes up. Laughter is contagious and a powerful tool. After this incident the diplomats became more discreet—dare I say more diplomatic.

In Copenhagen, though, political statements in the international section of the Programme of Action equating Zionism with racism prompted the U.S. to vote no on adoption of the document as a whole. Women in our delegation and others argued for a separate vote on the crucial national section that called on governments to take specific steps to improve the status of women in the fields of education, employment and health—the themes of the UN Decade for Women. We lost the argument and many of my friends went home disillusioned. I took solace in the fact that issues such as child care; migrant, rural, and young women; and my favorite, "women who alone are responsible for families" were in the document and that for the first time, domestic and sexual violence were explicitly mentioned and drew strong attention at the NGO Forum.

I felt especially good about the long section in the Programme on women's and grass roots organizations. It wasn't easy getting governments to admit that non-governmental organizations were important to the development of a country. As an American I had witnessed the power of local and national organizations to move governments. As a U.S. feminist I'd seen all the laws and policies that we got changed in the 1970s. Virtually everything Elsa and I had accomplished at AID had been undergirded by support from women's groups or women active in development organizations. The U.S. voting no was embarrassing, but it wasn't the end of the world. Most other countries voted yes. I thought women proved in Copenhagen that there was a truly international women's movement.

Before leaving Copenhagen, Jeannie, Yoyo and I celebrated with an evening at Tivoli, the amusement park in the heart of the city, enjoying the long twilight in this northern country where the sun barely went down in mid-summer. Yo seemed as satisfied working on the film as she ever could be about anything. She didn't tell me her name was on a credit line for the first time in her life. The next day Jeannie and I took a train to Oslo, and Yo went home via New York. Never satisfied to simply enjoy scenery, I took Jeannie to an Oslo museum commemorating the Norwegian underground activities during World War II and then on to visit a colleague who had been part of that resistance movement. The next day Jeannie and I took a train to Bergen and spent a few days at a seaside inn. Then I dropped Jeannie off in Copenhagen for her flight home and her summer life-guarding job, and I went on to visit our German friend, Stephanie Neunreither. I needed some down time to get ready for what faced me back in Washington, including a massive report to Congress on what we had accomplished in our WID office and in Copenhagen.

My future, and that of our family, also needed thought. Ronald Reagan was waging an aggressive campaign against President Carter. If Reagan won, I would have to find a new job. Would it be in Washington or Minneapolis? Don had run for the U.S. Senate in 1978 and lost. Now he was back in Minneapolis as mayor. Jeannie would be off to Yale in the fall and I'd be alone, living a commuter marriage with daily phone calls and weekend visits. And there was our constant worry about Yo. She needed help but neither Don nor I could figure out what kind. Moral support didn't dispel her sadness. She seemed so vulnerable, and yet disdained help.

After eighteen years in Washington, it, not Minneapolis, was home for me and Jeannie. To Don, Washington was never home. While in Congress, it was where he worked and his family lived. Politics was his life. Devastated by his narrow defeat in the 1978 primary, he served out his Congressional term, then took a temporary job with a foreign policy group and went through the motions of living. He came alive in May, 1979, when the incumbent Minneapolis mayor decided, on the day before the DFL Party's endorsing convention, not to run again. I didn't get much work done that day. On hearing the news, Don called me at my office. Should he go home to run? What did I think? It was up to me, he said, but his eagerness to run was in his voice.

"Let me think about it," was all I could muster. Jeannie still had a year of high school left. Who would support this family while Don campaigned? Yo couldn't be left alone. My stalling was an answer to his question, but not the answer he wanted. Late that afternoon, Jeannie, Don, and I sat out on our back patio nervously pondering our fates between phone calls from eager constituents and the media. As dusk hovered and with our conversation going nowhere, I finally said:

"If you're going to do this, you have to get on a plane." We lived only minutes from National Airport.

"If I get to New York by 9 o'clock, there's a plane to Minneapolis arriving about one in the morning. John will pick me up." Son John lived in our Minneapolis house. I couldn't say no. It was his life at stake. Jeannie and I would cope. I drove him to the airport, kissed him goodbye and wished him luck.

I had underestimated the effect of all this on Jeannie. She had not seemed upset during our discussions on the patio.

"He left us," she said sadly a day or so later. I tried to explain that politics was her father's life, that our family was not like others. Mature as she seemed, at sixteen she was too young to understand this. I should have realized her feeling of loss, and probably subconscious fear that our marriage was ending. She didn't understand that he respected and supported my need for my own independent career, after years of serving his. Now we had to respect his need.

In the '78 campaign, when his opponent made an issue of our somewhat unconventional lifestyle, he had vigorously defended my right to a separate career. His answer to that opponent still hangs proudly on my office wall. Son Tom had it copied in lovely calligraphy and framed. The last line, from my mild mannered husband who rarely swore, conveys the depth of his feeling and commitment to me and our marriage:

"You wanted to know what the combined salary of my wife and I is? I'm going to tell you something…My wife worked for twenty-five years raising the children. She served as my campaign manager…as a volunteer administrative assistant—unpaid—for at least fifteen years. Last year she went to work for President Carter… was the regional director for three states…When the campaign was over…she went to work on the personnel side of the White House. Today she's working as head of an office in the Agency for International Development…She's been active in the women's movement over the last ten years….

I have enormous respect for my wife as a person. You can go to hell before I'm going to start bringing her into the campaign."

That '78 campaign had been hard for all of us. As a federal employee, I could have no part in it, at least publicly. The Hatch Act prevented federal employees from engaging in partisan politics. That didn't prevent Don and me from talking about it at home. While I wished him well and was full of free advice, I wasn't as excited about this campaign as his others. Nevertheless, a Hatch Act violation was filed against me by a group Don had angered through his foreign affairs committee work. I could have lost my job and worse. Our friend Joe Rauh, one of Washington's most distinguished liberal lawyers, defended me, and eventually the charge was dismissed. At home in Washington with Don gone all the time, Jeannie and I became even closer. She seemed to accept his absence, perhaps secure in the thought that he would win and life would continue as she had always known it.

I went home to Minneapolis to be with Don for primary election night, September 12, and was distressed by his loss by less than one percent. Entering our Washington house a day later, a whiff of something like model airplane glue greeted me. Too busy and sad about Don's loss to investigate, I forgot about it. The following Sunday—Don still in Minneapolis—Jeannie and I were invited by Hal and Judy Wise, our favorite neighbors only three doors away, for an early dinner. When Jeannie went back to our house for a book she was reading, she returned within seconds exclaiming:

"Our house is on fire."

Hal and I rushed back to see flames spouting up the open stairwell.

"Turn on the hose," he yelled as he opened the sliding glass doors—never locked when we went to the Wises'—and pointed my patio garden hose toward the flames. Panicked, I turned the spigot left instead of right. Instantly sober—for he drank a lot—Hal pushed me aside, turned on the water and had the flames subdued before the fire department arrived.

Arson, the police and fire departments called it. One side of Yo's old piano and the linoleum tiled floor in the niche beneath the open stair-well showed signs of explo-sions. Only a few stairs were charred but smoke damage required repainting the whole house. The mystery about the fire was never solved. Arson cases rarely are.

I had long suspected our phone was tapped because of the crackling noises on the line, but this was Washington in the Nixon years. Liberals at parties made jokes about wire taps and FBI files. More than once I told the story

Where the explosion occurred that set our house on fire

about the men in phone company uniforms who appeared one late afternoon saying they'd come to fix our phones.

"I don't think there's anything wrong," I said.

"We got a call. We're here to fix them."

Busy with children and making dinner, I let them in. Later I wondered about the phone company truck I frequently saw across the street or at the side street with cables running down a manhole. But our neighborhood was full of politicians—Humphrey in Har-bour Square, House Speaker Foley next door for a year or two, and others in nearby complexes. I decided after the fire that our house had been constantly watched from across the street—perhaps from an apartment rented for that purpose. We were grateful, but our suspicions escalated, because the fire had been ignited when nobody was home. I never go out my back door, even now, without the feeling that someone is watching me.

Jeannie's feeling of abandonment by her father the following May changed somewhat after an incident at school. A teacher had asked her why she and her mother didn't go back to Minneapolis for Don's campaign for mayor. Apparently her schoolmates had been inquiring as well.

"Don't they understand who's supporting this family?" she exclaimed, breaking into tears. She had heard the same lament from me, probably too often. After Don was elected, Jeannie and I spent our vacations and holidays in Minneapolis. Don called every day. Jeannie excelled at school and shortly after the Copenhagen conference I drove her up to New Haven, Connecticut, for college, met her roommates, and cried half the way home. I was alone.

Carter's re-election campaign was not going well. If I lost my job Don's salary as mayor would not support us and pay Jeannie's college tuition. Like millions of other American families, we needed two incomes. I toyed with the idea of trying to convert to a senior civil service position until one day I saw a woman about my age coming toward me in one of those long, empty State Department halls. She looked drained of energy, ambling down the hall with little purpose in her step, and a slightly aggrieved expression on her face. Somehow, that did it. I might end up like her. Spoiled, a brother-in-law once called me, in a teasing voice but with a serious undertone. I want work I enjoy at least 75 percent of the time, work that is challenging, engrossing, and satisfying. I'd traveled from east to west across northern Africa, all over western Europe and the Caribbean, and become a committed internationalist. I felt good about what we had accomplished in the WID office in four years.

Reagan's election sealed my fate. My days at AID were numbered, but my experience in White House personnel taught me it took awhile to put a new administration in place. I had, perhaps, six months before I would be replaced. I was no longer anything like the timid woman who had walked into AID in 1977. I spent my short time left doing everything in my power to firmly institutionalize women in development at AID. Our office had made good progress in deeds as well as words. The required Report to Congress allowed us to show what we had accomplished.

My Republican successor, a bright and committed young woman, built on what we started. New ideas, if firmly planted, take on a life of their own.

Arvonne receiving an award from Charles Paolilo on her retirement from AID

In 2004 Irene Tinker and I co-edited a book that was eventually titled, *Developing Power: How Women Transformed International Development*. A collection of short memoirs written by colleagues in the early days of the women in development movement, it bristles with energy and accomplishment. Irene and I had a far less lofty title for the book, but our publisher thought this title fit. Former AID colleagues hosted a small seminar to celebrate the book's publication. I felt truly honored when Faye and Mary, the women who had welcomed me to AID and without whom I could not have done much, came to the 2004 seminar. I was equally thrilled when the Republican-appointed head of AID, in welcoming us, talked fervently about the importance of girls' education and how much AID was putting into that worldwide. Cynics might say he had been well briefed. I don't think so. Faking interest usually shows.

Chapter 11

Down and Out

In the spring of 1981, with Reagan president, Don, Jeannie, and my job gone, Minneapolis beckoned. The last year had been lonely. Even Yoyo had moved back to Minneapolis. I went back on weekends, and Don and I looked all over the city at houses. Nothing lived up to Tiber Island, those four stories of rooms a mile from the Capitol now filled only with memories. A complex of emotions, including plain sentimentality, drove us to buy a large old house two doors down 7th Street from the house we left in 1962. It was a mirror image of our old one in which Don and our children had been born and raised. Converting a rooming house into a large space for ourselves and two upstairs apartments for university students would be an exciting new project, we thought.

Mrs. Andersen, the seller of the house, had been our good neighbor throughout our children's lives. They called her "Mormor," Danish for grandmother, imitating her grandchildren. She wanted to stay in the neighborhood so we built her a small apartment upstairs. We had been landlords all our married life, renting whatever we weren't living in at the time. I functioned as property manager, Don as repairman and in-house lawyer. One of our renter-friends still laughs about Mayor Fraser appearing at 7 a.m., coveralls over his suit and tie, to fix an electrical problem at our St. Croix house before going to work.

Saying farewell to Washington was hard. Jeannie returned from college for summer break to help me move and get settled. Driving out to Chevy Chase, our original neighborhood in Washington, on a lovely May afternoon, nostalgia made me late for my final board meeting of our Washington Women's Network. Leisurely retracing the drive through Rock Creek Park and up Military Road, I smiled to myself as I recalled the time Don attempted to learn Spanish. Driving together to Capitol Hill, I sat with his book on my lap, drilling him on vocabulary and verb conjugations. Why did a man who was so good at math and music have such trouble learning another language, I wondered?

Nearing Chevy Chase, my thoughts turned to Annie and her accident, then to Yoyo, whom Don was helping find temporary jobs. The economy was in recession but she had done well, had found her own somewhat ramshackle apartment and furnished it. I worried about her having sold her piano before her move. She hadn't bought a new one. Concern about her was part of Don's and my daily phone conversations. I had even started smoking an occasional mini-cigar again, stanching my worries with nicotine. She seemed more content back in Minneapolis, was even dressing better when we all went out to dinner together. She didn't like her psychiatrist but said good things about her social worker. At my request, some of my good female friends took her to lunch. They weren't enthusiastic about her mental health but reported she was coping.

Parking near the large lovely white colonial home of our Network hostess, I cheered up, eager at the prospect of seeing good friends. Irene Tinker and I had started the Network when we discovered all of us—Carter administration appointees—were having trouble in our agencies. We decided we needed a support group where we could exchange stories about how our male peers and underlings treated—and mistreated—us, and how we coped. Even Cabinet members joined our group. Our meetings were often hilarious, sometimes deadly serious, and always therapeutic. It had been a remarkable four years. Carter's defeat had not dampened our camaraderie or the respect we had for the president who had appointed so many women to top administrative jobs and judgeships.

I rang the doorbell to no avail. Hearing familiar high-pitched female voices at the back of the house, I decided to go around to the back door. With all that noise, they probably couldn't hear the doorbell. As I walked into the back hall, the voices subsided abruptly. The hostess and Irene, their faces serious, came forward to greet me.

Yo (center) at a New York gathering.

offering condolences, asking what they could do to help, and plying me with vodka and tonics to calm me down. Lashing out in anger is common in grief. I privately consoled myself with this knowledge later when mentally revisiting my behavior. Gratified that so many friends turned up at this awful time, I was aware enough to know that Jeannie and I were in no condition to travel that night.

"We'll go on the first morning flight," I announced, after some good soul told us seats were ready for us on the last Northwest flight to Minneapolis that evening. That was the last decision I made until we got home to Minneapolis. Jeannie and I reversed roles that evening. Our eighteen-year-old college freshman was shocked into maturity, dealing with one more death. She and Yo had been with me when I found Don's sister Betty dead in a tent on the beach a year after Annie was killed. Then a few years later her Fraser grandmother, who then lived just across the courtyard from us in Tiber Island, died. Jeannie had once told me her recurring nightmare was that she would open a door and find a dead person. Now she had to manage this death. She got her abject mother to bed, to the airport next morning and, with the help of a sympathetic airline crew, into a window seat.

Staring blankly into the stratosphere until we landed, mutely grieving over one child, I neglected my youngest. By then we knew Yo's death had been peaceful. She had done what she wanted. I recalled over and over what she once said: "I just want to go to sleep and never wake up." Jeannie may have begun composing her brave memorial eulogy to Yo on that plane trip. They had been close, shared life-guarding duties at the Tiber Island pool and summer vacations at the St. Croix with Bonnie while I was at AID. Yo had come to New York with us the fall we lived there when Don was the congressional representative at the UN General Assembly session. Like Don and me, Jean had surely watched Yo's growing sadness, and probably sensed her parent's concern, but as a family we took respect for each other's private lives much too far.

Jeannie knew instinctively that I didn't want to be touched. I wanted family and friends around but all, except Don, at arms length. I still feel ashamed at how I fended off Tom, our oldest son, who attempted to hug me as we emerged from the airport gateway. Grief does terrible things to a person. I retreated into a shell from which I have never totally emerged.

I hadn't expected Don to meet us at the airport. He had found Yo, had dealt, along with Tom and John, with the police and media. His being mayor meant we were all on display, that there would be media at the airport when Jean and I arrived. He was in no condition for a public appearance. Coming off the plane I was aware enough to notice one of the city's star female newspaper photographers point her camera at me, then turn away without taking a shot. Respect is a sterling quality, manifested in many ways.

As we did when Annie died, Don, the children and I sat around the living room for hours both before and after Yo's memorial service. We talked—even laughed occasionally—about her, her idiosyncrasies and difficulties. We recalled memorable incidents. Our way of coping, and remembering her, was simply to be together.

Our new/old house was a mess. The renovation project started by Don and son John was abruptly halted. Thank goodness nobody took a picture of it. No one commented or complained about the ancient kitchen or worn carpeting as they brought in food or prepared it for the wake the non-religious Frasers wanted. Again, we pored over the hundreds of condolence messages that were exactly that, consoling. I still have most of them in a file cabinet in the basement, along with Annie's, even though I constantly complain about "too much stuff." Somehow I can't bring myself to throw them away.

We had little time for mourning. A few days after the memorial, Jeannie and I flew back to Washington to meet the previously-scheduled movers. Our dear German friend, Stephanie, living then in Miami in an elegant waterfront townhouse, insisted on coming up to help, even if she had "to sleep on the floor," she said. With friends like that, one manages. Having her there was good for both Jeannie and me. She was another of what Jeannie called her "other mothers." Stephanie's son, Stephan, had lived with us a couple of summers to practice his English. I'll never forget the morning he came downstairs, beaming, and announced: "Arvonne, I dreamt in English." Jeannie spent a winter semester in Luxembourg with Stephanie and her family, attended an international school, and was treated royally. Parting with another of Jeannie's extra mothers, our neighbor Judy Wise, was even harder.

I endured and was cheered by a large farewell party with friends from women's organizations, and was refreshed by an interview with a friend, a *Washington Post* reporter sympathetic to the women's movement. We laughed recalling that it hadn't been many years ago that the Style section of that paper—now second only in importance to the front page—was once the little-read Women's Section. A few days later I was splashed across its front page with my eternal cigarette and messy desk for all to see, but the article listed the accomplishments of the women's movement in Washington. Then, the house bare after the movers left, Jeannie and I packed up the remnants in my little blue Chevy and drove leisurely across country. We wanted back roads, trees, mountains, rivers to drive along. The movers would take time to get to Minneapolis. We could too. We were in no hurry now.

Don had been to Guatemala with a group of human rights activists shortly before Yo died, bringing home a gigantic plastic bag of cheap, hand-rolled cigars. I smoked every last one of them that summer, sitting on the sofa in our miserable house, looking out at the sky, with Jeannie beside me. All renovations on the house stopped. We lived with the mess. With our boys, we cleaned out Yo's apartment, sorting through her things, teary eyed, marveling at how she had cleaned her house, paid her bills. She left us only a tape recording that sounded serene and dream-like, as if she were reading something. I had called the public library to try to find out what she was reading from. The reference people kindly searched and searched, concluding finally that

Jean

the words were her own. We played it over and over for a few days. Now I can't bear to listen to it, nor can I destroy it.

About mid-July I picked myself up. Frasers, again, work to forget. Only in the car and in bed, when we were alone, did Don and I go over and over what we could have done, should have done....ultimately reconciling ourselves to the fact that there was nothing to do now but remember Yo. We respected her decision and the dignity with which she followed through with it. We added her name—her given name, Lois—to the memorial fund at the Minneapolis Public Library that had been established for Annie, specifying that it should include music and literature, in Yo's memory, as well as children's books.

I never could bring myself to go into the children's room of the old downtown library after Annie died. Too many memories came flooding back and I was afraid I would break into tears. One day a few years after Yo died, browsing the shelf of new books in the library's literature section, a biography of a writer I admired caught my eye. I opened the cover and there was the bookplate, a lovely Monarch butterfly above the names, Anne and Lois Fraser. I don't know who designed that bookplate but to me it was perfect. It said it all.

Chapter 12

Back to Work

Before I left Washington, I heard that Harlan Cleveland, dean of the newly established Humphrey Institute of Public Affairs at the University, might want me to join the Institute. He thought its academic faculty should be leavened with a few people who had practiced public affairs. Reflective practitioners, he called the two of us he recruited, although "senior fellows" was our official title. Our task was to reflect on our experiences in the public arena, share what we had learned with the Institute's students, and undertake a project. I thought this a grand opportunity to continue work on women's issues nationally and internationally. Dean Cleveland offered seed money to get our projects started, but we had to raise the serious money. I had raised money for campaigns and women's groups, and doled it out at AID. I recalled the advice of my Washington friend and neighbor, Jack Conway, a United Auto Workers union leader who later organized Common Cause and other liberal organizations.

Walking together down 4th Street in Washington one morning he had said: "If you know what you want to do and how to do it, you can raise money for it."

Senior fellows were invited to be part of another of Dean Cleveland's innovations, his reflective leadership seminar. I found the companionship and stimulus I needed after Yo's death in that seminar. The Monday nights during which it was held were the high point of my week—a welcome respite from living with the smell of lumber and plaster dust and dealing with contractors. Ruth Murphy, another seminar participant and political acquaintance, had also lost a son that year in a mysterious, violent, drug-related death. "How are you doing?" became our furtive, meaningful greeting each week. We often sat together during the seminar's supper hour. Seeing her brown eyes come alive when she was amused or irritated heartened me.

In the women's lavatory we deplored the sexism we perceived on the part of the men in the course, including Dean Cleveland. They assumed leaders were male, leadership characteristics masculine, and virtually all of the authors of our assigned readings were men, as were the speakers. Now strong members of what another friend called the Nothing to Lose Caucus, neither Ruth nor I was shy about expressing opinions. In response, Dean Cleveland suggested I prepare a set of readings on women and leadership and lead an evening's seminar. I tackled it with renewed energy. The night we discussed my readings, it was clear the men had only scanned the material. One honest soul, a fellow DFL Party activist, confessed that although he accepted many of the goals of the women's movement, he personally would have trouble working for a woman boss. I wonder whether he's escaped that fate.

I named my project Women, Public Policy and Development. I wanted to study the role and impact of women's organizations on public policy in the U.S. and abroad and to think more deeply—and write about—the world women's conferences. I soon discovered there was little money available from Minnesota foundations for international work, but what feminists laughingly called "the old girls network" came through for me. In the women's movement we campaigned hard against "the old boys network," symbolized by men-only social clubs where powerful males made decisions about affairs of state and community and helped each other and their younger peers in their careers and financial endeavors. Only recently had the prestigious Minneapolis Club opened its front door to women. Previously women had to enter by the back door. It seemed ironic that our women's support groups evolved into similar but more casual groups.

An earlier incident made my money-raising success even sweeter. The Institute's proposed budget for senior fellows' first year revealed that the male fellow was allotted a significantly larger grant of seed money than I.

"All they want is my name for their new institute. I'm a token, window dressing—and they give me chicken feed for the privilege," I ranted to Don over dinner, then loaded the dishwasher with such vehemence that he feared for the glassware. Waking in the middle of the night, I realized I couldn't let this go without challenge. My integrity and reputation were at stake. I recalled the Rajender case against the University of Minnesota that WEAL had supported. I couldn't live with myself if, having supported Rajender, I didn't speak up now.

Anger makes me articulate—and wordy. I strode to my typewriter in my nightgown and fired off a three-paged single spaced memo expressing my shock, anger, and dismay. What happened to my women's program budget, I wrote, was a first class "example of what my project is attempting to deal with and is symptomatic of women's problems in society.". Pointing out that my budget was cut seventy-seven percent while the male senior fellow's was cut only two, I added:"Some days I delude myself with the idea that the world is changing and that institutions such as this are dedicated to studying that change…" I went on to cite statistics, knowing how men loved statistics, showing that more than 50% of American women worked outside the home and that only 7% of the U.S. population lived in what is considered the traditional family—male breadwinner, dependent wife, and children. The memo's address list made it obvious that the budget committee was composed only of males.

Next morning, running full steam on fury, I ran off enough copies of my memo for the whole faculty and marched into Dean Cleveland's office, trembling. Either I get equal treatment or I'm out of here, I said to myself, wondering if I'd really have the courage to execute my own imperative. It took awhile, but I emerged victorious with an added benefit. My base salary would be the same as I had earned in government. The dean and I parted as colleagues, with a firm handshake and mutual respect. I destroyed all the copies of my memo to the faculty. My tantrum had served its purpose.

After that confrontation I decided that publicizing the facts of family economic and destroying the male breadwinner myth was a necessity. The two-earner family had become the successful norm. Working women—women employed outside the home, that is— were everywhere. The male faculty needed to open their eyes as well as their minds. Most of the senior men called me an "advocate," a denigrating term in academia. Somehow when one of them had an idea and testified before the Legislature or Congress that was public service, not advocacy. Serious academics were objective, they said. Feminism was subjective, therefore suspect. The fact that women were discriminated against, and had been for centuries, was not worthy research, they implied. Patriarchy was a dirty word when used by feminists but they rarely saw the anomaly when they proposed committees of wise men to solve a public affairs problem. There were exceptions, however. A male colleague, his wife a hospital executive, seconded the motion in faculty meeting when a female academic and I proposed establishing a Center on Women and Public Policy in the institute.

I was disturbed by the low status of women's work, paid or unpaid. It was irrational. Society depended on this work, but devalued it. When Aviva Breen, director of Minnesota's Commission on the Economic Status of Women, called me in 1982 and suggested we collaborate on a publication analyzing the 1980 Census data on women, I was intrigued. Together we published a booklet entitled *Women in Minnesota* that showed that among women aged 18 – 64, sixty-one percent were in the paid labor force. Among divorced, widowed, or separated women with no children under 18, the figure was 84%. Sixty percent of mothers with preschoolers were in the labor force and 78% of those with school aged children.

With the help of Tom Lehman, my very tall young Institute research assistant, we also published a pamphlet entitled "Worker, Mother, Wife: The Future of Today's Girls." It argued that while society and parents expected girls to become wives, mothers, and possibly workers outside the home, Census data drew another picture. Women, married and single, with or without children, were employed outside the home. I wanted women, myself included, to be recognized as independent citizens, not only as mothers and wives. The worldwide problem of women's economic and legal status became my primary concern. Subject of a myth that they were dependent beings, in reality women the world over carried a "double burden," as the Copenhagen conference document noted. Burdened by responsibilities for children and family, they were also economically active. Universally, they were paid less or not at all for their work. While at AID I had seen almost unspeakable poverty in the developing world. The 1980 Census statistics confirmed that women and children were the poorest of the poor. While social welfare is important, it is a temporary solution to poverty. My interest was in long-term solutions.

Another world women's conference loomed in 1985, the time in Nairobi, Kenya. Critics maintained that feminism was a Western idea. I had traveled enough, met enough women, to realize what we had in common far outweighed our differences. At the Commission on the Status of Women and at the world conferences I had met women like myself all over the world, women who believed in equality and were working for change. A few visited Minnesota under the auspices of the U.S. Information Agency (USIA), which supported international exchanges.

Miriam Habib of Pakistan, identified as "the Gloria Steinem of Pakistan" when USIA wanted me to meet with her, turned out to be as interested in women's education as I. And she educated me about women organizing to claim their rights in the more liberal parts of the Muslim world. Eddah Gachukia of Nairobi, another visitor, was a former member of Kenya's Parliament, and shared my interest in girls education and also women in politics. Eddah and her African colleagues had lobbied hard to host the 1985 world conference in Kenya, but they needed help. They didn't have access to the resources—money, information, or cheap communication—that we in the industrialized countries did, and the Kenyan government was concerned about the non-governmental forum. It wanted the prestige and money UN world conferences bring to a country, but it didn't want anything to do with feminists and feminism.

As a quasi-academic in the Humphrey Institute, I decided the best thing I could do in the international segment of my project was analyze and provide information about the world conferences and the influence they had—and could have—on government policy and individual behavior. After all, I was in the Humphrey Institute of Public Affairs. Humphrey had been an ardent internationalist, as was Dean Cleveland. Why not take a look at what women were doing and thinking and try to make people think about that? With the help of eager student research assistants and a colleague we did a worldwide informal survey of women's organizations. Most focused on social welfare projects, but a few worked for longer term change. Publishing and distributing this information, emphasizing what those groups accomplished would, I thought, encourage others. The implied message was that in groups there is power—the old adage that the whole is greater than the sums of its parts.

As in any campaign—and I was campaigning about women—mailing lists and attractive but substantive materials are important. I rarely drop a name from a list unless someone dies, and try to keep them updated. I had lists dating back to Mexico City and before. Anyone who contacted our office and seemed interested got added to our lists. And I worked at, and taught my workers, layout design—how to make our materials attract readers. An intriguing title and attractive cover on any publication were essential. The copy inside had to be factual but not deadly dull, and no typing, spelling or other errors were allowed; and the materials themselves had to be cheap to print and mail. "Looking to the Future: Equal Partnership between Women and Men in the 21st Century" was emblazened across the front cover of one early booklet in big blue letters on glossy white paper, with the symbol of the UN Decade for Women atop. It opened with: "This booklet is designed to provide information about an important series of events that have been overlooked by the media and by most scholars, and are not well known to the American public."

Read on, that said to anyone vaguely interested. In forty-five information-packed pages readers were told how individual women leaders and women's organizations had promoted women's interests ever since the UN was founded. It began with the UN Commission on the Status of Women, described the two world conferences, the NGO forums and the Convention on the Elimination of All Forms of Discrimination Against Women. The final section was on the effects of the UN Decade and preparations for the 1985 conference.

What I hoped readers would say to themselves: "My goodness. I didn't know all this had happened. Isn't this exciting. And there's another world conference coming up too. I have to tell my friends about this and maybe I better start doing something for women too." But the booklet also met academic standards. It was essentially a history and a handbook. It came from a university. It wasn't just American propaganda. And, like so many mail solicitations today, at the back of the booklet was our survey of women's organizations. It invited responses, saying the information received would help in preparing for the 1985 world conference, and respondents would receive updates about the conference. Our mailing lists grew.

The hard part was raising money to fund my project's staff, the publications and their distribution, and the travel involved in monitoring and contributing to preparations for the 1985 conference. But I kept my confidence at adequate heights by remembering my old friend, Jack Conway's, advice: *If you know what you want to do and how to do it, you can raise the money.* And it turned out that equal partnership—well, almost equal—between men and women worked. Dean Cleveland was happy to have another internationalist around, and the Humphrey Institute's development officer—a friendly male—

was a great help. He knew of an older woman, Kay Cram, who lived outside Minneapolis who was interested in women internationally. Her parents had been missionaries in China and she had run a very successful camp for girls in northern Minnesota. The development officer thought she might be interested in my project and suggested a lunch with her. We got along famously.

Sometime later Don met the University Foundation executive who had accompanied us to that lunch. This man reported his amazement at two women rambling away in a wide-ranging conversation that seemed to lead nowhere but ended up with Kay's donating a considerable sum to my project. Women communicate in circles; some things don't need to be said. Kay and I became friends because our interests intersected and we thought alike.

Then, in mid-1982, Sissy Farenthold, a longtime Washington colleague and friend, called me to say she had a client interested in women internationally. Could I advise her, she asked. The client was her cousin, Genevieve Vaughn, a Texas oil heiress who had lived in Italy and had been active in that country's feminist movement. Sissy, a former candidate for governor of Texas, and I had worked together when she headed the National Women's Political Caucus. We agreed to meet in Washington when we both had meetings there. This was the beginning of years of Gen Vaughn's generous support and collaboration.

I had met my third major international benefactor, Jill Sheffield, when I was at AID. Now a program officer at the Carnegie Corporation, a foundation with a major focus on Africa, she had lived and worked in Kenya and was passionate about helping African women. We both thought the 1985 conference—the first in the developing world—would draw media attention. Jill also called me for information and advice, and after prolonged negotiations, she convinced Carnegie to support my proposals for international work at the Institute.

With this financial and moral support, I thought the best thing my project could do would be to inform and educate women's groups worldwide on how to effectively participate in this 1985 conference. I had seen too many women at the previous world conferences who knew little about the UN system and its conferences but had great expectations of them. When those expectations were not met, they became frustrated or disillusioned. We all understood this first conference in the developing world was crucial. For the first time the majority of the attendees would be from developing countries. The culminating conference for the UN Decade for Women, it had to be successful. This meant providing an even better NGO Forum that most of the participants would attend. We wouldn't get any help from the U.S. or Kenyan governments. Kenya worried whether they had enough hotel rooms for both government delegations and thousands of forum participants. Would the forum women get out of hand and create expectations that Kenya and other African governments would not welcome? African women were eager to create demands on their governments but they had to be careful not to alienate them. Many were authoritarian and a backlash could be dangerous. We were on our own—*we* meaning the women who cared about the conference's success.

My colleagues and I were delighted when Eddah Gachukia was named head of the Kenya NGO Planning Committee. She shared our hopes and concerns, and was a strategic planner and organizer. In 1984, she invited me to Nairobi as a consultant for the committee's first planning meeting. My assignment was to set the context by describing the previous world conferences, explaining international NGO expectations, and answering questions. I learned much more than I gave, beginning with the weekend I spent with Eddah and her family. Her commitment to education was evident in the school she ran near her home. Daniel, her charming husband who had been President Jomo Kenyatta's protocol officer, entertained me with stories of that nation's transition from colonial rule to independence. Visits outside Nairobi on Sunday were like being in a latter-day scenic version—no romance or sex— Isak Dinesen/Karin Blixen's *Out of Africa*. On one huge farm, the wife raised flowers under massive plastic-roofed greenhouses and shipped them to Europe by air daily while the men in the family raised purebred cattle. My father would have thought he was in heaven had he been able to visit that farm. At another plantation I saw my first coffee tree/shrub growing on a hillside. Eddah was amused. Coffee to her was like corn and soybeans to me, so familiar everyone should recognize it. Pointing to the indentation on her forehead, Eddah explained it was from carrying huge loads, as a farm child, with a strap across her forehead to ease the burden. That evening we were wined and dined at a party with local farm owners and business people—black and white—from Kenya, Rhodesia (now Zimbabwe), and South Africa.

Monday morning Eddah and I set out early, driving across the Rift Valley with wildebeest and zebras along the roadside. Our destination was Egerton, an agricultural college campus built with U.S. assistance, where the meeting was to be held. Traditional African mud huts with thatched roofs bordered the college. Women of all ages, in Western and traditional dress, poured out of buses, vans, and cars for the two-day meeting. One young, seven-months pregnant woman from near the Sudan had ridden ten hours on various buses to attend the meeting. Other attendees ranged from women farmers to parliamentarians to college professors and students, all activists in various women's organizations. Their enthusiasm, power, and diversity confirmed my view that women's organizations were a key to success—of this conference and women's future.

One tall, lanky, farm woman, a heroine in Kenya's fight for independence from British rule, fascinated me. She reminded me of my beloved grandmother: the same build, almost the same color, and that old sweater held together with a big safety pin over a cotton print dress. The way she held herself and moved—despite the sweater and the fact she only spoke Swahili—conveyed a sense of confidence and strength. I sat for an hour with her and another Kenyan woman, a recent Harvard graduate who had heard about this woman's exploits all her life and was awed to be in her presence, and also a little sad that she had never learned Swahili and thus couldn't talk directly to the older woman. We three spent a lovely hour together, relaxing in the warm sun. Despite the language barrier, we quickly became friends, using body language and a volunteer translator.

"What would you like to see accomplished for women by July 1985 and by the year 2000?" was the question put to working groups at Egerton. The groups' answers to the question were published in a ten page report. It called on women to organize, to become more active in decision-making, for an end to polygamy, for closer government supervision of secondary schools, increased support for co-operatives, and a revolving credit fund to provide more economic opportunities for women. The report also asserted women's right to family planning and for women to "be educated to seek legal intervention rather than protect their husbands" in wife- and child-battering cases. Submitted to the government, Eddah reported this caused a furor. The political agility and sagacity of Kenyan leaders quieted the opposition and the preparations continued. I flew back home more determined than ever to do what I could to help make the conference and its NGO Forum a success.

Jill Sheffield, Sissy, Eddah, and I had numerous telephone conversations throughout the conference about the political eggshells we were tiptoeing across. There weren't enough hotel rooms. One night two other women shared my Hotel Stanley bed. A publication Jill Sheffield had commissioned didn't arrive until the last day of the conference, held up who knows why by port officials in Mombasa. But these and other obstacles notwithstanding, the University of Nairobi's campus, where the NGO Forum was held, vibrated with enthusiastic women from all over the world. The campus's central courtyard became a crafts and cultural marketplace while seminars and workshops were held in classrooms. Sissy's cousin, Gen Vaughn, underwrote the Peace Tent where women in chadors conversed with Israeli women, violence against women being the meeting ground. DAWN, a group of dedicated and enterprising developing country women, proposed "development alternatives for a new era," and drew great crowds to their workshops. Global issues discussed ranged from the debt crisis to environmental issues, religious fundamentalism, food security, and militarism.

Much of the credit for a successful conference and forum goes to Eddah and Dame Nita Barrow of Barbados, former head of the

World YWCA, who directed the NGO Forum. A large, calm, but no-nonsense black woman who began her career as a nurse-midwife, Nita had been granted the Dame honorific by the British government because of her work in public health in developing countries. Her race, background, and executive experience made her ideal for the job of organizing, funding, and managing the forum in a developing country with political, technological, and other infrastructural problems. Dealing with the anxious Kenyan government on all the logistical details took much of Nita's time and skills. Jill and I did as much as we could to help her and Eddah.

During 1984, as my Institute staff poured out materials about conference preparations and the Convention and mailed them all over the world, Jill Sheffield and I hosted a number of NGO preparatory meetings. In collaboration with women staffers at Wingspread Conference Center in Racine, Wisconsin, and the Bellagio Study and Conference Center in Italy, we brought leaders of women's organizations from all over the world and potential funders, including the Ford Foundation, to meet Nita and consult with her about the forum. I didn't worry about the crafts and cultural events. My concern was the workshops and seminars.

The enthusiasm, commitment, political sophistication and outspoken realism of the non-American participants was inspiring. At our first Wingspread conference, Carmen Barroso of Brazil made a major contribution to the education of potential participants when she said:

If women want to be decision-makers, they can't avoid politics… If we are to have an impact…we cannot repeat past errors of pretending to avoid political definitions, especially in an international forum. Instead of lamenting the politicization and engaging in the naïve hope of finding some trick to escape politics, we should try to understand that we have a common identity…We have rebelled against the current state of affairs in gender relations and helped to develop what is perhaps the most dynamic social movement of our times. We cannot ignore the fact that nuclear disarmament and the world economic crisis are two issues on which we cannot escape having at least a rough definition of our position. We can build upon our commonalities. They are crucial for survival and for the welfare of the poor and overworked women of the world. To search for a common ground outside politics is futile…

I thought this observation so important that I included it in one of my project's ever-expanding worldwide mailings. Carmen later became director of the MacArthur Foundation's program on population and reproductive health and now directs the Western Hemisphere Region of International Planned Parenthood Federation.

In early 1985, I began concentrating on the Convention on the Elimination of All Forms of Discrimination Against Women, the document I had been so thrilled to see signed in Copenhagen. Too few people knew about it. I was appalled that, now an international treaty, its significance and potential drew little interest and even less attention. Jill told me I had to meet Rebecca Cook, a lawyer with International Planned Parenthood Federation in London, who shared my interest, and Stephen Isaacs, a lawyer heading a development program at Columbia University in New York that Rebecca was to join. I had been collaborating with Dorienne Wilson Smillie, head of the British Commonwealth Secretariat's women in development office, and with the Commonwealth's Legal Unit. Together we published a book describing the progress made in changing laws concerning women in Commonwealth countries.

On a trip to London to confer with Dorienne, I scheduled a meeting with Rebecca and instantly knew I had a comrade. Walking around Regent's Park on a brilliant sunny day and later in my hotel room, we developed plans not only for a series of workshops on the Convention at the Nairobi conference, but also for an international network to publicize and encourage its implementation. The advantage of the Convention was that it laid out needed legislative changes in marriage and family law, education, employment, health, and every other field if discrimination was to be eliminated. Countries that ratified the Convention/treaty obligated themselves to make these changes. An international committee, called CEDAW, monitored national compliance.

Rebecca and I, with Jill's help, organized an international group of women lawyers, judges, legislators, and activists to lead our Nairobi conference workshops. Each day we drew standing room only crowds from countries around the world. Each evening we invited the most interested attendees to our hotel room to talk about the international network we wanted to create. By the time we left Nairobi we had over five hundred people who wanted to be part of our network. We decided to call it IWRAW—the International Women's Rights Action Watch. I was ecstatic. I would go home with a new endeavor. But first I wanted to see a bit more of East Africa and visit some local women's projects.

From Nairobi, I agreed to go to neighboring Uganda to see women's projects and meet with women leaders. I knew this was the country of Idi Amin, one of Africa's tyrants, but the current president, Obote, seemed more benign. The Ugandan women at our workshops had announced with pride that their country had recently ratified the Convention. I went to the consulate and got my visa, intending to spend only a couple of days.

Five days later I found myself in a huge convoy of Americans and other nationals being evacuated by land from Uganda back into Kenya. I should have gotten off the plane to Kampala when, from my window seat awaiting take off, I noticed two men in long white robes under the plane's wing of the plane conversing anxiously with a cabin attendant. Then I saw them slip her money. Small but heavy wooden boxes kept streaming up the cargo-loading conveyor belt. Ammunition, I now assume.

My itinerary included dinner with UN and American officials that evening and meetings with women's groups and tours of their projects the next two days. Settled in guest quarters, I had a swim in the pool that was part of the lovely compound, read my novel—I never travel without at least two—and chatted with Suzie, the charming fourteen-year-old daughter of my host. Under the warm African sun, I let the excitement of the conference drain from my mind and looked forward to the next days' activities and hopefully a sight of the Nile River's source.

Returning in the late afternoon, my grim-faced host announced that my dinner had been cancelled. Tensions were escalating; trouble was expected; a nighttime curfew had been established. Nobody knew what to expect, but Kampala was quiet. I spent an uneasy night. Next morning, under a tropical sky filled with fluffy white clouds, the world seemed serene, but eerily quiet. In the front courtyard after breakfast, I marveled at lemons and oranges growing on the trees and lush flower beds exploding with color. Then the whirring of a helicopter disturbed the serenity. It was President Obote fleeing the country, we later learned. We went inside.

Within minutes a jeep's brakes squealed and an FAO employee dashed in with news that there was fighting in downtown Kampala. My host tried to convince her to stay but she insisted on getting to her project outside the city. As she opened the door to leave, a breathless Ugandan burst in, seeking refuge. He said he had just sent his wife and children out of the country for their safety. Driving home a group of armed men commandeered his car. Seeing the UN flag outside the compound gate, he jumped over the wall, thinking it a safe haven. For the next two days, about twenty of us were imprisoned in the house, gunfire and mortars blasting in the distance. The UN short wave radio crackled with reports and instructions from UN security. "Farmer," the radio code word, seemed amusingly logical for the Food and Agriculture Organization compound.

"Internationals are in little danger during a coup," the burly UN senior security officer assured us, his very presence soothing. If he could navigate the streets, and had time to stop by, things couldn't be too bad. More than six feet tall, with dark hair and a hard glint in his eye, this Albanian exuded a don't-mess-with-me aura.

"Just follow instructions and stay calm," he ordered. "Stay inside, away from windows. Evacuation plans are underway for when things settle down."

My assignment was keeping the teenagers occupied and calm. Nothing like a responsibility to prevent panic. Playing Scrabble and rummy with only half a mind, pretending not to hear the rumble of gunfire, the teenagers and I became good friends. They observed the kitchen full of the servants' relatives seeking safe haven. One afternoon, during heavy gunfire close by, we quickly shoved the large dining room table against the wall, and scrambled under it, heads down in case the windows shattered. My host's son had rented two videos earlier. Evenings all of us, servants and their families included, sat before the TV in the darkened living room watching the videos. *Bonnie and Clyde* we decided was too bloody given our current situation. *My Brilliant Career*, the story of an Australian girl, we watched at least six times. Anything for diversion. When the house ran out of water, servants and neighbors began baling water out of the swimming pool. About day three, thankfully, it rained. Suzie and I cavorted in our swim suits with soap and shampoo, using the back roof overhang as our shower.

The telephone didn't work for outgoing calls but the second morning the household was roused by an international call. It was Don, worried, followed almost immediately by a call from Minneapolis media. Far more disconcerted than I conveyed, I assured everyone I was safe, despite the gunfire they could hear in the background. We had no news about what was happening outside. The airport was closed. UN offices and embassies were scrounging vehicles—jeeps, trucks and cars—and extra gas cans for the trek to the Kenyan border, some three hundred miles away, as soon as things calmed down.

On our last morning there we all assembled in a large courtyard and I watched UN, American, and European flags being secured over vehicle hoods and along their sides before we departed like refugees. Never in my life was I so glad to be surrounded by flags—the more the better. Our ticket to safe passage, I hoped. It would be a long, hot journey along tar and gravel roads, every vehicle crammed with people, baggage tied on roofs and in truck beds—but who cared?

The tension was palpable, especially when we passed small villages. The locals looked at us; we at them, hoping no armed men were behind the villagers. In the open countryside we simply stared as far as our eyes could see and sipped at our water bottles, mouths parched by dust. At roadside pit stops in assumed-to-be-safe territory, we got out and stretched our legs. At one stop I met a group of fellow Minnesotans, part of a medical aid organization. Crossing the origin of the Nile, a murmur of recognition passed along the entourage, but there was no inclination to stop. Escape was our goal.

At the border a barbed wire "no man's land" divided the two countries. Kenyan border guards, sitting in a trailer beside the gated road, weren't glad to see us. They took hours, meticulously checking every passport, vehicle, and piece of baggage. I suspect they were hoping for bribes to hasten the formalities. Over the border, we were taken to a resort hotel at Kisaui—with showers! Entering the hotel I felt my knees go weak, and my hands shook as I signed the register. With days of tension taking their toll, I told myself to shape up. I wasn't home yet. Early next morning we were driven to Nairobi and put on planes. Arriving home, I discovered what post-traumatic stress is. You can't concentrate, have nightmares, the slightest loud noise makes you jump or quiver. It took me a month before I was back to normal. I'm still gun shy and won't travel to any country I'm the least concerned about.

The events of 1985 convinced me that I had a whole new effort before me. Our seminars on the Convention at Nairobi had proved I was not alone in thinking that this document—the Convention on the Elimination of All Forms of Discrimination Against Women— had great possibilities.

Arvonne and St. Paul mayor George Latimer annouce Arvonne's candicacy as lieutenant governor. Her sons John (left) and Tom (right, with coat) are in the background.

Chapter 13

Latimer & Arvonne

All our married life Don and I have juggled vocations, avocations, and family life, supporting each other's interests and activities, but agreeing to disagree occasionally, sometimes even publicly. It has certainly given spice to our marriage. He seemed to enjoy my successes in the women's movement—and our arguments about candidates—or at least tolerate it all with good grace and wry jokes. In one bitter political fight in 1966 he supported Sandy Keith, the insurgent candidate for governor, and I supported the traditional choice, Governor Karl Rolvaag. (Neither won. A Republican—Harold LeVander—was elected that year.) Two years later, at the height of the Vietnam era, I supported Senator Gene McCarthy for president while he stayed loyal to Humphrey, although we both were ardent opponents of that war.

Don once observed that our interests seemed to criss-cross, converging sequentially rather than running parallel. In his congressional office he concentrated on foreign policy and I on domestic issues. Then I became more internationally minded, and he went home to be mayor. In the summer of 1986 I surprised everyone, including myself, when I took three months off from the Humphrey Institute to run for lieutenant governor of Minnesota with George Latimer, the mayor of St. Paul. As mayors of the Twin Cities, Fraser and Latimer often worked together and we saw the Latimers socially. George was full of ideas and had made Minneapolis's sister city wake up from its somewhat somnolent mix of old money and labor union dominance to become a much more lively metropolis. I especially admired what Latimer had done to renovate old housing stock in St. Paul. I thought the current governor, Rudy Perpich, also a DFLer, was tired and bored with the job after six years in office. Immersed in my Humphrey Institute projects, state politics was my after-hours avocation. I began attending Latimer for Governor meetings. At one gathering in the St. Paul Hotel, I asked him why he wanted to be governor. I considered that to be the crucial question for any candidate. I don't recall Latimer's exact response, but it sold me. He articulated his ideas forcefully, with boundless energy and good humor. Like any good politician, he could laugh at himself and was not mean about opponents. Governor Perpich had been good to women, had selected a woman as his lieutenant governor—a first for Minnesota. He had even called me in Washington to ask what I thought of his appointing Rosalie Wahl, an older woman who had gone to law school after raising children, to our state Supreme Court. But Perpich had run his course, I thought, and Latimer would bring fresh ideas and energy to the office. I joined Latimer's campaign advisory committee and was asked to be the main speaker at a women's fund raiser in May, held in a newly-renovated warehouse in Minneapolis.

All my women friends seemed to be there. Stirred by the huge attendance in this lovely new space, I gave a rousing speech and noticed Latimer looking at me not only pleased but a bit surprised. Audiences stir speakers as much as speakers stir audiences. Along with Marlene Johnson, Perpich's lieutenant governor, I had helped organize the Minnesota Women's Campaign Fund that supported pro-choice women candidates of both parties. I was as disturbed about women's assignment of major responsibility for children in this country as elsewhere. A colleague and I had developed a shared care of children project at the institute and I wrote frequently about that and women's employment issues. Some of my passion about these issues came through in my speech at this Latimer fund raiser organized by women.

In those days of intense feminist activity, and with Perpich having taken the lead in having a woman as lieutenant governor, Latimer was obligated to choose one too. I was helping him interview possible candidates. It was difficult because fewer than one in five state legislators were women, and few of them were from outside the metro area. A balanced ticket, which every gubernatorial candidate sought, meant putting together an urban/rural team. Some potential candidates didn't meet Latimer's qualifications. The one we wanted turned him down. Time was running out, but I wasn't worried about that when I spoke.

Early the next morning, Latimer called me up and said:

"I know this is unconventional…but how about you for lieutenant governor? You'll have a bigger platform for all your ideas…and I think we can win this thing."

I thought he was crazy. The Minneapolis mayor's wife, who many called a raging feminist, running with the mayor of St. Paul? That didn't make political sense in a state with a large rural population. I told him that, but he persisted. He argued I was a farmer's daughter and was known statewide. Finally, I said I would think about it and pledged myself to secrecy about the offer, except, I said, I had to tell Don. The DFL endorsing convention was just a week or so away and a decision had to be made soon. We had already decided that even if the convention didn't endorse Latimer, he would run in the primary.

I agonized. Honored and tempted, I worried about my IWRAW project. I had hired Marsha Freeman, a lawyer with a Ph.D. in English, but I wondered how she, and my New York colleagues on IWRAW, would carry the project on if Latimer and I were elected. Then, "quit flattering yourself," I mentally said. "You're not indispensable." I accompanied Don, a state DFL convention delegate, to Duluth. We stayed in a friend's empty house rather than in the convention hotel because I didn't want to be too visible. Some of Latimer's campaign staff and supporters knew I had been asked. They didn't like the idea, but Latimer never wavered. I had to make a decision. It wasn't fair to keep him waiting.

When Don, who understood my ambivalence, said the evening before the endorsement for governor vote: "You often regret the things you don't do," that did it. I called Latimer, went to the convention, and quietly watched his speech and the endorsement vote from the balcony of the convention hall. We knew that Perpich would probably get the endorsement. The plan was that before the vote on endorsement was announced, I would go out the back of the hall and be secretly whisked onto the small plane waiting at the airport. After the vote Latimer and one or two trusted staff would join me. It worked as planned. Latimer hadn't won the endorsement, but Perpich's support was not overwhelming for a sitting governor. We thought we had a chance to win the primary. We left the convention on Saturday and returned to the Twin Cities of Minneapolis and St. Paul. Latimer said we would announce on Monday.

Gathered on a brilliant summer afternoon in Latimer's backyard, were more media than we had ever anticipated. Word had leaked out. My sons Tom and John and their wives stood, smiling broadly, behind us as Latimer made the announcement. Don remained on the back side of the cameramen, part of the crowd. It was all unorthodox. Tradition out the window made news. Don had a statement ready saying that he had always supported the DFL's endorsement system and would remain neutral in this election. This added to the media excitement. "I'll keep the home fires burning," many newspapers quoted him as saying. He did just that. I'll never know who he voted for because I never asked. It didn't matter. This marvelous man I married is a rare one. We respected each other's beliefs and actions even when we disagreed.

The Latimer/Arvonne ticket—as our campaign stickers dubbed us—attracted many young people. I was blessed with two young women, Lucy Rogers and Chrissie Cammack, both from St. Paul, who became my advance team, occasional drivers, and constant helpers. They had been leaders in the women's fund raiser that started the whole adventure and continued to work the women's community for every vote they could get. I accompanied Latimer to many fund raisers and to some parades, but to cover a state as large Minnesota means everyone takes a bit of territory. Mine was primarily Minneapolis and my home farm area. Modesty goes out the window in a campaign. It took all the courage I had to stand on Minneapolis street corners, stick out my hand to shake that of any willing body and say:

"Hi, I'm Arvonne Fraser. I'm running for lieutenant governor with George Latimer, and hope you'll vote for us." I said "us" because Minnesota governors and lieutenant governors are not voted on separately, but run as a team. Minnesotans are friendly to candidates, even if they have no intention of voting for them. Daughter Jean, who came home to campaign for me, reported after a night of shaking hands along a parade route, that although people were nice to me, after I moved on, there were always comments, some not so friendly. Minnesota Nice is a face-to-face phenomenon. I had been in politics long enough to develop a thick skin.

Flying around our beautiful state in summer in a small plane, from media market to media market, was a feast for the senses. Vast expanses of forests with blue lakes glistening in sunshine in the northern part of the state, and fields of grain, corn, and soybeans in the western plains awed me. Looking down on isolated farmsteads with houses, silos, and barns surrounded by acres of land, I would wonder how we would get people in those houses to vote for us. It's a humbling thought, one I often had when I drove along city streets during Don's campaigns. It's the mystery of politics.

It wasn't always beautiful. Extreme weather thrills me when I'm on the ground and protected. In a plane it's a different story. On one trip to Duluth we ran into a wild thunderstorm. Our one engine plane was buffeted up, down, and sideways inside clouds as heavy rain and pellets of hail pelted the windshield. Latimer and the pilot, deathly silent, sat in the two front seats, staring into nothingness as the windshield wipers slapped back and forth. In the two back seats a young campaign aide and I gripped hands, white knuckled. This could be the end for all of us, I thought, picturing newspaper headlines: Latimer and Aides Killed in Crash. But Vern, the experienced pilot, never lost his cool. After what seemed hours but was only about fifteen minutes, we emerged from the clouds to see the airport below awash in a downpour. We landed safely. Senator Wellstone wasn't so lucky sixteen years later.

Visiting my family farm was a wrenching experience of another kind. I told Latimer, a New York city kid and lawyer, he had to see and feel this. It was also good politics. Again, weather delayed us. This time there was advance warning of a storm so, with a bevy of reporters, I twiddled my thumbs in a tiny suburban airport until the storm passed. Planned as a media event, we landed late in Springfield, but in sunshine, and drove the fifteen miles to the abandoned Skelton farm house. Farm prices were down. My farmer brother, like many of his peers, found he couldn't keep meeting the payments on the machinery needed for modern farming and sold out. We rented the land, and my mother, like so many farm widows, moved to town— rather, my sons Tom and John moved her.

I wouldn't let the reporters in the house, and I certainly didn't want to go in myself. The outside was bad enough with tall prairie grass threatening to engulf it. I had said goodbye to that house. It was now a symbol of what was happening across rural America. Standing in the tall grass with the wind blowing, as always, I looked down at the river where I had spent so many summers swimming. Filled with nostalgia, a lump in my throat, I spoke into a reporter's microphone about how sad it was that so many young rural families had to leave the land. Small towns were dying; nursing homes provided employment for farm women while their husbands struggled to make their share of the living on the land.

I was pleased that the newspapers mentioned my eighty-year-old mother had been a teacher, but she, too, was a symbol of what was happening in the world—women living to ripe old ages. Her mind was slipping. I worried about her attending the luncheon in Lamberton's lone café, surrounded by reporters and the campaign crew. I had warned the advance team about her condition, and told them to keep reporters away from her. She deserved respect for what she had been, not what she was now. Surrounded by reporters, former classmates, and onlookers, I couldn't give Mom the attention she deserved. But I was comforted by the protective solicitude of a childhood friend who shepherded her through the event. Sadly, she lived another decade and a half, bedridden and comatose the last years.

My mother and I were never close. I admired her sharp mind and many talents, but there was always tension between us. Her model of what a girl should be was not mine. I was a tomboy; she wanted a little lady, or at least a quiet child. Quiet I was not. I said what I thought, which horrified her. She worried about what other people would think. My father spoiled me, she said, enjoying my antics and telling others about them. I felt sorry for her, working so hard, worrying about my father and his drinking, taking care of his sister's children during summer vacations. She concealed Dad's alcoholism until hiding it was no longer possible. When she finally quit trying to pretend, she asked for help and then refused it. I gave up.

Sometime during my teenage years, I realized all her talk about her summer working in Minneapolis and her long-ago dream of becoming a doctor was an expression of a frustrated life. She was telling my sisters and me what might have been. In the 1920s, pregnancy required marriage, or at least so she thought. She loved my father, and he her. Each led frustrated lives. They were an example of what I never wanted to be, caught by circumstances and unwilling or unable to change them.

Yet I treasure my rural roots. I like big skies and open land. Being the daughter of farmers was also useful, not only in the campaign but in my work internationally. I understood rural life, people trying to make a living, feed their families, and, at least in my case, hoping to make life better for their children. Growing up surrounded by old people whose first language was not English, I developed a knack for understanding accented or mangled English as well as body language. I also knew what it was like for young women to come to the city, seek jobs and a husband, and make a new life unlike that of their parents. Being able to identify with a diversity of people is essential in campaigns and international work.

My rural roots were not enough. We carried Ramsey County, Latimer's home county, and won the seven county metro area by 53 to 47 percent, while Perpich carried the rest of Minnesota by 71 to 29 percent. The day after the election newspapers proclaimed Perpich won with a 57 to 41 percent majority. Way down in the polls when Latimer started his campaign, Governor Perpich came alive with our challenge and was a superb campaign strategist. I didn't help the ticket.

Losing an election is not the end of the world. When you put your ego on the line in a campaign, you know it's for a finite period. I was disappointed for Latimer. My admiration and respect for him only grew during the campaign. And Don was right. If I hadn't run, I would have regretted it. What gratifies me is that many of the young people in our campaign went on to their own careers in public life. Twenty years later Lucy, Chrissie, and I still enjoy lunching together, and George Latimer is a venerable public figure in Minnesota.

Chapter 14

The International Women's Rights Action Watch (IWRAW)

Turning sixty shortly after returning from Africa in 1985, I was asked by a reporter what I would tell young women of today. Without much thought, I responded: "You can do a lot in a lifetime, just not everything all at once." I didn't feel old. I felt free. All our children were out on their own, three of them married and the fourth well on her way to establishing a career and looking for the right husband. Mary Mac had produced our first grandchild. I looked forward to more. I was in good health, full of energy and upbeat about my new International Women's Rights Action Watch (IWRAW) project.

My new challenge—working to popularize and encourage implementation of the Convention on the Elimination of All Forms of Discrimination Against Women—fit nicely with what I had been doing and thinking about all my life. It tackled what I perceived to be unfairness. It involved governments and politics and set goals and standards for equality between men and women taking children and families into account. Now an international treaty, it was time women saw that governments lived up to it.

Its long name, the Convention on the Elimination of All Forms of Discrimination Against Women, was a problem. We began calling it simply the Women's Convention and, much later by its acronym CEDAW. To Americans, the word convention was misleading. We think of a convention as a large, deliberative meeting and build convention centers in cities for that purpose. Internationally, a convention is a document. It spells out an agreement between nations about basic principles. I wasn't too concerned about Americans, however. Thanks to two waves of the women's rights movement, we were on our way to achieving most of the rights covered by the convention. We had free, compulsory public education; rights in employment—not always obeyed but legally there; abortion was still an issue but the Supreme Court upheld that right in the *Roe v. Wade* decision. American women voted, participated in public life, and our thriving women's movement kept a watch on all the issues covered in the convention. President Carter submitted the convention to the U.S. Senate for ratification but the conservative chair of the Senate Foreign Relations Committee held it up.

My primary concern was women in developing countries. I was bent on moving the international women's movement approach from what I perceived as that of supplicant or victim to that of agent for change. As both a development and a rights document, the Convention was the ideal instrument around which to focus. Its sixteen substantive articles covered virtually every issue of interest to women's groups represented at the world conferences. If a country ratified the Convention, it obligated itself to conform its laws and policies to the provisions of the Convention. Enough countries had ratified so that it was an international treaty. Too many governments ratified more as a gesture than as a commitment. My worry was that unless a wide international audience knew of this convention, and used it, the energy generated by the world conferences would dissipate. The challenge for our International Women's Rights Action Watch, organized at the Nairobi conference, was to encourage women's and other organizations to understand the convention, press more governments to ratify it, and all governments to implement it.

This was no small task, but I had seen what we were able to do with the Sisterhood and WEAL, and with the world conferences. At Nairobi Rebecca Cook and I had found great partners. We had the beginnings of what we called our core network. Rebecca, a lawyer, had joined the Development Law and Policy program at Columbia University directed by Stephen Isaacs. Steve, I discovered, had worked overseas with AID and was a creative project manager and

Arvonne and Stephen Isaacs

how the international system of monitoring national implementation of the Convention worked.

With the excitement I always felt when beginning a campaign, I sat down at my Mac computer with the mental image of an educated woman in Nairobi already active in the women's movement in Kenya as one of the users of our campaign piece. I kept that woman in mind as I wrote:

The Convention...expands the concept of human rights by focusing on women. It is also an excellent framework for women's participation in the development process. The most concise and usable document adopted during the U.N. Decade for Women, it is the result of years of work by the U.N. Commission on the Status of Women and international women's organizations. As an international treaty...it spells out internationally accepted principles and standards for achieving equality between women and men taking children and families into account.

I recited the history of the Convention and explained that an international UN treaty committee received reports from ratifying countries on their progress with the convention, analyzed and commented on them. The final paragraph on the front page explained IWRAW and gave our address and telephone number. (We didn't yet have fax or email.) Condensing the convention's thirty articles took two and a half pages. I filled up the last of our four-paged brochure with additional information including how to get the full text of the Convention.

Using what my dear printer-friend Gerry Dillon taught me, in a few days I had what printers call "camera ready copy." I walked it to the university print shop myself. I didn't trust anyone else to deal with printers on this important run. A few days later I was like a child with a new toy when three thousand copies arrived.

It looked like this on page two:

THE INTERNATIONAL WOMEN'S RIGHTS CONVENTION

Countries that have ratified the Convention "condemn discrimination against women in all its forms" and "agree to pursue by all appropriate means and without delay a policy of eliminating discrimination against women" (Article 2). The first five articles of the Convention outline the general premises of eliminating discrimination..; the last thirteen articles detail the establishment, functioning and administration of the Committee on the Elimination of Discrimination. (for a more complete description of the articles contained in the document see Appendix I, page 29xxx)

I recruited everyone in the office to help stuff the envelopes addressed to those on our computerized data base—more than two thousand individuals and organizations around the world. Considering the world's population, this was the proverbial drop in a bucket but even a drop in the bucket generates a ripple effect. I wanted to make waves, not just ripples, but that would take time. There were moments when I sat at my desk in the Humphrey Institute and asked myself what a farm girl from Minnesota thought she was doing, trying to create an international constituency for a treaty few knew existed. And there were days and long, sleepless nights when I agonized over proposals to foundations and budgets, feeling overwhelmed. Those sleepless nights I'd finally get up, write out all my worries in my journal and invariably conclude with: "now I better get to work." Then I could sleep.

Raising money for this massive—and expensive—endeavor was a challenge. I never felt secure unless I had at least six month's or a year's funding in the projects accounts. What kept me going were my good colleagues and the accumulating evidence that we were making a difference. When I hadn't heard any good news for a while from either funders or women's groups, I would call Steve or Rebecca. They always made me feel better by commiserating or sharing a piece of good news. IWRAW had gotten notice in a publication in New York, Geneva, Tokyo, or Abidjan. Often we would end up laughing at the enormity of what we were trying to do. Other days, when my secretary came in smiling over a big check from a funder or word of an international call from a woman in a country she had never heard of, we exulted. And always there were my research assistants, bright-eyed students who relished our weekly staff meetings, especially when I went off on a tangent about how and why we were doing what we were trying to do.

The annual meetings of our IWRAW international core network were also a joy. Held in parallel with the meetings of the UN committee that monitored implementation of the convention—what we called the CEDAW Committee, this meant flying to New York or Vienna, Austria. The change of scenery, good for our morale, also contributed to the more academic side of our project. We studied how the committee functioned and how it might function more effectively. We both—the CEDAW Committee and IWRAW—were dealing with something totally new. My theory is that when people socialize, they work better together, so IWRAW hosted a reception for the committee members. They were UN officials, elected by governments; we were NGOs. Governments—especially non-democratic governments—are wary of non-governmental folks. What excited me was that I rarely saw such an intelligent, committed group of people from countries around the world in one room together. Still, it took a few years and a number of receptions before we reached what I thought was a satisfactory level of collegiality.

Our IWRAW group included Silvia Pimentel of Sao Paulo, Brazil, a vivacious, brilliant law professor and dedicated feminist; Texas-educated Isabel Plata of Colombia, who worked at Profamilia, Colombia's Planned Parenthood organization; and twenty or more women like them from Europe, Asia, and Africa. On the CEDAW Committee side were an intimidating judge from Australia, a former cabinet minister from Japan, an active feminist from Italy, a forceful but friendly official from Yugoslavia and twenty-three equally impressive women. Some of them were very suspicious of us. Would we be critical of their work? Interfere with it? Others, such as the Australian judge, thought she could give orders to us as she did in the court room. She thought we should be providing information about countries that the countries themselves didn't provide—what came to be called "shadow reports." She was right but we were just getting started and couldn't produce what she wanted so fast. The event was tense but it was a start.

In our separate IWRAW strategy sessions, Steve Isaac's insistence on "corridor time," as he called it—long coffee breaks where individuals got to know each other—helped immensely. Participants exchanged interests and expertise and shared their excitement about this new venture that was part campaign and legislative action workshop and part international law seminar. When Rebecca and Silvia talked about international jurisprudence, I was lost. When Isabel, Silvia, and others talked about the politics of modifying national constitutions and women's legal rights programs, I was in my element.

There was no way our U.S. based IWRAW secretariat could directly influence governments to make the changes called for in the Convention. That had to be done by their own citizens. IWRAW's job was to inform, motivate, and report on conformance—changes in law and policy and violations of women's rights. Never acknowledged but subconsciously understood was that we in the U.S., and others while they were in our country, could say and do what they might not be able to in their own countries. We had the freedom to organize, speak, print, and mail what some countries might consider subversive. Being based in academic institutions, and with an international network, gave our work and publications credence.

I was relieved when I was able to hire Marsha Freeman, a lawyer who was bored in a normal law office. I was not a lawyer and needed one for credibility on the Minneapolis end of our IWRAW triumvirate. Marsha, like me when I entered AID, knew little about international work but was a good feminist, an excellent writer, and a quick study. She could be demanding about what I considered trifles—quiet hotel rooms and good food, for example—but she tolerated, with a laugh, teasing about her idiosyncrasies.

Early in 1987 we launched *Women's Watch*, a quarterly newsletter. It brought the convention to life, with a blockbuster for our first issue. Wambui Otieno of Kenya had asked us for help. Her husband, a prominent lawyer, had died and his tribe claimed the body for burial on tribal land, according to custom. Married under civil law, and not of the same tribe, he and Wambui had agreed they would be buried in their family plot. I had met Wambui in 1984 in Kenya while preparing for the world conference. Her life story would make a great novel. The great-granddaughter of the Kikuyu tribe leader when the Europeans settled Kenya, as a young woman Wambui was deeply involved in the Kenya's independence movement. A spy for the Mau Mau, the guerilla organization, she created another stir after independence when she married a Luo tribesman, crossing tribal lines.

Wambui Otieno "is fighting for the right to have family life regulated by civil law rather than customary law," I wrote, quoting the Convention's provision on family law. "At stake is the right of women to assert themselves as equal partners in marriage and in widowhood." As a result of our publicity and Wambui's own efforts, her case became an international *cause celebre*. The body lay frozen for months in Nairobi's morgue as Wambui's case went up to the Kenya Court of Appeals. Although she lost her case, we made the point. Later, we learned a Tanzanian woman with a similar problem used the publicity given Wambui's battles to win in court.

Our first issue of *Women's Watch* also reported that a Zimbabwe law allowing women over age eighteen to arrange their own marriages and own property separately from their husband was still being resisted. We noted that Irish voters in June, 1986, overwhelmingly rejected a proposal to allow divorce—the only Western European country with that restriction; that Kenya's first Rhodes Scholar was a young woman; and that chador-clad women had been among those protesting the kidnapping of university teachers in Beirut. Other reports from every region in the world were grouped under headlines referring to relevant articles of the convention. Each issue began with an essay or a report on our annual IWRAW meeting.

Arvonne and Wambui Otieno at 1985 Nairobi conference

By our winter 1988 issue we were delighted to report that numerous groups were looking at the Convention as a whole. The Movimiento Feminists in Argentina proposed incorporating the entire text of the Convention into that country's constitution and was also protesting the Adidas company's practice of offering smaller prizes to women than men in a marathon it sponsored. The Women's Information Network for Asia and the Pacific was monitoring Convention compliance in that area. And both the Pakistan Committee on Women's Rights and Crimes Against Women and the Center on Research and Documentation in the University of Tunis Faculty of Law, held seminars on the Convention and Muslim law.

Information poured in from all over the world. Soon we found ourselves shortening items to squeeze more in. We tried for balance between the positive and negative, and between news from industrialized and developing countries. We also tried not to be too deadly serious. The Cup is Half Full headlined one issue followed by eight pages of mostly good news about women's groups in various countries. Another issue, headlined Women are People Too, began with: "Every woman is a citizen of some country, an individual whose human rights and potential are as important as those of her brother, father or husband." We wanted our readers to feel hopeful but challenged, to know that others like them were making progress. I found editing *Women's Watch* a great satisfaction but we were still only making ripples on the world scene, not waves.

While Marsha and I published *Women's Watch*, Steve and Rebecca put together a how-to guide called "Assessing the Status of Women" to teach individuals and groups how to prepare the "shadow reports" the Australian judge wanted. Governments tend to paint rosy pictures of themselves. CEDAW Committee members couldn't know what was going on in every country. They needed alternative or "shadow reports" from non-governmental groups. After our first IWRAW core network group meeting, I sat in on the CEDAW Committee's session and wrote a short report on it. It was the first of its kind, fifteen pages describing the committee's function and procedures. The UN published the committee's reports, but they were never widely circulated and were quite circumspect. The UN doesn't like to alienate its member governments. IWRAW had less compunction. We were bent on telling the world in simple language: "There's a new treaty on women's rights. A CEDAW Committee monitors its implementation. Here is information about that committee, who is on it, what it does and did this session." But there was no way we could afford to have someone sit through the committee's two-week long sessions every time it met.

Another Australian came to our rescue. His name was Andrew Byrnes. A lawyer, then studying in New York, he flew to Minneapolis to talk to me about the CEDAW Committee. I was startled and honored. He was cute, friendly, and smart, the age of my sons. He had seen my report and volunteered to observe the committee's next session and write a report for IWRAW. Looking at it now, printed on plain white copy machine paper, it is hardly the glossy product we later produced. I'm surprised it got the attention it did. What it lacked in appearance, it made up for in substance, including footnotes that impressed academics and UN specialists. We sent Andrew's report to libraries, human rights groups, and development organizations as well as our regular list. Known as the Byrnes report, it became a model for successive IWRAW reports and Andrew was welcomed into our core network.

From IWRAW's early days Steve Isaacs and I were determined to identify the Convention as a human rights instrument. The traditional human rights community concentrated on civil and political rights violation—torture, execution, and prolonged detention without trial of persons opposing authoritarian leaders. Steve and I tried to say politely that abrogations of women's rights were equally important. Women killed by husbands were as dead as men killed by dictator's death squads. Many countries justified or didn't punish the perpetrators of "honor" killings, such as murders of wives accused of adultery. The mutilations and killings of brides whose families reneged on dowry payments, or of women who had a child out of wedlock, or of girls who were victims of rape, were human rights violations. Governments turning a blind eye on such actions reinforced the idea that how men ruled the family was a family matter, not one for police. This was unconscionable, we argued.

By 1990 we had gained support among women in human rights groups and in Congress. When I was invited to testify before the House Foreign Affairs Committee's Subcommittee on Human Rights, I jumped at the chance. I sweated for days over my statement for the committee's hearings record. As usual, I asked Marsha to edit my draft. Returning it to me with a quizzical look on her face, she said: "This isn't the way you usually write."

"Well, now you hear my formal testimony voice. Hundreds of copies of these hearings will be printed and circulated. Every human rights guy worth his salt is going to have to read this, because it comes from the committee. I've got to prove our case using their language, not my usual rousing or cajoling the troops language."

Rereading the hearings record today, I still feel good. It shows why it's important to have women in Congress. Representative Pat Schroeder of Colorado, a Democrat and the first witness, expressed the regrets of Representative Olympia Snowe, a Republican who could not appear that day. "She feels very strongly about this issue too," Schroeder said. I am also pleased that both Congressman Yatron, chair of the committee, and Representative Schroeder linked human rights to democratic institution building. I believed all IWRAW's work was building that base. We were promoting the rule of law and teaching women how to deal with governments respectfully and responsibly. In my testimony I argued that human rights were to protect the integrity of the individual regardless of sex, race, national origin, or religion. The view that the private sphere—home and family—was out of bounds, and of no concern to the legal system, denied the integrity of women and made them second-class citizens. The idea that custom should be venerated and have the force of law needed to be put into proper context. Dowries, bride prices and purdah—condoned by custom and adversely affecting women—were, I wrote, violations of the Universal Declaration of Human Rights, the Convention, and the International Covenant on Civil and Political Rights. Just as the world discarded the vile custom of slavery, we ought to get rid of customs harmful to women.

I learned a great deal heading IWRAW. As a Midwestern American, even though I traveled widely, I rarely thought about Article Nine of the Convention, on nationality, until Unity Dow of Botswana faxed us. I had to look on a map to know where Botswana was. She wanted help. Unity married an American Peace Corps worker and had two children who were considered American citizens, although the family lived in Botswana and the children were born there. If she took her children outside the country she couldn't get them back in unless accompanied by her husband. The children were denied many other rights Botswana children had. Unity, a lawyer herself, was suing and needed information about American law on nationality. Marsha found a Minneapolis law firm willing to do a bit of pro bono work and we expressed a box of materials to Unity.

She lost her case on the first round and appealed. Ultimately, the Botswana supreme court ruled that, even though Botswana hadn't ratified the Convention, under international customary law, children had the right to the nationality of both parents until they reached the age of majority.

Our whole office broke into triumphal cries when we learned of this ground-breaking verdict. The Convention did make a difference! With almost a hundred countries ratifying by 1989, courts were treating the Convention as international customary law. The irony was that while national and local customary law was often a problem for women, international customary law was a boon. As late as 1981, I had my own experience with the customary law idea that men headed families. I paid income taxes on my salary to the District of Columbia the year after Don went home to Minneapolis. When I returned to Minnesota, and paid Minnesota taxes, someone in the state revenue department decided since Don lived in Minnesota, I owed Minnesota taxes on my D.C. salary. I disputed their claim, and won.

Each IWRAW conference drew new people with new ideas and experiences. Young legal scholars and activists from developing countries were a special joy. Although I thought of them as peers, I was occasionally brought up short, realizing by something they said that I was the age of their mother or sometimes grandmother. My maternal instincts were stirred. These idealistic young people were at the beginning of their careers. I sensed many were future leaders in their country or were legal scholars who would teach new generations of students about rights and not incidentally, democracy and tolerance.

Now, some twenty years later, I click on Google and exult in finding Chaloka Beyani of Zambia, a bright, young lawyer whose intelligence shone at our conferences, is now at the London School of Economics, affiliated with the Centre for the Study of Human Rights. I will never forget the startled expression on Chaloka's face when I gave him two volumes of family law history he had admired on my book shelves. In his country books were a precious commodity; in mine easily replaced. I thought he might become prime minister or a member of parliament someday. Sadly his country turned anti-democratic.

Another Google click shows Andrew Byrnes is professor of law at the University of New South Wales in Sydney, Australia; on IWRAW Asia/Pacific advisory committee; and chair of the Australian Centre for Human Rights. Thandabantu Nhlapo of South Africa is now on the University of Cape Town law faculty. Her served on the South African Law Commission and pushed for the Recognition of Customary Marriages Act passed by that country's parliament in 1998. If we did nothing but provide a platform for young achievers, show them how democratic institutions work and encourage them to be bold and think hard, that would be satisfaction enough for me.

From the beginning, I urged our network participants to either run for election to the CEDAW Committee or find and promote good candidates. This seemed to fall on deaf ears. The elections are complicated, a kind of international balancing act. The committee must have representatives from every UN region and the world's different legal systems. The U.S. isn't involved because we haven't yet ratified the Convention, sad to say. A few years ago I was overjoyed to learn that two of our IWRAW core network members had taken my advice. Shanthi Diariam of Malaysia and Silvia Pimentel of Brazil were elected to the committee. Shanthi founded IWRAW Asia/Pacific and spent years training others on how to use the Convention. Silvia, now a proud grandmother like me, is still on the law faculty at the University of Sao Paulo and hasn't lost any of her energy.

Isabel Plata now heads Profamilia in Bogota and Rebecca Cook is Chair of the International Human Rights Law at the University of Toronto in Canada. Those two are close friends, and also big names in the reproductive rights field. They see each other often at international meetings. Unfortunately, Farida Shaheed of Pakistan, a distinguished writer active with the group, Women Living Under Muslim Laws, has been impeded—but not stopped—by the aggressive Islamic fundamentalists in her part of the world. I console myself with small stories I read about women leaders working under the political radar in that part of the world. But I worry about them. Shirin Ebadi's receiving the Nobel Peace prize in 2003 for her work on women's and children's rights in Iran cheered me, but Ayaan Hirsi Ali's 2007 book, *Infidel*, illustrates how much remains to be done. Religious fundamentalism denies women's integrity. It kills their spirit, enslaves them, hides them, and too often mutilates or kills them in body as well as mind. It is the very antithesis of human rights.

Despite my deep fear that we are in a worldwide struggle between religious fundamentalism and human rights that is not yet fully recognized, I remain optimistic. Organizing and leading IWRAW was a high point of my life. It proved that collaboration generates power. The whole *is* greater—far greater—than the sum of its parts. Very little is accomplished alone.

Arvonne with members of IWRAW at the Fraser's St. Croix house.

The U. S. Delegation to the Asia-Pacific Conference in 1994

Chapter 15

Winning and Losing

The 1992 elections were coming up, and it looked like it might be a Democratic year. IWRAW had made its mark. Hundreds, if not thousands of women worldwide, were using the Convention and working with the CEDAW Committee. This was great, but I was getting restless. Was I just tired of the constant fundraising? (We now had a good-sized staff, and our publications, mailings, travel, and network meetings cost hundreds of thousands annually.) Or was I just looking for a new and different challenge? At a recent national seminar of women who had started feminist non-profits, I was a bit startled at the observation: "We're just a bunch of entrepreneurs. We enjoy the challenge of starting something new." And as Elsa Chaney, my former deputy at AID, had pointed out: "But when you have something up and running and about to be institutionalized, you are ready to move on." Marsha could take IWRAW in new directions. I was itching at the bit—an old farm expression meaning restless, eager to move on.

When Bill Clinton won the presidential election, I was ready for one last fling at government. NGOs push for change. Governments make it happen. Three more world conferences were coming up: human rights in 1993, population in 1994; and a fourth world women's conference in 1995. I decided to seek appointment as U.S. representative to the UN Commission on the Status of Women and as part of the U.S. delegation to the 1993 world human rights conference. The Commission would set the tenor and stage for the women's conference and draft the document to be adopted at it. That document and resolutions of the Commission would go to the UN General Assembly for debate and adoption. As U.S. representative I could push for women's legal rights even though the U.S. hadn't ratified the Convention. Inside government I could push to get the Convention re-submitted for ratification.

I was tired of woman-as-victim. That mentality is disabling. It was time we were acting like agents, not victims. If we really meant what we said, that women's rights were an integral part of human rights, then the human rights conference was the place to make that a reality, to settle the question. I didn't worry too much about the population conference. It was in good hands. Friends and colleagues of mine were already scheming about how to confront—and defeat—the religious fundamentalists and powerful others who believed women's reproductive rights—birth control and abortion—were anathema.

I saw these conferences as a continuum, with synergistic possibilities. If women were successful in 1993 at the human rights conference, we would be building momentum for the 1994 and 1995 conferences. I felt that I could be far more effective inside government, rather than standing outside trying to convince women to convince their governments to do x, y or z. I knew the Commission would begin preparing for the 1995 conference in 1993 and that it would be watching carefully to see what was happening at the other conferences.

I hadn't been very active in the Clinton campaign, but I still had contacts in the national political world. Shortly after the election, I found a colleague on the Clinton transition team and told her of my interests. A quick listen on the political grapevine told me I didn't have too much competition for the post. I figured if I got the Commission post, I could get on the human rights delegation. But I had to campaign for these jobs—and campaign hard. My days in the Carter administration, and especially in the White House Office of Personnel, had taught me that appointments went to seekers, not to those who waited to be called. The job I wanted was far down on the list of presidential appointments, but I trusted nothing to chance.

I called the National Women's Political Caucus next to seek its support. Their support was crucial and my contacts there confirmed what I'd heard on the political grapevine. Most women were concentrating on the top jobs, but I knew some active Clinton campaigner who wanted a government job might be reduced to thinking about the one I wanted. Having been in the Carter campaign would help me, I thought, and I was known in feminist and political circles. I threw modesty to the winds, polished and beefed up my resume, gritted my teeth—for I hated campaigning for myself—and asked anyone who might carry weight with the Clinton team for a recommendation. I lobbied hard, but made sure I wasn't a pain in the neck to anyone. That never paid off. If I'd been a nail biter, I would have chewed to the nub. Instead, alas, I just smoked more and drowned myself in IWRAW work while waiting and hoping for word about the appointments.

Our January 1993 *Women's Watch* carried the headline Women Are People Too, with pages of information about all the conferences. One hundred nineteen countries had ratified the Convention, a real tribute to the momentum of the international women's movement. We were making an impact, but the laws of physics—for every action there is an equal and opposite reaction—applied to the women's movement as well. I worried in print and in speeches about the rise of religious fundamentalism.

The more I thought about it, the more I wanted the Commission job. It would set the stage and tenor for the 1995 women's conference scheduled to be held in Beijing, China. Closed for so many years under its Communist regime, China was at last opening up. Having the conference in China would mean increased worldwide attention on the part of media and governments. I also believed this would probably be the last world women's conference—or human rights or population conference—for a good while. UN world conferences were getting too big, difficult for any country to accommodate, and expensive. As a U.S. delegate, I wouldn't be able to speak directly about the Convention because we hadn't ratified it yet. But my IWRAW and women in development work was widely known, so I was confident I could figure out ways to bring attention to women's legal rights and the particular articles of the Convention. My friends in ratifying countries could take it from there. I also knew that the Commission would begin work on the women's conference in 1993, so time was of the essence.

I whooped with glee when I received a copy of a letter Congressman Jim Oberstar, from Minnesota's Eight District, sent to the White House on my behalf. He and I disagreed on the abortion issue, but we shared international interests and were both good liberals. We had talked often when I lived in Washington about his work in Haiti as a Peace Corps volunteer, and I admired his fluency in French. His letter reaffirmed my conviction that in politics, as in life, you can respect, and even be helped by, an individual, with whom you differ. I'm certain Oberstar's letter helped my nomination immensely, as did the endorsement of the Women's Political Caucus. Having been a member of previous U.S. delegations and at AID was also in my favor. After many anxious weeks, I finally got the call in early February, 1993, saying the job was mine. It was part-time, on a per-diem-when-employed, reimbursement-of-expenses basis. The first Commission meeting would be in March.

For months I and many other appointees worked for expenses only until all our papers were processed and clearances obtained. It is difficult to put a new administration together, especially for a former governor with no Washington experience. Although the position had the rank of ambassador, requiring confirmation by the Senate, I could fill the position as I filled out the last of the required papers and sent them on through the complicated clearance process. I was full of ideas about what could be done and happily commuted to Washington and back, working part-time at the Humphrey Institute and part-time at the State Department. Actually, I gladly worked double—and sometimes triple—time, at IWRAW, at the State Department, and on my clearance papers, which eventually filled a three-inch three-ring binder. One glitch was agony, costing me time, money, and sleepless nights when the media made a big deal of finding another potential appointee who had employed an undocumented household worker. That ended her career in government. Another had not paid Social Security for a household worker. The media were having a field day. I had a Native American cleaning woman for years, whom we had agreed was an independent contractor, but I was taking no chances. I hired a lawyer and an accountant, went through my old financial files and checkbooks and paid all back Social Security taxes—for employer and employee. Documenting every country I had ever visited was another pain. Luckily, I had saved my Carter administration clearance papers and kept old passports. But, with the European Community, my passports had no enter and exit stamps designating the various European countries I visited when I traveled within that community. Another big job, combing my IWRAW records. Where the heck had I gone on this or that trip?

Meanwhile, my immediate concern was the March, 1993, meeting of the Commission in Vienna, Austria, with a briefing book at least three inches thick and a ten-member delegation to manage. Four of our delegation were political appointees, all good feminists, including Veronica Biggins, originally from Georgia but now on the White House staff; Caroline Croft, who had been instrumental in my appointment; Dottie Lamm, an activist interested in women's reproductive rights who was also the wife of Colorado's governor; and Nancy Rubin, a consummate fundraiser for women's causes and the Democratic Party. This was their first Commission meeting and they were as anxious as I about the whole experience. The other five on the delegation were State Department employees including the assistant assigned to me and a bright young lawyer, Kathy Skipper, who, I discovered, was a strong advocate for women's legal rights.

I was thrilled to see "Increased awareness by women of their rights, including legal literacy "on the Commission's agenda. Our earlier work at IWRAW and at the 1985 conference had borne fruit, but we couldn't take all the credit. The Commission, from its inception in 1945, had been criticized for concentrating on women's legal, educational, and economic status. To me this was right; others, whom I mentally—but never publicly!—characterized as women-as-victim, social welfare types, looked for more programmatic, rather than policy, alternatives. At the State Department, before departing for Vienna, we drafted a resolution on legal literacy and speeches for me to deliver in support of the resolution.

If I accomplished nothing else, I wanted to make women's legal rights—and hopefully the Convention—priorities at both the Commission and the world conference. Any resolution or speech needed various State Department clearances to make sure it conformed to U.S. policy. Patience is not my long suit. In this staid bureaucracy—the worst I'd encountered in government—I kept my temper and tongue in place by leaving clearances to my assistant. When my drafts came back with at least some of my wording remaining, I was relieved. Sometimes, I was pleased and a bit chagrined to see that my drafts were improved with references to previous relevant UN actions that I knew little or nothing about.

I don't recall now who wrote the paragraph about 1992 being "called 'the year of the women' in the United States…because so many more women—and minorities—were elected" to what the UN called "decision-making posts" at the local, state, and national level. In that speech I, and my unknown assistant speech writers, went on to say: "These groups not only worked to change and apply laws, using both our legislative and judicial systems, but in the process conducted what might well be called legal literacy and service campaigns…legal service to poor and disadvantaged groups."

Scratch me deep enough, and you will find a blue-blooded patriot. Every government at the UN likes to put its best foot forward, linking what they have done in their country to the subject on the agenda. I thoroughly enjoyed reading those words before the Commission. The speech went on to give credit to women in developing countries and NGOs for their work on legal literacy. We then introduced the subject of gender sensitivity in the whole legal system. Minnesota had pioneered in this effort. Rosalie Wahl, our first woman Supreme Court judge, had been a leader in this. Judges, lawyers, and police in rape cases would often require the woman to prove she hadn't tempted her abuser. Studies found pretty young women were given an especially hard time. In divorce cases a judge might be more sympathetic to the husband—allowing payments on his boat before deciding how much he could afford for child support. And officials might call a woman "girl" when they would never dare call a man "boy." This led women lawyers and judges to develop gender training courses and manuals for all legal personnel.

Our legal literacy resolution was a real triumph, thanks to the hard work of Kathy Skipper and others on our delegation. They scurried around to find other national delegations as co-sponsors. Co-sponsors tinker with wording, some substantive, some only rhetorical. With pride in my country, my delegation, and my anonymous speech writers back in State, I was delighted to formally introduce our resolution with thirty-one cosponsors. In my firmest voice, trying not to reveal my delight, I read:

"This resolution underscores the importance of the pursuit of equal rights for women. Raising awareness of women's rights under international conventions and national law is a central part of the larger process of empowerment of women." This seems like an innocuous statement, but everyone in the room knew that the U.S. had not ratified the Convention and most were aware of my IWRAW work. This subtly announced that the Clinton administration was going to submit the Convention to the U.S. Senate again for ratification.

The next paragraph in our statement also had hidden meanings: "We note that a few technical corrections were made to improve the draft before it was tabled yesterday following consultations with many interested delegations." That said the resolution wasn't just a U.S. initiative; others had input. Hop on the bandwagon was the implication. By the time the resolution was adopted we had close to fifty co-sponsors ranging from Australia and Austria to Zaire, Zambia, and Zimbabwe. Kathy Skipper proved tireless as the consummate negotiator both with countries and with our backup team in Washington, which had to approve every word added to the resolution. Equally heartening was that the political-appointee members of our delegation discovered their political skills were as useful at the international level as at home. Individuals do make a difference even in the United Nations where we all speak for our governments. And thank goodness there are nameless women and men in government who care about issues and know how to work the system.

Another great coup was getting rape in war recognized as a war crime. Nobody had expected the war in the former Yugoslavia to be raging in Vienna's backyard when the agenda was set but it proved, sad to say, timely. Although I got credit in the UN news sheet for introducing a resolution on "rape and abuse of women in the former Yugoslavia," I had little to do with it. Again it was our diligent State Department staff. When our resolution was debated, I gladly relinquished the chair to Tom Martin, the DCM—deputy chief of mission at the U.S. embassy in Vienna—to ride out the storm. Debating international law about war was out of my territory. Passions were high for war crimes that could be prosecuted. Finally, the resolution was put to a vote—a rare event at the UN—with 38 in favor, none opposed and one abstention. Wow, I thought, we're making history.

There was no good news when I got back to Washington. My papers still languished in the bowels of the bureaucracy, in some nameless soul's in-box. I was happy to have the job but being on the payroll would be nice too. I had no idea how to mine this department. My assistant was either too busy or unconcerned. Finally one day an office secretary, on hearing me complain, took pity on me.

Using her secretarial network and her knowledge of the department, she found my papers and got them processed. Within days my work for expenses only was over. Never underestimate the power of networks or of secretaries. This time it was a Mary or Jane or Suzie, not Mohammed, that moved the bureaucratic mountain.

Soon after I returned from Vienna, Madeline Albright, US ambassador to the UN, invited me to New York to report to the NGO community there. I had known Madeleine slightly in the Carter Administration. A good feminist, during the Reagan years she asked me to speak to a university class she taught in Washington. I was delighted when she was appointed ambassador. With interest in the 1995 world conference growing, NGOs were eager to hear what had happened in Vienna. Ambassador Albright, in good diplomatic fashion, hosted an evening reception for me with the New York-based NGOs. The next morning we both spoke at a briefing hosted by our mutual friend, Vivian Derryck, who headed the African-American Institute, just down the street from the U.S. embassy to the UN.

It was a celebratory couple of days. Walking down the street with the ambassador, whom many people recognized, I felt the old girls network had arrived. Women were in decision-making posts. Topping off the trip was a luncheon in the ambassador's official quarters at the top of the Waldorf-Astoria Hotel. My New York colleagues were invited, but the ambassador had invited Barbra Streisand and other prominent women. Looking around the elegant room I marveled at what my friends had achieved in two decades. There was Jill Sheffield, my Carnegie Corporation program officer, now heading Family Care International. Joan Dunlop, who had supported my popular version of the World Plan of Action after the 1975 world conference, now headed an international population organization. Vivian Derryck and I had worked together at AID. Michaela Walsh, another Mexico City friend, had founded Women's World Banking to help women entrepreneurs globally. It was doing magnificently.

I was overwhelmed and suddenly uncomfortable. That old "What's this Minnesota farm girl doing here?" feeling came over me. What would I say to Barbra Streisand? Which fork am I supposed to pick up for dessert and which for salad? Formal social affairs in elegant surroundings sometimes throw me. I resisted Mom's instructions about being a little lady—etiquette was for sissies. But the niceties of life do have their place and function. I never took the time to learn them. Don has said I get out of a car or leave a party as if there's a fire, too often forgetting social amenities.

Back in the State Department, I felt much more secure working with the lawyer putting together the President's submission to the Senate on ratifying the Convention. The legal niceties of conforming the Convention's provisions to our Constitution and national laws intrigued me. Ratifying countries can attach reservations and understandings, indicating that they cannot agree to conform to certain articles of the Convention. The U.S. reservations were on assigning women in the military to direct combat, comparable worth in employment, and paid maternity leave. I remembered our WEAL committee on women in the military and how pleased we were when, in 1976, Congress authorized the admission of women to the military academies. Now we were worrying about women in combat. I was also proud of our reservation on "private conduct," once it was explained to me that our Constitution's freedom of speech clause was involved. We allow people to say what they think even if it's derogatory. Sadly, our work was for naught. Senator Jesse Helms nixed ratification.

One good thing Karen Nussbaum, head of the Women's Bureau in the Department of Labor, and I did was host a series of regional conferences to inform American women about the 1995 conference. UN conferences are complicated affairs. Americans get confused about the government meeting and the parallel NGO forum. Karen and I thought women across the country should know what was going on in Washington and New York about this world conference. We also needed to hear what women across the country thought the major issues were. Bill Gallston in the White House Domestic Council's office shared our view. With Bill's help, the White House approved our proposal, the Women's Bureau regional offices organized and hosted the forums, and my office in State provided the background and informational materials.

Traveling around the country for these meetings gave me new insights into the problems of America's employed women. I remember especially a South Dakotan describing how farm women commuted hundreds of miles weekly to office jobs in cities and towns. Though well educated, they worked for low wages because jobs were so scarce in that sparsely populated state. Farming often didn't pay enough to support families. What irritated me was that my State Department staff only volunteered to attend the New York or Boston meetings. I don't think the old joke that the U.S. heartland is flyover country is funny. After these regional meetings I was not shy about announcing around State that more than 5000 people attended them.

Most satisfying and usually enjoyable, though, were the Commission meetings where I also saw and caught up with old friends from abroad who were either delegates or NGOs. Formality prevailed during the sessions and at official luncheons and receptions— somehow I absorbed that protocol—but during coffee breaks and after hours it was like old home week. NGO friends and colleagues might lobby me hard for language on their favorite issue, but we could also laugh and joke about past exploits and catch up on each other's lives and pass along information about absent mutual friends. It was my insider/outsider theory about government being played out. We informed, lobbied, and taught each other while respecting the constraints inherent in our different roles. Confidences were respected and rules obeyed. The deepest friendships are between those who have been both government insiders and outsiders. We relish the freedom when we are NGOs, and, frankly, relish our power in government.

The insider/outsider idea worked at the 1993 world conference on human rights as well. Again, the meeting was in Vienna. I was aware that activists whose focus was violence against women would demand attention. Making rape a war crime at the women's meeting only spurred the NGOs on. Although I thought these groups concentrated too much on women as victims, I knew the violence against women problem helped make the case for women's rights as human rights. It showed how bad things could become when women were considered lesser beings. The conference was an upstairs/downstairs operation with the NGO forum on the ground floor, the UN conference up the escalator on the main floor.

The NGOs were smart. They made the most of their relegation downstairs. They put TV monitors right beside the escalator that depicted horrible scenes of bride burnings in South Asia, stonings of pregnant women in the Middle East, the results of rape in Bosnia, and domestic violence in neighborhoods around the globe. Government delegates couldn't avoid these monitors and their horrors. The TV scenes were dramatic, attention-grabbing. Upstairs in the government meeting every country allotted some time in their opening speech to the violence against women question.

My cynical self recognized that many of the countries talking about the problem might not do much to alleviate it, but lip service was a start. Violence makes news and TV makes the violence issue much more graphic. One of our senior U.S. delegates, standing before a TV monitor in the NGO Forum during a break in the upstairs sessions, was aghast at the pictures he saw and words he heard.

"I never knew all this was going on," he said, shaking his head as he turned to go upstairs.

The NGOs not only depicted and dramatized the problem, they had amendments ready for the conference document. By this time the traditional human rights organizations, responding to their membership and contributors, had added women's rights advocates to their staffs. Dorothy Thomas of Human Rights Watch was one of the smartest and most strategic. Eventually language was included urging the UN Human Rights Commission to appoint a special rapporteur on violence against women, along with a full section on women's rights as human rights.

I came home from that conference feeling triumphant. Women had gained recognition as a political force. It had taken two hundred years but at last the theory of the rights of man included women.

Thomas Jefferson in the Declaration of Independence and the French revolutionaries who penned the Declaration of the Rights of Man in 1789 had articulated the theory that individual citizens had rights, but it was for men only. Who doesn't remember the phrase "all men are created equal." Two months after the French had declared these Rights of Men, the women of Paris staged a march on Versailles and presented a Women's declaration to the all-male National Assembly, but it wasn't even brought up for discussion. Three years later Mary Wollstonecraft's *Vindication of the Rights of Women,* appeared. Now these and many similar efforts were at last bearing fruit. The Convention had been cited by country after country, but it was women organizing in local communities around the world that did it. They told their stories. The world's dirty little secret, that violence against women—especially in the home, but in war and many other places—was tolerated, even by those who professed to believe in human rights, was no longer a secret. At last, women were recognized as equals, people with rights.

This whole endeavor—being on the Commission and at the human rights conference—made me think even harder about the history of women's emancipation. Why did it take so long? Did we do it backwards or the only way we could—the "we" meaning women over the centuries? I had been reading—and filling my bookshelves—with the explosion of feminist literature that was part of the twentieth-century women's movement, especially that of feminist historians. I treasured the book, *Woman Into Citizen,* published in England and given to me by my Sri Lankan friend, executive director of the International Alliance of Women, which was founded in Berlin in 1904. That book embarrassed and thrilled me. What I had thought were new ideas of my generation had been expressed and worked on before I was even born. But these thoughts were for my spare time. I kept reading; my suitcase and briefcase always had a book or two, a novel to turn off my head and get me to sleep after a busy day, and, increasingly, a biographies or feminist history.

Now I had to face a "murder board." My clearances were in order, approved. A State Department "murder board" prepared candidates for Senate confirmation hearings. I was up for confirmation as U.S. ambassador to the Commission. I considered this board a waste of taxpayers' money, but rules are rules. This practice question and answer session might be important for nominees as Secretary of State and assistant secretaries, but my view was that senators have better things to do than question the appointee to UN Commission on the Status of Women about U.S. foreign policy. And I certainly believed State employees had better things to do than run me through this exercise. I was known on the Hill. Senator Wellstone introduced me and Senators Kerry, Sarbanes, and Simon all praised Don and me in nice senatorial language. Don had been their colleague in Congress. Minnesota TV and newspaper reporters ran "local girl makes good" stories—it was a dull news day—and I became Madame Ambassador.

Finally, in 1994, I began working full time, flying to Jakarta, Buenos Aires, Vienna, and New York for meetings. At the Southeast Asia and Pacific meeting in Jakarta our U.S. delegation was criticized for attending. We were lumped with other "colonial powers" such as the Netherlands, which had been Indonesia's colonial power in Indonesia. I could have countered that the U.S. bordered the Pacific and Hawaii was a state but I didn't think it worth wasting delegates' time. The U.S., for once, could just listen. I was all ears, as the Philippine delegation complained about their migrant women who, as household workers in other Southeast Asian countries, were often sexually or financially abused by employers. These workers' remittances supported families back home and were a huge contribution to the national income, much as those of Mexican and Caribbean men and women working in the U.S. are today.

In Latin America, I was ashamed that we North Americans know so little about our southern neighbors' history and internal politics. We are all nations of immigrants who displaced indigenous populations and imported slaves. We all have histories of discrimination. At the Latin American meeting, the creation of civil societies was a major topic for many countries who were transitioning from authoritarian regimes and re-emerging as democracies. Hearing them talk about creating political will, teaching women how to make government work for them, and using the media effectively, made me wish our U.S. women's movement did more of that. And, of course, most of them spoke fluent English while my Spanish did not go much beyond "gracias" and "por favor."

This was my first trip so far south. From my airplane window, I gazed out over the vast Argentinean pampas and saw gauchos herding masses of cattle as we flew from Buenos Aires to the meeting site at Mar del Plata. One unforgettable luncheon for delegates featured a beef-roast picnic at a ranch. We sat outdoors at long tables covered by bright red-and-white checkered tablecloths, hardly the formal luncheon of Europe or Asia. American informality pervades our two continents. Seeing massive carcasses roasting on spits or, once done, spread on long tables and sliced into slabs turned my stomach but I couldn't resist the mouth-watering smell. I turned my back to the carcasses and enjoyed the succulent meat and accompanying vegetables.

At the next Commission meeting my dealings with the Chinese ambassador made me even more aware of democratic principles. He was aggressive and demanding about the conditions under which his nation would host the world conference. I don't trust repressive regimes. In 1993 Don and I had traveled to Beijing and Harbin in northern China on an official sister city visit. I resented the regimentation and control I saw and felt beneath the surface cordiality. It took me awhile during that visit to realize how regimented we were. Through the Ford Foundation's Beijing office, I arranged two private meetings and skipped a dinner meeting I was supposed to attend. My independent activity angered, and probably frightened, our local hosts. When I visited the All China Women's Organization, it was clear that the extra woman in the room was present to report everything that was said to the government.

On this sister-city trip, we were supposed to do everything as a group and were constantly escorted by numerous people. Only when we were alone on a bus, being taken from one place to another, did our young interpreters open up. They were eager to learn about America. They were careful about what they said but we did learn a bit about the very repressive days of Chairman Mao's regime. We got the sense, never in explicit language, that life had been harsh. Now China was loosening up a bit because it was desperate to industrialize and join the wider world.

One ever-present young man in our escort group drew my attention because he was the only one who never wore a suit. Naïve me. I mentally identified him as a political hanger-on. He seemed to have no official function. My ignorance was revealed one day when it became clear he was our undercover security officer. Outside a new department store one morning, in the midst of a crowd, this young man abruptly took my arm and hustled me along, telling me in perfect English to hold my purse tightly as they sometimes had a problem with pickpockets. That was the only time in the whole trip that anyone admitted China was anything but perfect and the only time I ever heard the man speak.

This trip made me wary in dealing with the Chinese ambassador at the Commission. I knew that China had recently lost a bid for the Olympics and took the women's conference to save face and bring them tourist dollars and world acceptance. What they didn't want were NGOs—thousands of unattached, free women—wandering around their country. At Commission meetings, the ambassador tried to put as many logistical constraints on the conference as he could. It seemed the Dutch ambassador and I were the only ones willing to take him on. We were a bit indignant that our other industrialized country counterparts were unwilling to challenge China. I finally decided their countries were eager to establish trade relations with this newly opening country and told their delegates not to offend the ambassador.

I was astounded when the ambassador asked that countries submit to China lists of every NGO in their country. They needed this information to grant NGO visas he said. I almost laughed, but one doesn't laugh at the UN, nor does one humiliate another delegate. This poor man had no comprehension of how democracies operated. In the kindest formal words I could think of I responded that our government maintained no such list and therefore could not provide it. Privately I imagined the uproar if every PTA or YWCA or Girl Scout troop had to register with some federal authority and send a list of their members to it.

The expression on the Chinese ambassador's face indicated he thought I was just an obstructionist. Other delegations may have thought so too, but I didn't care. I resisted telling him that in the United States we allow people to organize freely. This was incomprehensible to China and to other nations that required government permission before an NGO can be organized. I did what I could but China ultimately put the 1995 NGO Forum out in the proverbial woods, in a new suburb miles from the official conference site in Beijing, and many American women had trouble getting their visas to attend the conference.

My crowning achievement, I believe, though some may laugh, was to succeed in including the girl child as one of the critical areas of concern in the Beijing Platform for Action. Early in the preparatory meetings, I had convinced the State Department that a speech emphasizing education for girls would be a contribution to the dialogue on the Platform's education and training section. I felt strongly about education of girls. Where would I be if my parents or my country hadn't valued educating girls? Although there was evidence in reports from developing countries that more girls were attending school, worldwide statistics still showed that women were the majority of the world's illiterates.

At a Commission's session in New York, I noticed a group of African delegates huddled at the back of our meeting room. Huddles like that always meant something was up. I asked an assistant to find out what was going on. She returned saying the African group wanted to add the girl child to the list of critical areas of concern. These were the essence of the Platform. Each concern was to be diagnosed, strategic objectives were to be set out, and concrete actions to be taken by governments, the UN, and civil society—meaning NGOs and the private sector—were to be spelled out. Women's education, employment, and health continued to take priority as they had in previous conferences. The developing countries added poverty to the list. Violence, women in armed conflict, and women's human rights were also added, as were women and the media and women and the environment. Nations began to worry that the list was getting too long.

I agreed, but I also felt that girls the world over got the short end of the stick. I even saw it at times in my own household, despite my feminism, and in my own country. Traditions are very hard to change. If we didn't put more emphasis on girls we would never achieve equality between men and women. I knew Gertrude Mongella of Tanzania, UN Secretary General for the conference, also felt strongly about girls. I didn't think she would object if the girl child were added to the critical concerns list.

I went back to the African group and said if you propose adding the girl child to the critical concerns list, the U.S. will support you. I had no authority to do this. State Department approval was required for any new initiatives or changes in policy and I feared, if we called back for approval, the answer would be "No, the list is too long already." It was now or never. I gambled, thinking we, the U.S., had made a statement on girls and education, so why not. Over 80 million girls worldwide had no access to primary school; where there were schools too many girls were forced to drop out because their families thought they were needed at home to care for smaller siblings. In some countries female fetuses were aborted—boys being preferred; in others, girls were sold young into marriage because marriage was their livelihood. The worst picture I'd ever seen at AID was of a mother with two small children, brother and sister. The boy was well fed; the girl was malnourished, dying of hunger. All these justifications went through my head as I realized I might be in trouble.

I didn't tell anyone what I was going to do, figuring once the deed was done no one could publicly object. As the African delegate began speaking, I waved the U.S. wooden nameplate indicating I wanted to speak next. Shaking with trepidation, I punched the red button to turn my microphone on, and in my most commanding voice I simply said:

"Madame chair. The United States supports the African proposal." Ordinarily such a statement would have been the opening line of a speech giving reasons for our support. I didn't think this was necessary or wise. As I was speaking, out of the corner of my eye, I saw Sweden raise its sign. It was a lovely moment. Their delegate gave the same short statement. A flurry of signs went up, each affirming support and no more. The girl child was in. Formality was out. The room broke into applause and smiles. Almost everyone in the room had been a girl once.

Meanwhile, intrigues were brewing back at the State Department. Interest in the Beijing conference was escalating. A trip to China was a rare opportunity. Very few living Americans had been to China. The conference would be a big media event and State assistant secretaries and underlings were struggling over which bureau was going to run the U.S. show in Beijing and who would get a trip to China. These power struggles are not pretty. I could feel the tension in the air; watched faces when certain people—including myself—entered a room where clearly plots were being devised, and gossip exchanged. Earlier, when people suggested that Hillary Clinton should lead the delegation, I demurred, saying if she announced she would go every president and premier's wife in the world would feel obligated to attend. This would spoil the whole idea of the conference. It was about women, not wives. If she did go—and I thought she should because she was a good feminist—she ought to announce it at the last minute.

All this and more contributed to my downfall. In November, 1994, Newt Gingrich and a new generation of conservatives were elected to Congress. The Clinton administration was shaken. It now had to deal with a very conservative Republican House of Representatives. In December the U.S. lost its seat on the UN Commission on the Status of Women. The European group nominated two candidates, couldn't agree on one and ended up electing both, thus deposing the U.S. I didn't feel personally offended. Seats on the commission and other UN bodies are allotted by region. The U.S. lost it by neglect and perhaps gender politics. They—I should say we—put too many candidates for elective positions on various UN bodies and lost the Commission seat because the man who was supposed to attend the regional caucus where the deal to elect Commission members was made, missed the meeting. Was this deliberate? Part of the power struggle? Who knows.

The morning of December 13 I was called to the White House, thinking it was to consult on the conference. Instead, Veronica Biggins, who had been part of our delegation to Vienna in 1993, had been assigned the job of telling me I was no longer needed. She didn't use the word fired, and she looked miserable. Despite my anger and dismay, I felt sorry for her because I had fired people and knew it was no fun. She did offer that I could be a member of the delegation to China. I didn't exactly say, "no thanks," but she got the message. I was both furious and felt strangely liberated.

Earlier, I had scheduled a lunch for that noon with the lawyer I had worked with on U.S. ratification of the Convention. The White House had sent it to the Senate in September and we were going to discuss its prospects. I debated canceling the lunch, but I hated returning to the State Department. This man was a good soul. I could tell him what had happened, thereby practicing what I would tell others. I leisurely walked from the White House to the restaurant we had agreed on. My colleague listened quietly as I vented my anger and all the frustration I'd felt with the escalating power struggles. Talking it out helped me conquer my dismay until I walked into my office and learned that my assistant and others already knew what I had been told but the assistant secretary I reported to, Doug Bennett, didn't. That said more about the power struggles than I wanted to know.

No one had informed or consulted that good man. He poured out his anguish and shocked me when he hugged and kissed me as our meeting ended. I treasure the wonderful letter I got from him later. We hadn't known each other all that well when we had both been in the Carter Administration. I admired him as a knowledgeable and compassionate person who cared deeply about international affairs. I'll always remember one noontime seminar he held on the then-new topic of HIV/AIDs. Deeply concerned about this new epidemic, he tried to explain what it might mean in the future only to be pooh-poohed by a senior diplomat who predicted only a few thousand people in Africa would ever be affected. The grace with which Bennett handled this effrontery was impressive and consistent with all his actions.

The next day I signed numerous papers, and made the rounds to say goodbye to the people I had grown to like and enjoyed working with. Then I packed up a box of papers and personal belongings, turned in my badge, and went back to the apartment Don and I had rented four months earlier. I was a free woman again. No more bureaucracy, no more infighting. It had been a sometimes glorious, sometimes frustrating adventure, but it was over. The Platform was drafted. Issues I wanted in it were there. Now the only question was who would carry the U.S. banner, who would be on the delegation or its support staff, and how many problems would NGOs have in getting to China. But that wasn't my problem. I could go home to Minneapolis to my new "home office," and to the list of things I wanted to do in retirement.

Chapter 16

Summing Up

Glide ratio, Don called it, musing about our future as we began the drive home to Minneapolis from Washington.

"You work along, reach retirement age and then begin the downward glide to extinction. Let's just hope the glide ratio is a long one," he said with a grin. And so we embarked on a thirteen-hundred-mile conversation about our past and future, pausing from time to time as we nervously passed trucks on slippery mountain roads. Finally facing retirement, we were in no hurry. We had plenty to think and talk about. Don was seventy and I was sixty-nine. We had been married forty-four years. We had driven between these two cities countless times when he was in Congress. Forget the Pennsylvania Turnpike and busy freeways, we decided before we left Washington. This time we can just wander home.

We were what a friend called "golden oldies," physically healthy with IRAs, pensions, Social Security, and no pressing obligations. Yes, our Washington adventure had ended prematurely, but with few regrets. We had seen old friends and enjoyed our cozy apartment, but with Newt Gingrich and the conservatives taking control of Congress, going home was appealing. We mused about what we were going to do with the rest of our lives. I'm sure some gas station attendant in Indiana or Illinois wondered why that old couple in their Honda, with Minnesota license plates and a backseat packed with stuff, was going northwest in winter instead of south. Moving south for the winter had never been on our agenda. We had often gone to Florida for a week's vacation. By Thursdays we were usually bored, eager to get home and back to real life and work. This time we had no work to get back to, but neither of us was ready for indolence. Our minds were too full of things that needed doing.

I wrote later in our traditional holiday letter—usually late—that work is our religion. Neither Don nor I are content unless we have activities that engage us and, to be frank, keep us out of each other's way at least part of every weekday. Too much togetherness is dangerous for any marriage. I had encouraged Don—pushed is a better word—to accept the invitation for a semester at Harvard's Kennedy School immediately after he retired as mayor. Staying in Minneapolis, picking up the paper and worrying about what his successor and the new city council were doing, did not seem like a good idea. Since I was commuting to Washington then, Cambridge, Massachusetts was closer to Washington than Minneapolis. At the Kennedy School, Don returned to his old interest in Congress, international human rights, and even had me up one week to lecture on women's rights.

While he was mayor, the Minneapolis school superintendent had interested Don in the need for more and better early childhood education. He was anxious to work on this again, and I had no intention of giving up on women's issues. I looked forward to getting back to writing again. My December 1993 article in the *Foreign Service Journal*, "Women's Rights are Human Rights," had been well received. I bored Don for miles talking about my idea for an article on the history of women's human rights. By the time we got home, three days later, we were both glad to get out of the car and on to our individual projects.

Now, twelve years later, we are often too busy to muse. The glide has been a long one and it isn't over yet. Before we got married, lying one starry night on a blanket above the Mississippi, we agreed Don would not be a lawyer whose major goal was to make money. We were not going to spend a lot of time entertaining prospective clients nor were we going to live in the suburbs. Our focus was on the large family we had already decided we were going to have and on the old house we were inheriting. Politics would be our avocation. Making politics your livelihood is dangerous. Having another occupation to fall back on is freeing. I feel the same way about marriage. Making it the sole focus of a life can be disastrous for women—and probably for men, though I don't think that idea often occurs to them. The basic understanding, that neither Don nor I would be or do the conventional, has been the theme of our lives.

I now realize that decision had a liberating quality that sustained us through some very trying times, the worst of which, of course, were the losses of Annie and Yo. In a strange and terrible way, we were strengthened by those losses. When you've endured the worst, lesser losses don't hurt as much and minor mistakes become trivial. OK. I goofed, you say to yourself and others. We bury ourselves in, are sustained by, and get great satisfaction from our work. Daughter Mary Mac said it best one evening when we were all sitting around after dinner on our St. Croix porch:

"What would a Fraser be without projects? Answer: dead." Greeted with guffaws, everyone recognized this family trait. From their infancy, our children have been involved in what we call our projects. Maintaining or renovating old houses, repairing boats, moving back and forth between Minneapolis and Washington, sewing for me, fixing any household appliance for Don and, of course, community activities. Having a project seems to be genetic. All our children have bought old houses—with the "Bank of Mom's" help—and fixed them up. Mary Mac has made a career out of it, becoming a mini-developer and now a commercial property manager. John and Tom resurrected an old Mercedes while they were in college with the help of a handy neighbor. John discovered computers and has started two business ventures—one a success, the other now in the "you may lose your shirt" phase. Tom discovered the satisfaction of pro-bono legal work while in law school, and sustains it as a trial lawyer and arbitrator. Jean, our other lawyer now in health care, crusades about biking to work and, like her mother, can't stay at one job more than a decade. All this makes for lively conversation and "can you help me…?" requests.

Having a sense of humor about life while also being deadly serious is what Mark Twain must have meant when he said that the "secret source of humor itself is not joy but sorrow." When a project goes wrong, we can laugh about it. Reinhold Neibuhr's statement, "Humor is a prelude to faith and Laughter is the beginning of prayer," characterizes us. I suspect that is why I was a misfit at State, and felt liberated when I was terminated. Humor is not the State Department's strong suit; diplomacy is deadly serious business and intrigue a part of the whole.

My home office was the blessing I had hoped, lined with full bookshelves, files beneath a long worktop, computer and printer in another cozy corner. We had dispossessed a tenant as a celebratory act once the mortgage was paid off and converted her apartment to office and family room. Rocking chairs face the TV with my sewing area behind them. Sometimes I think we might as well rent out the rest of the house, except for the kitchen.

By 1995, my chapter on the history of the Convention was published in *Women and Politics in the United Nations,* and I was immersed in research and writing another piece of women's history. To me history is very personal. How and why am I here? What happened before me? Who made what happen, and how is that influencing what is happening now? History has fascinated me ever since, as a child, I listened to my grandparents' stories. At the university, my Social and Intellectual History class professor lectured us on the importance of historical records and the danger of losing them, given modern technology. Marrying Don and his family's old house, its attic filled with boxes of papers, I recalled my professor's words and began an association with the Minnesota Historical Society.

This lead, in the 1970s, to my co-authoring a chapter on the first women elected to the Minnesota legislature. Myrtle Cain was one of four who were elected immediately after women were allowed to vote and hold office. I had worked with her in the DFL office where she opened my eyes—and mind—with stories about being part of the women suffrage movement in Washington, D.C. Earlier, in the 1970s, devouring all the new literature about women that I found in bookstores, I discovered Gerda Lerner's book, *The*

Grimke Sisters from South Carolina: Rebels Against Slavery, published in 1975. To me it read like a novel and gave added meaning to my women's movement activities.

Writing that book, Lerner had a similar reaction, for in 1979 she published, *The Majority Finds Its Past: Placing Women in History.* In its foreword, which she titled "Autobiographical Notes, by way of an introduction," she says writing about the Grimke sisters sent her off, as a mature woman, to get an MA and PhD in history. Lerner is now one of the country's leading feminist historians. I became a devotee of and, as any reader can see, a nut about women's history. My exposure to Lerner, and to the history of the International Alliance of Women that my SriLankan friend gave me, made me determined to add whatever I could to the historical record. What really convinced me was Lerner's later book, *The Creation of Feminist Consciousness.* Don't let the words "feminist" and "consciousness" scare you off. This is important stuff. Lerner argues that women are intellectually—and essentially politically—hampered by lack of their sex's history. Women who don't know much or anything about their foremothers are "overwhelmed by the sense of their own inferiority or, conversely, the sense of the dangers of their daring to be different...For thinking women, the absence of Women's History was perhaps the most serious obstacle of all to their intellectual growth."

Overwhelmed by my reading and research, it took me five years—interspersed between other projects—to research and write an article I called, "Becoming Human: the origins and development of women's human rights," but it was worth it. The research was like solving a mystery. From an earlier chapter I did on the history of the drafting of the Women's Convention, I sensed a pattern I had seen in Mary Wollstonecraft's *Vindication of the Rights of Women,* which I read in the 1970's when that book enjoyed a resurgence of interest. I also recalled reading somewhere that Lucretia Mott, a Quaker elder who was Elizabeth Cady Stanton's mentor, kept a copy of Wollstonecraft's book tucked in her baby's cradle. I thought that lovely, and was beginning to sense a pattern and a continuum.

So what happened between 1792 and the 1860s when Mott, Stanton, and the Grimke sisters were anti-slavery and then women's rights activists, I asked myself. One book led to another and another and soon I had notebooks, file folders, and bookcases jammed. Eventually I was back to the fifteenth-century reading Christine de Pizan's *City of Ladies*. Four themes emerged. Education was first. Illiterate women are at the mercy of those who speak to them. Literate women can explore other worlds through the printed word. "Teach girls to think," was Wollstonecraft's admonition. Second is employment, the ability to make a living outside marriage. All marriages end, either in death or divorce, and what girl or woman hasn't read about English governesses? Third is legal rights, the right to be seen as an individual citizen, not simply a subordinate member of a family whose ordinate was male—husband or father. Fourth was the organizing—collective action, working with others—for change. From these four, all other efforts and issues flowed, including birth control.

Women, centuries ago, worked to educate girls. Banned from speaking in public, they wrote, often using men's pseudonyms to get published. Think George Sand and George Eliot. Others sued to be guardians of their own children and had to fight for the right to own property, appear in court, be lawyers. American women were the best at organizing, beginning with anti-slavery organizations and moving on to women's rights. Every article in the Convention on the Elimination of All Forms of Discrimination reflects this history and is a testament to the years—nay, centuries—of work and advocacy by women and women's groups that preceded its drafting. I thoroughly enjoyed writing that article on the history of women's rights, and it has proved well worth the time and effort. Published in 1999 in the *Human Rights Quarterly*, it has been reprinted as lead chapter in two other books on women's human rights.

Leadership, especially women's leadership—or lack thereof—has intrigued and puzzled me ever since I was in Dean Cleveland's leadership program in 1981. I have come to believe that in girlhood, we are taught by our mothers and society to ignore, fear, and deny exercising power directly. What's even worse, we are subtly encouraged to use it indirectly. When teaching and in meetings, I noticed that women tended to hang back, to fear speaking out and taking leadership.. To allay this fear, in speeches and meetings, I often used electricity as an example of power. It's inert until you use it. Turn on a light switch, plug in an appliance and *voila!* This wasn't the perfect analogy but it made my point. It was time, I emphasized, that women plugged themselves in to government, community affairs or wherever, time to make their interests known and use their talents and experience.

I also noticed that many women let men dominate in conversations or spoke in timid voices.

"Project," I would say in class, especially when I began to get hard of hearing. "Pretend you are scolding a child or trying to get the attention of someone across the street. I know you can do that." Almost in exasperation, I organized a series of women and leadership seminars at the Humphrey Institute. A child of World War II, I understood the fear of the word leader. Hitler had called himself Der Furhrer, the leader. But I couldn't think of a better synonym. In the seminar I posed questions: Do women have different styles of leadership? How do they become leaders in a world where the very word leadership connotes men? What are the characteristics of women leaders? We pondered those questions, told life stories and had a great time. I surprised myself. The subject of leadership is tricky. I never wanted to be called a leader, nor do I think of myself as one. I told people I was an educator, an organizer, a feminist, a politician. I do feel complimented when someone says, on seeing me after an interval of time: "Still making trouble, Arvonne?" I laugh. One day it occurred to me that no one asks that question of men.

In my international work I had the same problem. Women were exercising leadership but few would admit it, or consciously teach younger women to lead. I began introducing the topic at our IWRAW conferences gently, hosting a small workshop at our 1991 seminar. Only African women attended. On reflection I thought, of course. They didn't fear the word or the idea or speak in soft voices. They understood the subtle difference between calling your-self a leader and exercising leadership. We had a good time in that workshop, laughing hilariously as one of the participants mimicked a pompous male who called himself a leader but hadn't a clue about the responsibilities that went with leadership.

Women have the same problem in writing about themselves as Jill Ker Conway says in her *When Memory Speaks: Exploring the Art of Autobiography*. She writes about women's fear of expressing agency, of acknowledging effectiveness, of admitting we exercise leadership and power. This is the result of centuries of conditioning, Conway argues. Analyzing women's writing about themselves in the past, she says they conform to "the romantic heroine" model, the social norms of their time. When Irene Tinker and I co-edited our *Developing Power*, we encountered that problem. Too often we women either don't write about our efforts and successes or disguise them in passive voices and ascribe them to luck rather than effort. (Note to readers: if you got this far, am I guilty too?)

Women candidates also walk a fine line. They can't appear to be aggressive and yet have to portray themselves as substantial enough to carry out the duties of the office they seek. That isn't fair but it's a fact. It took two tries by women before we elected a U.S. Senator from Minnesota in 2006. Amy Klobuchar, Minnesota's first elected woman senator, always started her campaign speeches with homey or feminine anecdotes. But the world may be changing. I was all smiles one day when Kate, my youngest grandchild, announced she was going to be president when she grows up. There's hope.

Times have changed, but not fast enough. Nancy Pelosi, the first woman Speaker of the U.S. House of Representatives, when questioned about whether she was strong or tough enough for that office, made much of using her "mother of five voice," if necessary. On her inauguration, front page and TV pictures of her surround-ed by a bevy of small children—her own grandchildren and oth-ers—were both heart-warming and politically effective. She's a great role model, I think. And I always admired Minneapolis' first woman mayor, Sharon Sayles Belton, a black woman, who was pregnant with her third child when she was president of the city council. She knew how to project her voice, but Don, who was mayor when she was council president, also found her a great collaborator who knew how to get things done on the council.

I take special pride in Nancy Pelosi's rise to the speakership because it links back to the Nameless Sisterhood. Widely reported when Pelosi became speaker was that her initial candidacy for Congress was promoted by Congresswoman Sala Burton of San Francisco. Sala, a Sisterhood member, credited the Sisterhood publicly with giving her the confidence needed to run for Congress after her husband, Congressman Phil Burton, died. Reportedly, on her deathbed, Sala urged that Nancy Pelosi be her successor. This is a fine illustration of the old slogan, "sisterhood is powerful." Linkages such as these—from Sisterhood to Sala to Pelosi as speaker—give me immense satisfaction.

I was also pleased to discover, when writing about women legislators, that the districts that elected the first women, in 1922, have all had more women elected since than other districts. Our first congresswoman, Coya Knutson, was a legislator came from one of those districts in northwestern Minnesota; my legislative district in Minneapolis with Myrtle Cain, Alpha Smaby, and Phyllis Kahn, must be nearing a cumulative total of half a century of female representation. And both women Speakers of our Minnesota House have come from the district that elected Mabeth Hurd Paige in 1922. So what we need are more barrier breakers and role models.

In this era of celebrity worship, I'm reminded of what Dean Cleveland tried to teach us in his leadership seminar. He gave credit to General, later President, Eisenhower for saying what I recall went something like this:"You can get a lot done in the world if you don't worry about getting credit for it." In other words, leadership doesn't mean getting your name in the paper, it's what one does that counts. Anonymity has its uses. Private satisfaction can be sweeter than reading your name in the paper. It's like having a lovely secret. But women, as Gerda Lerner and Jill Ker Conway emphasize, carry this being in the background far too far. It disempowers future generations of women. If there is one thing I want younger women to learn, it is that women before them accomplished a great deal. The important thing about women writing history—including their own history as a woman—is to show that ordinary women can make a difference in their communities and the world.

O ne of my great regrets is that I didn't defend U.S. Representative Coya Knutson when she was attacked, and ultimately defeated for re-election, by members of my own party. The first woman elected to Congress from Minnesota, she came from the 9th district, the remote northwestern corner of the state. She had defeated the party's endorsed candidate to win her congressional seat in 1954, and two years later, as a congresswoman, led the Kefauver for President campaign in Minnesota primaries. Party loyalists—myself among them—supported Adlai Stevenson for president. Male party leaders never forgave her. The endorsement system was sacrosanct. Her defeat came when a few party leaders conspired with her derelict husband to issue a "Coya, Come Home" letter just before the 1958 election which got immense publicity in her district, the state, and the nation. It played into the traditional "man of the house" sensibilities in her district and the wider world.

This took place a decade before my consciousness about women was raised, but I still feel guilty. At the time I felt sorry for Coya, thought she was treated badly, but I did nothing. A sin of omission. Instead of speaking out, I hewed to the party line as did other political women. Our crime was silence. I hope I've learned that when something needs saying, say it, even if no one else does.

Coya did not fit the image of a lady held by the DFL political leaders of her time. She was a farm woman, a rural school teacher, and, although she had spent a year at New York's Juillard School of Music and had a liberal voting record, hers was a sin of commission. She took on the party's endorsed candidates and won. This was unforgivable, many party leaders thought. The result was that Odin Langen, a Republican, was elected in Coya's place. I'm sure her fate is one of the reasons we had to wait more than forty years before sending another Minnesota woman to Congress.

During the five years I was writing my "On Becoming Human" article, I also taught at the Humphrey Institute and with IWRAW; spoke around the country on women's rights, leadership, and politics; wrote a number of other articles; spent four months in Sweden where Don taught an American law course; renovated our St. Croix kitchen; and had more grandchildren. The last was the easiest and the most joyful. I used to think grandparents were a little silly, carrying around and showing pictures of their little darlings. Then I became one. As a contemporary said, "Having grandchildren is like being in love all over again." Nice. Few things are more rewarding than having a little one yell, "Grandma!" either in joy at seeing you again or in need of help or solace.

Writing is a lonely, solitary endeavor. My mental health demands balancing it with physical and social activities, but finding the right balance is tricky. I can get so immersed in writing—living in the world of my head and page—that I lose track of time. I may sit down

Arvonne amd Don surrounded by family and friends at their fiftieth wedding anniversary party on the St. Croix

at nine, think I've written for an hour or so, and find it's almost noon and I have a lunch date somewhere. Other days, I'll get engrossed in a project or the demands of a household and don't get to writing. Retirement makes it all worse. No external office schedule for discipline. I'm beginning to think what saves me, and other women, is that from childhood on we watch our mothers tend children, manage a household, and make time for individual interests. We are trained in multi-tasking, become jugglers of time. Don is amazed that when I put my coffee cup in the microwave for reheating, I run out to empty the garbage or load the dishwasher.

Once, overwhelmed with too many commitments, I complained to a male colleague.

"What you need to do is set priorities," he said and walked off as if that was simple. I also remember Don's father saying: "This one thing I do," as an explanation of his success. Men of my generation and the previous one too often assume others—meaning wives—will take care of the trivia of living. And we do, by multi-tasking. This has its benefits. We make good managers. Consultants make money teaching male managers how to multi-task. They should just watch their wives and mothers.

I realize that I create—or let happen—the demands on my time. Though I prize solitude, I need people, a social life. In retirement, unlike having a job or office to go to, you have to get out and make a social life. Never one for chit-chat and married to a man who is even worse at it, we find our sociability—and keep our minds functioning—in community activities and, as always, in politics. As a public member of the Minnesota Board of Law Examiners, my respect for the rule of law and about 99.8 percent of lawyers increased. The .2 percent of those who passed their bar exams, but had too little respect for the law, or had made mistakes in their young life, made service on that board awesome. I combined my interest in libraries with politics by working with the local Friends of the Library to pass a referendum to support a new downtown library. With overwhelming support, a spectacular new library was built, but the dot com stock market bubble burst, state aid was cut, and we were back to square one, enmeshed again in politics.

I've come full circle, from neighborhood to international work and back again to the point where, sitting on my neighborhood organization's land use committee, I am learning about real estate and economic development, planning growth, and changes I may never live to see. Ours is a neighborhood in transition. The oldest section of the city, across the Mississippi from downtown and abutting the University of Minnesota, many big old houses are either stuffed with students, have oldsters like us living in them, or are renovated back to their past glory. Industrial buildings on the periphery are being renovated or leveled, and new high-rise condos are planned. How to blend historic properties with modern architecture is an on-going argument. Should you emulate the old or highlight it by contrast with ultra-modern? Whether to demolish historic properties or find someone to renovate them is a question neighbors and preservations get passionate about. I come home from meetings stimulated by the discussions. The nights I'm embarrassed because I talked too much at the meeting I console myself with the idea that I'm fending off dementia. Keep your mind busy, all the studies and reports say. I hope it's my mind that is busy, not just my mouth. I remember old folks who talked too much. Am I becoming one of them?

The older I get, the more there is to think about. I look around, read the papers and compare what's happening with what went before and what I foresee. Traditionalists think American society is or should be composed of a man and woman, married with children, living in a single-family house and speaking English. That is not the world we live in now. Census statistics paint a very different picture. Simply walk down the street or go into a school if you want to see the real world or the future.

Even conservative writers are recognizing—usually as an aside—that the twentieth-century women's movement, the civil rights movement, and immigration reshaped modern life. I would like to think that while the twentieth-century was about securing rights, the twenty-first century will be one in which we emphasize responsibility. I'm honored that my old friend Garrison Keillor jokes about Sister Arvonne, of Our Lady of Perpetual Responsibility Church. It has always seemed to me that rights imply responsibilities. As the Universal Declaration of Human Rights says in its penultimate article: "Everyone has duties to the community in which alone the free and full development of his (sic) personality is possible."

It may take a century for this idea to gain worldwide acceptance. People who have been subjugated, whether they be women or citizens of a country with autocratic rulers, begin to see themselves as victims and lash out at whatever is available, including their neighbors. Often they dare not lash out at autocratic rulers. They deflect their anger. I'm thinking now of the young men in the Middle East without employment who are led to believe that it is America and Western ways that are the cause of their plight. Some American leaders believe that only force can liberate peoples. People have to liberate themselves, hard as that is. Liberation means defying culture and traditions that smother initiative and subjugate peoples. But it also means accepting responsibility for one's self and the world. I feel good every Monday and Tuesday on my morning walk when I see all the recycling people put out for collection. Small acts by lots of people make a difference.

I continue to worry about religious fundamentalism turned political. Human rights are anathema to fundamentalists. The terrible irony is that belief in old texts is too often enforced with the latest in arms technology. Politicizing religion denies free and open discussion of valued texts that should be interpreted in the context of the times—our times and the times in which those texts were written.

I wonder often why young American women with children, including my own daughters, tolerate their work load. Why should young parents alone bear the physical and financial burdens of bearing and raising the next generation of workers and citizens? Why should young mothers have to get up early every morning, feed children, get them off to school or day care, then get themselves "off to work." They have been working. Then they come home and make meals, do the laundry, help children with their homework and get them off to bed without much help from the children's father or society. On top of that, hiring household help—without which I never could have done what I have done—is too often considered an abrogation of responsibility by those who hire it, and a demeaning occupation for those who do it. This, it seems to me, is carrying the idea of responsibility quite a bit too far.

Reporters used to ask me what I was most proud of in all my work. I hated that question. One thing? Everything I did was related. How could I single out the one thing? One little success here and a little one there and soon you have a movement. Finally, one day, in exasperation—with a bit of malicious delight, but in all sincerity—I responded: "I raised good kids." That was not the answer any reporter wanted. Raising children is no accomplishment in the eyes of the world. But the next generation is the future. Are they violent or fair-minded? Are they able to make a living as well as sound judgments? Are they honest? Can they admit big mistakes and laugh at little ones?

To be truthful, I didn't raise my children alone. There was my sister, Bonnie, a significant presence always with as much concern for them as I had—and sometimes more. There was Rosetta, our maid and cleaning woman for years in Washington, who taught the children what life was like for minorities, and who earned and demanded respect for the work she did. (She once told me she wouldn't work for a certain friend of mine because that woman treated her like dirt. I knew then why my friend had so much trouble keeping help, and why I liked Rosetta so much. She might be illiterate, but she had backbone.) And there were my woman friends and neighbors, and a number of men, who paid attention to our children as individuals and gave them advice they never would have taken from Don and me. Friendship is so undervalued—and unexamined.

One of my current joys is watching my children raising theirs. Mary Mac, our most difficult teenager, is now dealing with her own. She says I once said, when she was reporting her travails:

"Retribution time." I can't believe I said that. She must have read my mind. At least we can laugh together now. The compliment she gave me shortly after her first was born was: "Mom, I never appreciated you until I had Allison." Then, a Sunday or so ago, our son Tom had his children all to himself. His wife was visiting friends in California. I remember winter Sundays alone, with bored children and work to be done around the house.

"We had a family meeting," Tom reported over the phone, "and made a to-do list with assignments for everybody." I suspect all the tasks didn't get done—they never did after our family meetings when he was young. But his reporting they had a family meeting made me happy all day. Mothers delight in small consolations like that.

Small consolations added up make a life worthwhile. I could write pages about them: notes on cards from former students, research assistants, and interns recounting a good memory; women I don't know or recognize who see me on the street or at events and thank me for what I did in the women's movement; a workman who remembers a project he or his father did at our house; a old colleague who finds my email and writes me a note reminding me what we did together. Every time I read about President Carter or see former Vice President Mondale, I feel proud that I played a bit in helping them get elected. Or I'm asked to give a lecture in Texas by a young woman the age of my granddaughter.

Lately I've been gratified to see on my computer—along with requests for contributions—that two major international women's groups, the Global Fund and ICRW, the International Research Center for Research on Women, are mounting significant programs on behalf of the girl child. Yeah, I say to myself. I helped make the girl child a critical area of concern at the last world women's conference and groups are taking up the cause. I'm especially gratified because friends of mine started both of those international women's organizations. It's news like that that makes this old woman's day. But I got my come-uppance recently when grandson Jack, on seeing my picture in the local paper, asked: "Grandma, are you important?" Then he beat me at rummy.

I don't want a tombstone. I go to funerals these days and think of my own mortality. What I would like after I die is for my children, a month or so later, to throw a big party for my friends, relatives, and colleagues. I went to such an event recently. (Some weeks I think our whole social life is funerals and fundraisers.) At this memorial event, stories were told, idiosyncrasies laughed at, friendships and good memories extolled. That's for me, I thought. Meanwhile, there's this book to finish editing—I've only been at it often and on for a decade. There's my to-do list demanding attention, emails to answer. And I'm late for a meeting!

© 1998, Dan Marshall

Appendix

(For background see Chapter 14, page 240)

A condensed version of the Convention on the Elimination of All Forms of Discrimination Against Women (CEDAW), the international women's human rights treaty. (For full text, contact the United Nations Department of Public Information.)

ARTICLE I: DEFINITION OF DISCRIMANATION

Any distinction, exclusion or restriction made on the basis of sex, which has the purpose or effect of denying equal exercise of human rights and fundamental freedoms in all fields of human endeavor.

ARTICLE 2: POLICY MEASURES TO BE UNDERTAKEN TO ELIMINATE DISCRIMINATION

Embody the principle of equality in national constitutions, codes or other laws, and ensure its practical realization. Establish institutions to protect against discrimination. Ensure that public authorities and institutions refrain from discrimination. Abolish all existing laws, customs and regulations that discriminate against women

ARTICLE 3: GUARANTEES BASIC HUMAN RIGHTS AND FUNDAMENTAL FREEDOMS ON AN EQUAL BASIS WITH MEN

ARTICLE 4: TEMPORARY SPECIAL MEASURES TO ACHIEVE EQUALITY

Temporary special measures may be adopted and must be discontinued when equality is achieved. Special measures to protect maternity are not considered discriminatory. Practices based on the inferiority or superiority of either sex shall be eliminated. Ensure that family education teaches that both men and women share a common role in raising children

ARTICLE 5:Sex Roles And Stereotyping

Social and cultural patterns must be modified to eliminate sex-role stereotypes and notions of the inferiority or superiority of either sex. Family education shall teach that men and women share a common responsibility in the raising of children

ARTICLE 6:Prostitution

Measures shall be taken to suppress all forms of traffic in women and exploitation of prostitution

ARTICLE 7: Political And Public Life

The right to vote in all elections and be eligible for election to all elected bodies. To participate in formulation of government policy and hold office at all levels of government. To participate in non-governmental organizations

ARTICLE 8: Participation At The International Level

The opportunity to represent their country at the international level and to participate in international organizations

ARTICLE 9: Nationality

Equal rights to acquire, change or retain their nationality. Equal rights to the nationality of their children

ARTICLE 10: Education

Equal access to education and vocational guidance. The same curricula, examinations, standards for teaching and equipment. Equal opportunity to scholarships and grants. Equal access to continuing education, including literacy programs. For elimination of stereotyping in education and textbooks. Measures for reduction of female dropout rates. Equal participation in sports and physical education. Equal access to health and family planning information

ARTICLE 11: Employment

The same employment rights as men. Free choice of profession, employment and training. Equal remuneration,and benefits, including equal treatment as to work of equal value. Social security. Ooccupational health and safety protection. Prohibition of dismissal on the basis of pregnancy or marital status. Maternity leave. Provision of social services encouraged, including child care. Special protection against harmful work during pregnancy

ARTICLE 12: Health Care And Family Planning

-equal access to; appropriate pregnancy services

ARTICLE 13: Economic And Social Benefits

Equal access to family benefits; loans and credit. Equal right to participate in recreational activities, sports, cultural life.

ARTICLE 14: Rural Women

Recognition of the particular problems of rural women, the special roles they play in economic survival of families and of their unpaid work. Ensure their equal participation in development. Right to participate in development planning and implementation. Access to health care and family planning services. Right to benefit directly from social security. Right to training and education. Right to organize self-help groups and cooperatives

ARTICLE 15: Equality Before the Law

Guarantee of same legal capacity as men—to contract, administer property, appear in court or before tribunals. Freedom of movement, right to choose residence and domicile. Contractual and other private restrictions on legal capacity of women shall be declared null and void

ARTICLE 16: Marriage and Family Law

Equal rights and responsibilities with men in marriage and family relations. The right to freely enter into marriage and choose a spouse. Equality during marriage and at its dissolution. The right to choose freely the number and spacing of children; access to information, education, and means to make that choice. Equal rights to guardianship and adoption of children. The same personal rights as husband; Right to choose family name, profession or occupation. Equal rights and responsibilities regarding ownership, management and disposition of property. A minimum age and registration of marriage

ARTICLES 17-22: Detail the Establish and Function of the Cedaw Committee

ARTICLES 23-30: Detail the Administration of the Convention

INDEX